The
Controversial
Pivot

The Controversial Pivot

The U.S. Congress and North America

ROBERT A. PASTOR
RAFAEL FERNANDEZ DE CASTRO
Editors

Brookings Institution Press
Washington, D.C.

ABOUT BROOKINGS

The Brookings Institution is a private nonprofit organization devoted to research, education, and publication on important issues of domestic and foreign policy. Its principal purpose is to bring knowledge to bear on current and emerging policy problems. The Institution maintains a position of neutrality on issues of public policy. Interpretations or conclusions in publications of the Brookings Institution Press should be understood to be solely those of the authors.

Library of Congress Cataloging-in-Publication data

The controversial pivot : The U.S. Congress and North America /
Robert A. Pastor and Rafael Fernandez de Castro, editors.
    p.   cm.
  Includes bibliographical references.
  ISBN 0-8157-6924-5 (cloth : alk. paper)
  ISBN 0-8157-6923-7 (pbk. : alk. paper)
    1. United States—Foreign economic relations—Mexico.   2. Mexico—
Foreign economic relations—United States.   3. United States—Foreign
economic relations—Canada.   4. Canada—Foreign economic relations—
United States.   5. United States. Congress.   6. United States—Commercial
policy.   7. North America—Politics and government.   I. Pastor, Robert A.
II. Fernandez de Castro, Rafael.
  HF1455.Z4 M493   1998
  337.7307—ddc21
                                                                    98-25372
                                                                    CIP

9 8 7 6 5 4 3 2 1

The paper used in this publication meets the minimum requirements of the American National Standard for Information Sciences—Permanence of Paper for Printed Library Materials, ANSI Z39.48-1984.

Typeset in Palatino

Composition by Princeton Editorial Associates
Scottsdale, Arizona, and Roosevelt, New Jersey

Printed by R. R. Donnelley & Sons
Harrisonburg, Virginia

belief that a clearer
ing that goal. Dur-
ved our chapters
was in October
, the second in
he first drafts,
e Association

htful com-
ecialist at
the Mex-
(CSIS);
olar of
osner,
rico
in
se

after two events occurred in
en inconceivable just five years
ching of the North American Free
n aimed to bind the economies of the
anada. It ended with the Republicans'
ngress for the first time in forty years. Led
Newt Gingrich, the 104th Congress was dedi-
as' "Contract with America," a "revolutionary"
ationalism and lacking a spirit of neighborliness
oligation. The neighbors to the north and south of
es were deeply concerned about the implications for
e new inward-focused mood of America that was reflected
ange in Congress. Would the new Congress undermine
before it had a chance to begin? Was it possible to advance the
ration process if the U.S. Congress stepped on the brakes?

One of us, Rafael Fernandez de Castro, took the initiative in recruiting the other, Robert Pastor, and the contributors to answer these questions and to develop a book that would enable readers to better understand the politics and the policy of North American integration. For
reasons that we develop in the first chapter, we have chosen to look at
the integration process by focusing on the U.S. Congress because we
believe that institution has played a pivotal role in North American
politics and is likely to continue to play such a role.

Our hypothesis about Congress's importance has withstood recent
unanticipatetd events, and our research supports our observation that
not only is the U.S. Congress more independent and influential than the
Canadian Parliament or the Mexican legislatures, it shapes the banks
within which the river of North American integration runs its course.

This book represents the work of scholars from Mexico, Canada, and
the United States who want to foster a mutually beneficial process of

integration within North America. We share the
understanding of the U.S. Congress is key to achiev
ing the past four years we developed ideas and impr
at three formal meetings in Washington, D.C. The firs
1995 at a Latin American Studies Association conventio
June 1996 at the American Enterprise Institute to review
and the last in August 1997 at an American Political Scien
convention, to review the penultimate drafts.

At the second meeting we were fortunate to receive thou
mentaries on our chapters from Raymond Ahearn, a trade sp
the Congressional Research Service; Delal Baer, the director of
ico Project at the Center for Strategic and International Studie
Charles F. Doran of the Johns Hopkins University, a leading sch
Canada; Thomas E. Mann of the Brookings Institution; Jeremy R
then of the Carnegie Endowment for International Peace; and Fede
Salas, minister for congressional affairs at the Mexican Embass
Washington. We also benefited from the advice and comments of J
Ignacio Madrazo and Arturo Sarukham of the Mexican Embass
Demetrios Papademetriou, director of the International Migration Pol-
icy Program at the Carnegie Endowment; Christopher Sands of the
Canada Project at CSIS; Dhalia Stein of the National Planning Associa-
tion; and Sidney Weintraub of CSIS. Ambassador Jesus Silva Herzog of
Mexico also provided us with vivid pictures of how a foreign diplomat
sees the U.S. Congress.

At the final meeting of the authors in August 1997, we appreciated
further comments by Federico Salas and José Ignacio Madrazo of the
Mexican Embassy, Frederick Mayer of Duke University, and Todd
Eisenstadt of the University of California, San Diego. We are very grateful to Nancy Davidson, Brookings Institution Press editor, for her very
helpful suggestions and editing. (We are, after all, interested in integration not only among the three countries of North America, but also
among the eight chapters of our book.) Finally, we express our appreciation for the detailed and constructive criticisms of three anonymous
readers whose comments helped us to improve the book. We accept
responsibility for any remaining errors.

This process and the book would not have been possible without the
support and generous contribution of the Ford Foundation's Mexico
City office. Norman Collins, director of the office, has been a key supporter of the Instituto Tecnológico Autónomo de México (ITAM), the

institution that received the original grant. We also thank Miguel Cornejo, Shannon Culbertson, the Carter Center, and Emory University for helping us coordinate this project in the United States. Princeton Editorial Associates provided editorial and composition services and prepared the index.

The views expressed are those of the authors alone and should not be attributed to those acknowledged or to the trustees, officers, or staff members of the Brookings Institution.

Contents

Tables

Figures

integration within North America. We share the belief that a clearer understanding of the U.S. Congress is key to achieving that goal. During the past four years we developed ideas and improved our chapters at three formal meetings in Washington, D.C. The first was in October 1995 at a Latin American Studies Association convention, the second in June 1996 at the American Enterprise Institute to review the first drafts, and the last in August 1997 at an American Political Science Association convention, to review the penultimate drafts.

At the second meeting we were fortunate to receive thoughtful commentaries on our chapters from Raymond Ahearn, a trade specialist at the Congressional Research Service; Delal Baer, the director of the Mexico Project at the Center for Strategic and International Studies (CSIS); Charles F. Doran of the Johns Hopkins University, a leading scholar of Canada; Thomas E. Mann of the Brookings Institution; Jeremy Rosner, then of the Carnegie Endowment for International Peace; and Federico Salas, minister for congressional affairs at the Mexican Embassy in Washington. We also benefited from the advice and comments of José Ignacio Madrazo and Arturo Sarukham of the Mexican Embassy; Demetrios Papademetriou, director of the International Migration Policy Program at the Carnegie Endowment; Christopher Sands of the Canada Project at CSIS; Dhalia Stein of the National Planning Association; and Sidney Weintraub of CSIS. Ambassador Jesus Silva Herzog of Mexico also provided us with vivid pictures of how a foreign diplomat sees the U.S. Congress.

At the final meeting of the authors in August 1997, we appreciated further comments by Federico Salas and José Ignacio Madrazo of the Mexican Embassy, Frederick Mayer of Duke University, and Todd Eisenstadt of the University of California, San Diego. We are very grateful to Nancy Davidson, Brookings Institution Press editor, for her very helpful suggestions and editing. (We are, after all, interested in integration not only among the three countries of North America, but also among the eight chapters of our book.) Finally, we express our appreciation for the detailed and constructive criticisms of three anonymous readers whose comments helped us to improve the book. We accept responsibility for any remaining errors.

This process and the book would not have been possible without the support and generous contribution of the Ford Foundation's Mexico City office. Norman Collins, director of the office, has been a key supporter of the Instituto Tecnológico Autónomo de México (ITAM), the

Preface

THIS BOOK was conceived after two events occurred in 1994 that would have been inconceivable just five years before. The year began with the launching of the North American Free Trade Agreement (NAFTA), which aimed to bind the economies of the United States, Mexico, and Canada. It ended with the Republicans' taking control of the U.S. Congress for the first time in forty years. Led by Speaker of the House Newt Gingrich, the 104th Congress was dedicated to the Republicans' "Contract with America," a "revolutionary" agenda laden with nationalism and lacking a spirit of neighborliness or international obligation. The neighbors to the north and south of the United States were deeply concerned about the implications for NAFTA of the new inward-focused mood of America that was reflected by the change in Congress. Would the new Congress undermine NAFTA before it had a chance to begin? Was it possible to advance the integration process if the U.S. Congress stepped on the brakes?

One of us, Rafael Fernandez de Castro, took the initiative in recruiting the other, Robert Pastor, and the contributors to answer these questions and to develop a book that would enable readers to better understand the politics and the policy of North American integration. For reasons that we develop in the first chapter, we have chosen to look at the integration process by focusing on the U.S. Congress because we believe that institution has played a pivotal role in North American politics and is likely to continue to play such a role.

Our hypothesis about Congress's importance has withstood recent unanticipatetd events, and our research supports our observation that not only is the U.S. Congress more independent and influential than the Canadian Parliament or the Mexican legislatures, it shapes the banks within which the river of North American integration runs its course.

This book represents the work of scholars from Mexico, Canada, and the United States who want to foster a mutually beneficial process of

Chapter 1

National Legislatures within North America

Robert A. Pastor and Rafael Fernandez de Castro

A FTER LISTENING to an address on democracy by Mexico's President Ernesto Zedillo during a conference at the Carter Center on April 28, 1997, Newt Gingrich, the speaker of the U.S. House of Representatives, praised Zedillo and his speech as "remarkable" and said:

> You are to be commended not only for your courage in implementing the policies you described but for the international clarity you gave tonight in explaining where I think the entire human race has to go—toward accountability—through honest elections, so that every citizen has the opportunity and the right to measure those to whom they loan power. I thank you for coming here to Atlanta to share with us what you are courageously implementing in your country.[1]

Four days later, as U.S. President Bill Clinton was leaving for Mexico, Gingrich sent him a letter that accused Zedillo of not showing the "resolve to halt the production and transit of illegal drugs" to the United States, concluding that that was because of "corruption or a lack of political will." Gingrich demanded that Clinton extract six commitments from Zedillo, including giving the U.S. Drug Enforcement Administration agents in Mexico "immunities [and] the necessary means to defend themselves," allowing extradition of Mexican nationals, and granting the U.S. Coast Guard and aircraft rights to "hot pursuit" into Mexican waters and territory.[2] Each of these demands was

We express our appreciation to Jason Mack and Robin Gault Moriarty for compiling the tables and data used in this chapter.

viewed as interventionist and insulting by the Mexicans, who questioned, with justification, whether the United States would accept them if Mexico were proposing them.[3]

Between the adulation and the accusation heaped on President Zedillo sat four days in the life of the same speaker, which illustrate the contradictory way in which the U.S. Congress has always treated its North American neighbors. Gingrich's comments reflect the two sides of a three-sided North American relationship. Congress can be statesmanlike, as Gingrich was in Atlanta, or it can be parochial and acerbic, as he was four days later. It is rare that a single person is both in so short a time, but the chapters in this book on Mexico and Canada amply document the capacity of Congress to speak out of both sides of its mouth.

The premise of this book is that the North American Free Trade Agreement (NAFTA) represents a genuine watershed in U.S.-Mexican-Canadian relations, allowing the three governments to move from a relationship of paternalism to one of partnership. NAFTA also offers North Americans the chance to construct a regional entity that could be a model for industrialized and developing nations and could be as integrated as but more powerful than the European Union.

NAFTA can be viewed as a strategic response by the three governments of North America to the compression of the world by technology, migration, and economic competition. Although these forces are pushing the three countries of North America together, other institutions and concerns in each of the three countries are pulling them apart. For reasons of culture, traditional nationalism, or fear that integration can blur one's identity or eliminate one's job, some groups in these countries either reject or reluctantly acquiesce to the integration process. This ambivalence is reflected in the different relationships among institutions in the three countries. Due to NAFTA and the integration process that it accelerated, the three heads of government have grown closer, although the three legislatures have grown more distant.

For constitutional and political reasons, the U.S. Congress is the most independent—and at times appears to be the most insular—of the three bodies. Why is it that the strongest nation has the most parochial legislature? The legislators in each of the three countries are elected by smaller constituencies than the executive, but in Mexico and Canada the parties can impose discipline and a wider perspective on individual members. In the United States the political parties are weaker; legislators run for office on their own and are therefore more sensitive to the concerns of their constituents and less to those of their party or to their nation's collective interest. That is why the U.S. Congress is the center of this book and the pivot of the relationship. If one visualizes each state as a car and the legislatures as trying to steer their nations' cars so that they travel smoothly without fear of collision, the U.S. Congress can be seen as having a heavy foot, alternately, on the brakes or the accelerator. Successful integration is not possible unless one finds a way to persuade Congress to moderate its approach to driving.

There are many ways to understand the contemporary political and economic landscape of North America. In this book the authors try to do so by analyzing the role of the U.S. Congress in policies that affect its two neighbors and in responding to concerns from them. In this chapter we begin by examining the contradictory pressures of history, geography, and economics, which bring the three countries together and pull them apart at the same time. We also analyze the changes in the world, particularly the end of the cold war, that allowed North America to emerge as the second most integrated region, behind the European Union but ahead of east Asia. Next we compare the mechanics of governing in each of the three North American governments as a way to see why we have selected the U.S. Congress as the window on North America. And finally we summarize the contributions of each of the authors.

Both Sides of the North American Watershed

Between the conclusion of the Canadian-U.S. Free Trade Agreement (CUFTA) in 1988 and NAFTA in 1992, the three governments crossed a genuine watershed in their relations. Canada and Mexico felt the change most profoundly because of the dominant role that the United States has played in their economies and affairs. But the fact that the U.S. debate on NAFTA did not end with congressional approval of the agreement in November 1993 is just one of many signs that the United States is growing increasingly aware of its neighbors' impact on its society, economy, and politics.

The three nations of North America were drawn together by migration, trade, and geography, and they are separated by their views of history and their differing economic and political systems. In the first half of the nineteenth century, the United States seized almost half of

Mexico and tried unsuccessfully to acquire Canada. Those two events are remembered as well in Mexico and Canada as they are forgotten in the United States. That history explains why both Canadian and Mexican leaders have tried to keep their powerful neighbor at arm's length lest they lose some of their independence.

During the dictatorship of Porfirio Diaz (1877–1910), Mexico opened its doors to foreign investment, modern technology, and trade. The result was a period of rapid industrialization, but also widening social inequalities and growing international influence. The revolution in the second decade of the twentieth century that swept away Diaz seemed aimed at the United States as much as against this old regime. When it was over Mexico built strong, high, and sturdy walls to separate itself from the United States, defining the "limits to friendship."[4] No Mexican president dared to change that until Carlos Salinas proposed a free trade agreement seventy years later.

Canadians also developed a historical wariness of their neighbor to the south, in part because they feared that some Americans really believed their "manifest destiny" was to acquire their neighbor to the north. But there was a more subtle concern, according to James M. Minifie, the Canadian Broadcasting Corporation's radio correspondent in Washington, that a "too-close alliance" would convey "the appearance of subordination to the United States."[5] Economic nationalism was viewed as a critical line of defense to preclude American domination.

Since 1947 the United States, a country more confident of its power and more focused on the future than preoccupied with the past, repeatedly implored its neighbors to reduce their trade and investment barriers. Neither Mexico nor Canada was much interested in opening its trade to the United States, but repeated rejection did not discourage U.S. presidents from asking.

Canada was the first to risk a change in direction. In the late 1950s it embraced a limited free trade agreement in the area of defense procurement. This was followed in 1965 with a free trade agreement in the area of automobiles and auto parts. But it was not until the 1980s that the Progressive Conservative government of Brian Mulroney proposed a comprehensive free trade agreement with the United States. An agreement was concluded in 1988. Although the U.S. Senate Committee on Finance came close to rejecting the agreement, in fact it was far more controversial in Canada.

Two years later Mexico's Salinas took an even greater risk by proposing a free trade agreement from a weaker position but with a similar purpose. Both Canada and Mexico had become so dependent on trade with the United States that arbitrary trade barriers adversely affected their economies. A proposal of freer trade was not only a path into the world's largest market; it was also a way to secure the market and minimize trade disruptions. A regional trade agreement also represented a departure for the United States from its global trade policy; however, because the United States had an economy twenty times that of Mexico and ten times that of Canada, the impact on the United States would not be as great as on its neighbors.

North America constitutes a formidable land mass and with a total population of 391 million in 1996, having more than doubled since 1950. Immigration has been an important cause of the rise in population in the United States and Canada, and improved health care has been the primary reason in Mexico. Although the rate of population growth in Mexico declined sharply after that country introduced family planning in 1972, the rate is still about twice that of its neighbors to the north. The result is a much younger population in Mexico and an age distribution profile that complements those of the United States and Canada. In 1990 over 36 percent of Mexico's population was under age fifteen, as compared with about 21 percent of the populations of its two northern neighbors (see table 1-1).

Since 1970 North America's gross domestic product has increased nearly eight times—from $1.1 to $8.3 trillion (see table 1-2). The region's exports have grown twice as fast—from $61 billion to $919 billion—and trade among the three nations has grown faster than their world trade, tying the economies closer together (see tables 1-3 and 1-4). Intraregional exports in North America as a fraction of total exports rose from less than a third in 1980 to nearly half in 1996 (see table 1-4).

The United States is the largest foreign investor in both of its neighbors, and the rate of investment has increased since NAFTA came into force. By the end of 1996 U.S. investment accounted for approximately 60 percent of the total foreign direct investment of about $73 billion in Mexico. The annual direct investment in Mexico has been roughly four times higher in the years since NAFTA than in the 1980s.[6] U.S. direct investment in Canada reached $92 billion in 1996, representing a 16 percent increase over the previous year.[7]

TABLE 1-1. *North America: Population and Age Distribution Profiles, 1950–2000*

Category	United States	Mexico	Canada	North America (average)
Population (millions)				
1950	152.27	26.28	13.74	192.29
1970	205.05	51.18	21.32	277.55
1990	250.00	86.20	26.50	362.70
2000	276.62	102.91	29.99	409.52
Age distribution (percent of population)				
Under 15				
1950	26.87	45.60	33.50	35.32
1970	28.26	46.50	30.20	34.99
1990	21.57	36.50	21.40	26.49
2000	19.70	25.00	19.30	21.20
16–60				
1950	58.25	49.30	58.20	55.25
1970	57.71	50.00	61.90	56.54
1990	61.20	60.50	68/60	63.43
2000	62.50	66.00	63.50	64.00
Over 61				
1950	14.88	5.10	8.30	9.43
1970	14.04	3.50	7.90	8.48
1990	17.22	3.00	10.00	10.07
2000	18.20	9.00	17.20	14.80

Sources: U.S. Department of Commerce, Bureau of the Census, *1996 Statistical Abstract of the U.S.* (1997); World Bank, *World Tables* (1984 and 1991), *World Tables—Social Data* (1984), and *World Development Report* (1992). U.S. data for the year 2000 are projections from the U.S. Bureau of the Census; the projections for Canada and Mexico are based on World Bank estimates.

Mexico's direct investment in the United States has also increased since NAFTA; it doubled from 1993 to 1994 to about $2 billion. Of course, that is trivial compared with the Canadian investment in the United States of $60 billion, which makes Canada the fifth largest direct investor in the United States.[8] Canadian investment has boomed in Mexico since NAFTA, but it represents less than 2 percent of total foreign direct investment there.

The intensity of contact between the United States and Mexico is unlike any other between a developed nation and a developing nation. In 1996 alone, 254 million people, 75 million cars, and 3.5 million trucks and rail cars entered the United States from Mexico through thirty-nine legal crossing points along the frontier.[9] Binational trade has surged 122 percent since 1990, reaching nearly $150 billion in 1996 (see table 1-5). Mexico's peso crisis of 1994–95 had little impact on the total amount of U.S.-Mexican trade; U.S. exports to Mexico declined by only 1.8 percent in 1995. In contrast, Mexico's imports from Japan dropped 25 percent, and those from the European Union dropped by 26 percent. NAFTA, in brief, secured the U.S. market for Mexican goods and the Mexican market for goods from the United States.

The world's largest bilateral trading relationship is that between Canada and the United States. In 1985, when negotiations for a free trade agreement began, the United States was exporting $47 billion of goods and services and importing $69 billion. In one decade, total trade more than doubled (see table 1-5).

In terms of population, Mexican Americans represent 65 percent of Hispanics in the United States. Of the 27 million Hispanics in the United States, 18 million are of Mexican origin, and a third (6 million) were born in Mexico. By 2010, if the current rate of population growth and migration continues at the same rate, Hispanics will constitute the largest U.S. minority group, outnumbering the African American population.

Because the majority of Canadians live in urban centers located within 100 kilometers of the Canada-U.S. border, a string of important regional market clusters has been created along the border. Therefore, Canadians tend to look south more than they do east or west. Companies based in east central Canada often view the northeastern United States as their primary market. Companies in Vancouver look south to U.S. states such as Washington, Oregon, and California for market opportunities.

TABLE 1-2. *North America: Economic Indicators, 1970–96*

Indicator	United States	Mexico	Canada	North America
GNP (billions of current U.S. dollars)				
1970	1,018.58	37.87	83.15	1,139.60
1990	5,519.60	238.43	547.62	6,305.65
1995	6,952.86	237.09	548.81	7,738.76
1996	7,433.50	341.70	569.90	8,345.10
GNP per capita (current U.S. dollars)[a]				
1970	4,960	730	3,840	3,177
1990	22,350	2,630	19,630	14,870
1995	26,980	3,320	19,380	16,560
1996	27,990	3,690	19,110	16,930
Exports (basis, fob, millions of current U.S. dollars/percentages)[b]				
1970	43,220	1,205	16,185	60,610
	71.31	1.99	26.70	37.34
1990	393,106	27,167	126,447	546,720
	71.90	4.97	23.13	39.76
1995	582,526	79,541	190,187	852,254
	68.35	9.33	22.32	46.86
1996	622,945	95,991	200,146	919,082
	67.78	10.44	21.78	48.50

Imports (basis, cif, millions of current U.S. dollars/percentages)[b]

Year				
1970	39,950	2,461	14,256	56,667
				40.61
1990	517,018	30,014	119,673	666,705
	21.78	67.75	70.56	32.61
1995	770,947	72,452	163,288	1,006,687
	27.86	75.61	79.49	39.67
1996	817,785	89,464	170,038	1,077,287
	29.40	76.55	80.49	41.38

Sources: World Bank, *World Tables* (1984, 1991), *World Development Report* (1992, 1995, 1998), and *World Development Indicators* (1998); OECD, *Monthly Statistics on Foreign Trade* (July 1972); International Monetary Fund, *Direction of Trade Statistics Yearbook* (1992, 1997).

a. North American GNP per capita is an average of the three countries.

b. The percentages under Exports and Imports reflect each country's exports (or imports) to its North American neighbors as percentages of its total trade.

TABLE 1-3. *Intraregional Trade in North America, 1980–96*
Millions of current U.S. dollars

Exporter	Importer	Exports				Imports			
		1980	*1990*	*1995*	*1996*	*1980*	*1990*	*1995*	*1996*
Canada	Mexico	419	488	786	855	295	1,483	3,774	4,281
	United States	41,999	93,780	148,304	159,746	35,395	82,959	126,024	132,584
Total Canadian intraregional trade		42,418	94,268	149,090	160,601	35,690	84,442	129,798	136,865
Mexico	Canada	295	1,483	3,774	4,281	419	488	786	855
	United States	10,072	18,837	66,475	80,663	10,890	19,846	53,995	67,629
Total Mexican intraregional trade		10,367	20,320	70,249	84,944	11,309	20,334	54,781	68,484
United States	Canada	35,395	82,959	126,024	132,584	41,999	93,780	148,304	159,746
	Mexico	10,890	19,846	53,995	67,629	10,072	18,837	66,475	80,663
Total U.S. intraregional trade		46,285	102,805	180,019	200,213	52,071	112,617	214,779	240,409

Source: International Monetary Fund, *Direction of Trade Statistics Yearbook* (1987, 1997).

TABLE 1-4. *North American World Trade, 1980–96*
Millions of current U.S. dollars

	Exports				Imports			
	1980	1990	1995	1996	1980	1990	1995	1996
North American worldwide trade values								
Canada	67,730	126,447	190,187	200,146	61,004	119,673	163,288	170,038
Mexico	15,557	27,167	79,541	95,991	17,687	30,014	72,452	89,464
United States	220,781	393,106	582,526	622,945	256,959	517,018	770,947	817,785
Totals	304,068	546,720	852,254	919,082	335,650	666,705	1,006,687	1,077,287
Intraregional trade as a percentage of world trade								
Canada	62.63	74.55	78.39	80.24	58.50	70.56	79.49	80.49
Mexico	66.64	74.80	88.32	88.49	63.94	67.75	75.61	76.55
United States	20.96	26.15	30.90	32.14	20.26	21.78	27.86	29.40
Trade within North America as a percentage of region's trade with the world	32.58	39.76	46.86	48.50	29.52	32.61	39.67	41.38

Source: International Monetary Fund, *Direction of Trade Statistics Yearbook* (1987, 1997).

TABLE 1-5. *Trade among the United States, Mexico, and Canada, 1980–96*

Millions of current U.S. dollars

Year	Exports	Imports	Total	Percentage of exports	Percentage of imports
U.S. trade with Mexico					
1980	10,890	10,072	20,962	4.93	61.57
1985	8,954	13,341	22,295	4.20	66.62
1990	19,846	18,837	38,683	5.05	66.12
1995	53,995	66,475	120,470	9.27	74.53
1996	67,629	80,663	148,292	10.86	75.59
U.S. trade with Canada					
1980	35,395	41,999	77,394	16.03	58.02
1985	47,251	69,427	116,678	22.17	60.06
1990	82,959	93,780	176,739	21.10	69.32
1995	126,024	148,304	274,328	21.63	77.18
1996	132,584	159,746	292,330	21.28	77.97
Mexican trade with Canada					
1980	295	419	714	1.90	0.48
1985	976	287	1,263	4.42	1.24
1990	226	391	617	0.83	0.19
1995	1,979	1,374	3,353	2.49	1.21
1996	1,181	1,744	2,925	1.23	0.69

Sources: U.S. Department of Commerce, Bureau of the Census, *Statistical Abstract of the U.S.* (1950–1991); International Monetary Fund, *Direction of Trade Statistics Yearbook* (1987, 1992, 1994, 1995, 1997).

Cultural influence originates in each of the three countries and extends to the others, enriching and sometimes unsettling communities. Mexicans now share consumer habits with Americans and Canadians, and Mexican food and culture can be found in the most remote areas of Canada and the United States, with perhaps a dominant presence in the southwestern part of the United States. Although Canadians feature prominently in the most important nightly news programs in the United States, Canadians, with good reason, are much more concerned about the disproportionate influence of U.S. movies and publications in their country. This concern was reflected in CUFTA, which exempts the cultural industries from free trade.

Few bilateral relations involve as many actors and issues as the U.S.-Mexican and U.S.-Canadian relationships. In each area—trade, cultural exchange, migration, and drug trafficking, for instance—different constellations of groups and leaders shape the decisions. Some of these groups, such as businesses and environmentalists, form transnational coalitions, having more in common with like-minded groups in the other countries. Other groups, such as labor unions, have more difficulty relating to their counterparts in the other countries because they view the relationships between the countries as more of a zero-sum game; job growth in one country is at the expense of that in the other.[10] The management of bilateral affairs has therefore become much more difficult. Moreover, on the border three levels of government officials—local, state (or province), and national—coincide and sometimes collide.

Asymmetry defines the special nature of a relationship that is weak on its third side. Until NAFTA, Canada and Mexico had minimal economic and political relations. What they share is a deep dependence on the U.S. economy. In 1996 the United States absorbed more than 80 percent of Mexican and Canadian exports. From the other direction, the top two largest markets for U.S. exports are Canada and Mexico, but the United States is much less dependent on Canada (accounting for 21 percent of its exports in 1996) or on Mexico (11 percent) than its neighbors are on the U.S. market (see table 1-4).[11] However, Canada and Mexico are more important markets to the United States today than before NAFTA, and nearly a third of total U.S. trade is with its two closest neighbors. The fact that half the world trade of the three countries of North America is with each other confirms the depth of regional integration, but the asymmetric dependence explains why Canadians and Mexicans are more attentive to U.S. affairs than vice versa.

The End of the Cold War and the Emergence of Regions

The cold war ended without a battlefield victory or the signing of a peace treaty, but when it was over the international landscape changed as radically as it had after the two cataclysmic world wars. World power was redistributed as the Soviet Union imploded and the economies of its former constituent republics slid down to third world levels. The ideological struggle between communism and capitalism or democracy disappeared, leaving democracy and market economics as the reigning political and economic ideas. Traditional security issues declined in importance relative to economic issues. The most important

FIGURE 1-1. *The World's Three Main Regions: Indicators, 1996*

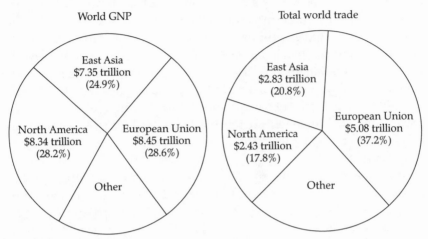

World GNP

East Asia
$7.35 trillion
(24.9%)

North America
$8.34 trillion
(28.2%)

European Union
$8.45 trillion
(28.6%)

Other

Total world trade

East Asia
$2.83 trillion
(20.8%)

North America
$2.43 trillion
(17.8%)

European Union
$5.08 trillion
(37.2%)

Other

Source: World Bank, *World Development Indicators* (1998).
Notes: Total trade is total of exports and imports of goods and services. *North America:* Canada, Mexico, United States (population 388 million). *European Union:* Austria, Belgium, Denmark, Finland, France, Germany, Greece, Ireland, Italy, Luxembourg, Netherlands, Portugal, Spain, Sweden, United Kingdom (population 373 billion). *East Asia:* Brunei, China, Hong Kong, Indonesia, Japan, Malaysia, Philippines, Singapore, South Korea, Taiwan, Thailand (population 1.72 billion).

actors were the United States, Japan, and Germany as leaders of the three major regions of the world (see figure 1-1).

The spine of the new world order seems to be trade. Since the first General Agreement on Tariffs and Trade (GATT) was negotiated in 1947, world trade has expanded more rapidly—sometimes two or three times faster—than world production almost every year. Today the World Trade Organization that replaced GATT has 132 members, and it negotiates issues in areas as varied as investments, intellectual property rights, services, communications, the environment, and labor.

Trading patterns changed because of the end of colonialism and the emergence of a single set of global rules. Both of these changes made geography and proximity more important determinants of trading patterns today than before World War II. For example, until World War II the United Kingdom was Canada's most important trading partner. In 1938 Canada's exports to the United Kingdom were almost twice those to the United States.[12] A single set of global trading rules meant that a country would naturally expect to trade more with its neighbors than with distant political allies, and this had the somewhat paradoxical effect of encouraging the development of regional trading areas.[13]

Two scholars of geography summarized the overall effect of these changes: "While the technical impediments to trade over long distances have largely been overcome, intense (macro-) regional trade relations, mainly shaped by a limited number of dominating centres, are becoming an increasingly salient feature of the global trade map."[14] The three leading trading nations in the world were also the center of three regional trading areas—the United States in the Americas, Germany in Europe, and Japan in Asia. Today there is more world trade within than between the three regions.

The most integrated and developed region is in Europe. The Treaty of Maastricht, signed in December 1991, committed the twelve governments of the European Community (EC) to become a European Union (EU) with a single currency and unified foreign and defense policies. One year later, on December 31, 1992, the EU eliminated all its internal barriers. With the cold war's demise, the EU faced a double challenge: to deepen economic relations among its fifteen members while widening to integrate eastern Europe.

There is no single east Asian region, nor is it as easy to locate its center as it is in Europe or North America. Nonetheless, through its multinational corporations Japan has built the railroad connecting many of the Asian economies, and it was the region's engine until it stalled in the early 1990s. Japan's trade with Asia doubled in the 1980s, and its multinationals tripled their foreign output. At the same time Japan established itself as the unquestioned leader in the region in terms of technology, capital goods, and foreign aid.[15] Still, all of Asia depends increasingly on the United States and the European markets, and with China competing with Japan and the Association of Southeast Asian Nations still trying to define the terms of its own integration, any reference to an Asian trading region is an overstatement.

The three nations of North America do not really see themselves as part of a region, but the statistics on trade, migration, investment, and tourism suggest that something more than a trading area exists. If the EU's mistake was to overinstitutionalize, however, North America made the opposite mistake; there are few if any institutions that examine North American problems and opportunities from a regional perspective. Although the United States is a superpower, its two neighbors are its two most important markets; the United States exports more to them (a third of its total trade) than it does to the EU or to Japan and east Asia.

In December 1994 President Bill Clinton hosted the first Summit of the Americas in Miami, and the thirty-four presidents and prime ministers assembled pledged to pursue the establishment of a Free Trade Area of the Americas (FTAA) by the year 2005. Whether that deadline can be met or not, the nature of U.S. integration with South America is of a different order than it is with North America. Indeed, during the 1990s U.S. trade with Mexico alone was roughly equivalent to its trade with the rest of Latin America. NAFTA's extension to an FTAA would expand U.S. exports and regional trade, and over the long term it would integrate the hemisphere. But the really hard social and economic issues of integration that the United States faces in the next decade will have to do with its two closest neighbors. For that reason, in this book we are concentrating on North America.

The increased trade in goods and services among the three diverse countries of North America is just one element of a vast, complicated project of economic and social integration. Before too long North America will be compelled, just as the EC was, to follow the functional logic from reducing tariffs to negotiating standards and fiscal policies. There is nothing inevitable or irreversible about the process, as the EC learned. The question is whether the North American governments can learn from the EC's experience.

The U.S. Congress has a central role in the forging of a North American community because the domestic issues that are at the center of the integration process are those in which it has authority and special interest. But Congress has a short-term, constituency-servicing orientation, and the delicate process of integrating three such different countries often requires a long and broad perspective.

The Three National Legislatures

The three North American countries all have federal governments with substantial powers delegated to the states (or provinces). All are democracies that derive their powers from the consent of the governed by means of free elections, although until very recently most Mexicans had little confidence in the fairness of their electoral process. All three governments have legislatures, but only the U.S. Congress has been independent of the executive branch of government.

Formally, Mexico shares with the United States a presidential system with checks and balances provided by the legislature and the courts. In practice, however, for most of the twentieth century the Mexican president has had almost monarchical power.[16] His powers derived from several sources, but probably the most important was his power to appoint. As long as the Institutional Revolutionary Party (PRI) has ruled, since 1929, the president could appoint not just his cabinet and the justices who headed the courts, but virtually the entire government—the Congress, the governors, and the mayors—because nomination by the PRI was tantamount to winning election. Deputies serve one term, so any future position in the government depended not on their ties to their constituencies, but on whether they pleased the president.

The interplay between the executive and legislative branches of government in Mexico was altered somewhat by the midterm election of 1997. For the first time in its history, the ruling PRI lost its majority in the Chamber of Deputies. The four opposition parties, the Democratic Revolutionary Party (PRD), the National Action Party (PAN), and two smaller parties, the Green Party (PVEM) and the Labor Party (PT), forged a fragile coalition with eleven more votes than the PRI. They then organized the legislature, chairing fourteen of twenty-four committees. The new Mexican Congress therefore emerged as a potentially autonomous political actor. The opposition parties compelled the executive, for the first time, to debate the budget and respond to hostile questions from Congress. Legislation no longer exclusively reflects the preferences of the executive.

The Mexican Senate has constitutional powers similar to those of the U.S. Senate in the area of foreign affairs, but in practice the Mexican Senate has followed the president. Appointments were routinely confirmed; treaties were approved automatically. The PRI still holds an ample majority of 76 of 128 in the Senate, but the opposition has more seats and stronger, more independent voices than before.

In 1993, while the U.S. Congress was arguing the merits and costs of NAFTA, the Mexican Congress passed it virtually without any debate. The gradual democratization of the Mexican political system means that the private debates that have long characterized Mexico's approach to policymaking are likely to become more public and contentious. Important elements in the PRI and the two major opposition parties believe that the Mexican government has been too accommodating to the United States. Although the new Mexican legislature is unlikely to be as independent or critical of the president as the U.S. Congress has been, it might force the president to be more confrontational with the United States.

Canada's parliamentary tradition has remained remarkably stable since its inception in 1867. Two major political parties, the Liberals and the Progressive Conservatives, alternated in power until 1993, when the ruling Conservative Party suffered a devastating defeat, losing all but two seats of their 155-seat majority. The Liberal Party won the election and faced an opposition of two regional parties, the separatist Bloc Quebeçois and the western-based Reform Party.

Unlike in the U.S. and Mexican presidential models, there is no separation between the executive and legislative branches in the parliamentary system. Cabinet ministers are chosen by the prime minister from the members of the governing party. Moreover, party discipline means that the government's agenda is routinely approved by the House of Commons. The Canadian upper house, the Senate, has very different roles than the Senate in either the United States or Mexico. All its members are personal appointments of the prime minister and, once chosen, serve until they are seventy-five years old. As a consequence, the Canadian Senate lacks legitimacy as a legislative body and plays little part in policymaking. In foreign affairs, neither the House of Commons nor the Senate has a profound impact. That is the responsibility of the prime minister and the cabinet.

This is not to suggest that members of Parliament have no influence on Canada's relationships with the United States and Mexico. Members of the governing party may have more influence on Canada's foreign policy than any single member of the U.S. Congress has on U.S. foreign policy, but the influence of members of Parliament (MPs) is channeled individually, not institutionally, through the cabinet, the party, and the foreign policy leadership. Members of the opposition serve as channels through which diverse pressures in the domestic community are conveyed to the government. One vehicle for conveying these concerns is the question period, a time when individual MPs pose questions directly to the prime minister or members of the cabinet.

Members of the opposition have become more aggressive in raising issues in Parliament, but one can identify only a few cases in which a formal parliamentary debate can be said to have had a decisive impact on government behavior in the foreign affairs field.[17] One example was the debate on allegations that members of the Canadian peacekeeping mission in Somalia had tortured and murdered a Somalian youth. The government was forced into lengthy and politically costly hearings into the affair, and the issue dominated the question period for many months.

As for the United States, it is not happenstance that the first article in the U.S. Constitution defines the powers of Congress, the second those of the executive branch of government. A revolution had just been fought against tyranny, and the principal purpose of the Constitution was to protect liberty by limiting, checking, and balancing the executive. Congress was granted the power to tax and spend, to consent to treaties and confirm appointments, to regulate commerce and provide for the common defense. Abraham Soafer, the Reagan administration's legal advisor, wrote:

> The ratification debates confirm what the Constitution suggests—that Congress was to have the final say in foreign and military affairs. The President was to manage diplomatic intercourse and negotiations and to conduct all authorized military operations. But Congress, and especially the Senate, would be able to approve or reject foreign policy in exercising their powers over treaties, appointments, and appropriations.[18]

The view that a docile Congress followed the president in a blissful spirit of bipartisanship before the Vietnam War fractured the national consensus is a myth. Congress has rarely been reticent in using its powers either directly or by encouraging the president to use his.[19] The natural tension between the two branches is exacerbated when each branch is controlled by a different party. For all these reasons Congress is the most open and caustic window on the major debates on the future directions of North America. Whether on an issue of salmon with Canada or an issue of drugs with Mexico, Congress has often preempted presidential "quiet diplomacy" by publicly shaping the debate and making the policy.

But although Congress does admonish the United States' neighbors, it also plays a number of constructive roles in foreign affairs. It establishes new priorities and insists that specific interests be pursued by the executive branch with more forcefulness. These interests usually originate from some domestic source. For example, the human rights policy originated in Congress in the mid-1970s, reflecting a public mood that our foreign policymakers had become too cozy with dictators. In the 1980s Congress insisted on a tougher policy against apartheid and also against drug traffickers; both interests were deeply held, albeit by different constituencies. In some ways, as we point out later, the new congressional assertiveness against Mexico and Canada has less to do with these two countries than it has to do with the fact that they collide against salient U.S. interests.

Relatively recently, Mexico and Canada have begun to follow the activities of the U.S. Congress more than Americans have. To take one illustration, it is far easier to learn about U.S. congressional hearings on Mexico and Canada in those countries than in the United States. And even the blandest statements made in the halls of the U.S. Congress are more likely to provoke attention in our neighbors than if the same comments were made in their own legislatures. This pattern has always been true of U.S. congressional hearings on Mexico, but it is also true of hearings on Canada. In September 1996 the House Foreign Affairs Committee held a hearing on the security and economic implications of a secession by Quebec. University of Toronto Professor Mel Watkins acknowledged the absurdity that no Canadian testified, "and though it was supposed to be for the benefit of the United States, the hearing room was filled with only Canadian journalists."[20] Congress, in brief, has become the pivot around which our neighbors circle.

Organization of This Book

This book is organized in two parts. The first addresses the question of how Congress's activities affect Mexico and Canada and how those two governments have tried recently to influence Congress. The second part explores whether the 103d through 105th Congresses have been different from those in the past, how Congress's influence on trade policy has affected and is likely to affect Mexico and Canada, and how people in the three North American countries view themselves and each other.

In chapter 2 we examine ten cases of how Congress has dealt with Mexico from the U.S.-Mexican War of 1846 through the current debates on drug and immigration issues. In the following chapter Kim Richard Nossal asks a similar set of questions, but these are about Congress's effect on relations with Canada. He also surveys the historical terrain from the Continental Congress's efforts to coerce loyalists in British North America to join the republican experiment to the passage of the Helms-Burton Law of 1996.

Both chapters have similar answers. Both report that Congress has always been deeply involved in trying to influence Mexico and Canada, that the degree of involvement is greater on economic than on security issues, and that Congress is capable of both parochial and statesmanlike behavior. The progressive economic and social integration of North America has apparently not affected the way in which Congress behaves toward its neighbors or toward the issues that concern them. Congress treats both Canada and Mexico the same, usually with little respect.

So what have the Canadians and the Mexicans done about it? Have they timidly accepted congressional insults, or have they lobbied back? George Grayson answers those questions. With very few exceptions, Canada and Mexico followed the diplomatic rule: they conveyed their concerns through the State Department.[21] The two governments changed the rule only when the two free trade agreements came before Congress. The Canadians were first in lobbying for the CUFTA. The Mexicans then followed with an even more elaborate campaign to gain approval of NAFTA. In comparing both countries' lobbying, Grayson finds that they followed the same formula with trivial differences. The Canadian Embassy centralized its campaign, whereas Mexico's was run by its Trade Ministry, and its consulates played an important role. Mexicans also tried to mobilize Mexican Americans, while Canadians focused on Congress.

Have the Congresses of the United States elected since 1992 been different from those in the past? Norman Ornstein, one of America's most perceptive students of American government, answers that question. Like the Congresses elected after World Wars I and II, the post–cold war Congresses (the 104th in 1994 and the 105th in 1996) have been Republican. They have been confronting a Democratic president, have been preoccupied with domestic concerns, and have been uninterested in the world. Only about a fifth of the freshman class of the 105th Congress had served in the armed forces, and a third never had a passport. The turnover also was stunning; 62 percent of those in Congress had been elected since the Berlin Wall fell in 1989, and 42 percent of those in the Senate were serving their first term. Is it surprising that this new Congress has been particularly insensitive to the perspectives of Canada and Mexico?

Congress has changed, but has it changed the way that it deals with the defining issue of North American relations, trade? I. M. Destler concludes that the basic pattern of U.S. trade policy that was established in the 1934 Reciprocal Trade Agreements Act remains unchanged. That pattern involves considerable congressional influence on trade policy, but if the executive branch is responsive to the concerns of Congress, Congress delegates negotiating authority to the president. Destler, however, is concerned about the recent stalemate in trade policy, and he is uncertain whether past patterns of trade policymaking will be able to withstand the increasing weight of ancillary issues such as labor, the environment, and human rights. In brief, Destler provides just one more example as to why Congress is not ready to manage a complex North American integration process. The failure of Congress to approve fast-track negotiating authority for the president before its recess in November 1997 certainly appears to confirm Destler's point.

In the next chapter Neil Nevitte and Miguel Basañez explore the attitudinal parameters of North America by examining the perceptions of people in all three countries on values, each other, and NAFTA. Quite surprisingly, they have found that the values of Canadians, Mexicans, and Americans began to converge in the 1980s in rather important ways. They have documented increasing support for political liberalization, a free market although "not" laissez-faire economic policy, and more autonomy and self-expression in all spheres of life. Moreover, the convergence is not toward an "Americanized system." All three peoples have changed. These surveys suggest that there is a solid foundation that undergirds the movement toward a North American community.

Despite the deep-seated nationalism in all three countries, the people in each like each other. And their views of NAFTA have changed over time. The change is partly due to perceptions of their economies. Not surprisingly, Mexican views of NAFTA declined rather precipitously after the peso crisis. Canadians grew more favorable toward NAFTA after their economy picked itself out of a serious recession in 1993. U.S. views have remained modestly favorable, with intense pockets of opposition in certain sectors. The authors have discovered two other important factors that explain support for NAFTA in all three countries: the trust that people have in their neighbors and the degree to which they value economic individualism. The higher the degree of their trust and regard for economic individualism, the greater their support for NAFTA.

The Pivot

Before 1990 Mexico had its foot on the brake of progress toward integration with the United States, and to a certain extent Canada did before 1988. Theoretically, NAFTA should have changed the relationships, but the tensions continue, and the U.S. Congress has become the controversial pivot. Why? First, the United States is the most powerful partner, and its decisions therefore have a larger effect on its neighbors than they have on the United States. Second, as the agenda of North American integration becomes more domestic, Congress's role increases. Third, as the integration process advances, more problems will be brought before Congress. Fourth, Congress works in the open, and its job is to impress its constituents, often at the price of severely criticizing foreign governments, even those of our neighbors. And fifth, this all sums to an uneasy relationship and an uncertain, ad hoc integration process.

Some of the problems in the relationships can be solved; others just need to be managed better. Each country offers its people a chance to replace their leaders at periodic intervals, and when a large number of new and inexperienced people are elected there is unquestionably a period in which our countries may collide with our neighbors. Each country also has its own style, and it will take time for all of us to learn to adjust to each other. It is our view that awareness of both the complications and the importance of a successful integration process might provide the lubricants that the governments of the United States, Mexico, and Canada need to prevent the gears of the interaction from grinding to a halt.

Notes

1. The Carter Center, "Remarks by Newt Gingrich," in *Final Report: Agenda for the Americas for the 21st Century,* Atlanta, April 28–29, 1997, pp. 20–25.

2. Unpublished letter from Newt Gingrich, House speaker, and Richard Armey, House majority leader, to President Bill Clinton, May 2, 1997.

3. "Rechaza la Comision Permanente el Processo Aplicado por Washington," *La Jornada,* 26 February 1998, p. 40.

4. Robert A. Pastor and Jorge G. Castañeda, *Limits to Friendship: The United States and Mexico* (Knopf, 1988).

5. Cited by Denis Stairs, "The Canadian Dilemma in North America," in Joyce Hoebing, Sidney Weintraub, and M. Delal Baer, eds., *NAFTA and Sovereignty: Trade-offs for Canada, Mexico, and the United States* (Washington, D.C.: Center for Strategic and International Studies, 1996), p. 6.

6. The average annual increase in foreign direct investment in Mexico in 1994–97, despite the economic crisis, was $10 billion, compared with the average in the 1980s of about $2.4 billion. BANAMEX, *Review of the Economic Situation of Mexico*, "Direct Foreign Investment in Mexico," vol. 73, no. 861 (August 1997), pp. 328–32; U.S. Embassy, Mexico City, *Foreign Investment Report, 1996–97*; for 1997, United Nations Economic Commission for Latin America and the Caribbean, *Preliminary Overview of the Economy of Latin America and the Caribbean, 1997* (Santiago, 1997), p. 57.

7. Robert G. Wright, Canadian deputy minister of international trade, "Should NAFTA Be Expanded?" transcript of an address at the Carter Center, Atlanta, September 23, 1997, p. 2.

8. U.S. Government, *Study on the Operation and Effects of the North American Free Trade Agreement*, July 1997, pp. 22–25; Wright, "Should NAFTA Be Expanded?" p. 2.

9. Executive Office of the President, Office of National Drug Control Policy, *Report to Congress: U.S. and Mexico Counterdrug Cooperation*, September 1997, p. 1.

10. See Edward J. Williams, "Discord in U.S.-Mexican Labor Relations and the North American Agreement on Labor Cooperation," in *Bridging the Border: Transforming Mexico-U.S. Relations* (New York: Rowman and Littlefield, 1997); George W. Grayson, "Mexico's Old-Line Union Bosses Are Under Siege," *Wall Street Journal*, February 6, 1998, p. A23.

11. Pastor and Castañeda, *Limits to Friendship*, p. iv.

12. Murray G. Smith, "Canada and Economic Sovereignty," in *NAFTA and Sovereignty*, p. 41.

13. T. Nierop and S. de Vos, "Of Shrinking Empires and Changing Roles: World Trade Patterns in the Postwar Period," *Tijdschrift voor Econ. en Soc. Geografie* (Amsterdam, Netherlands), vol. 79, no. 5 (1988), pp. 343–64. See also Robert A. Pastor, "The North American Free Trade Agreement: Hemispheric and Global Implications," *The International Executive*, vol. 36, no. 1 (January/ February 1994), pp. 3–31.

14. Nierop and de Vos, "Of Shrinking Empires," p. 362.

15. See Peter J. Katzenstein and Takashi Shiraishi, eds., *Network Power: Japan and Asia* (Cornell University Press, 1997), pp. 345–47.

16. The Mexican historian Daniel Cosio Villegas described the Mexican president as "a six-year monarch." See his *El Sistema Politico Mexicano* (Mexico, D.F.: Joaquin Mortiz, 1982), p. 31.

17. R. J. and D. Jackson, *Politics in Canada* (Scarborough: Prentice Hall, 1994), pp. 598–99.

18. Cited in Anthony Lewis, "President and Congress," *New York Times,* December 6, 1988, p. 31.

19. See Robert A. Pastor, "The President versus Congress," in Robert J. Art and Seyom Brown, eds., *U.S. Foreign Policy: The Search for a New Role* (Macmillan, 1992), and "Congress and U.S. Foreign Policy: Comparative Advantage or Disadvantage?" *Washington Quarterly,* vol. 14, no. 4 (Autumn 1991), pp. 101–14.

20. Anthony De Palma, "For Canada, Is U.S. Gaze Offensive or Friendly?" *New York Times,* September 28, 1996, p. 4.

21. In chapter 2 we describe one exception to that rule during the Civil War when Mexican Ambassador Matias Romero lobbied Congress to liberate Mexico from French rule. When he failed he conspired with some in Congress against President Lincoln. After Lincoln's death Romero tried to get General Ulysses S. Grant to invade even though President Andrew Johnson ruled it out.

PART ONE

Congressional Policy toward North America

Chapter 2

Congress and Mexico

Robert A. Pastor and Rafael Fernandez de Castro

M EXICO WAS THE ONLY major country in Latin America
that was wary of the seductive invitation of President
John Kennedy for a share of Alliance for Progress funds. The Mexicans
understood a simple lesson that the rest of Latin America would learn
and that Mexico would forget and then relearn: if a country accepts aid
from the United States, it also has to accept questions, exhortations, and
conditions from the U.S. Congress.

That lesson was brought home to Mexico in 1986 as it was emerging,
hurt and humiliated, from a debt crisis. The United States had stepped
in to help both Mexico and U.S. banks, and in a hearing of the Senate
Foreign Relations Committee Jesse Helms, in his special way, explained
the implications to Mexico:

> If the United States is called upon, both directly and indirectly, to bolster
> the faltering Mexican economy, we have the right to inquire to what extent
> our assistance might be stablilizing or destabilizing. . . . If Mexico wants
> United States help, the Mexican people have no choice, it seems to me, but
> to bring about fundamental political reform. I would say to the Mexican
> government, open up your electoral process to review and inspection. . . .
> Let the press in Mexico speak with an open mind. . . . Let all of the political
> parties in Mexico criticize the process and recommend reforms.[1]

This is the equation that Mexico had tried to avoid: in exchange for
help, and whether with cause or without, the United States was going to
tell Mexico what it needed to do. This came about because of weakness

We express our appreciation to Robin Gault Moriarty for the research we used
in developing the case studies and to Frederick Mayer for his helpful comments
on an earlier draft.

and poor economic policy, but many Mexicans felt it was because of the arrogance and insensitivity of the United States.

Ten years later, on January 17, 1995, Representative David Bonior, a Democratic leader in the House of Representatives whose views are at the opposite end of the political spectrum from those of Helms, nonetheless conveyed a message similar to that of Helms: "If the American people are going to be asked to guarantee up to $40 billion in loans to Mexico, we have a right to demand that Mexico meet certain conditions in return." Bonior wanted to tie Mexican wages to production. His Senate colleagues Alfonse D'Amato and Diane Feinstein wanted to use the loan to stop drugs and illegal aliens. Their colleagues had other demands.

The U.S.-Mexican relationship was supposed to change after passage of the North American Free Trade Agreement (NAFTA) in 1994. The paternalism of the past was expected to be replaced by respect and a new partnership. NAFTA was supposed to lift Mexico into the "first world" economically and politically. None of this happened, and although many in the United States blame it on the collapse of the peso and the corruption of an obsolete system, many in Mexico simply blamed the U.S. Congress.

Despite the best intentions of the two countries' Yale-educated presidents, Bill Clinton and Ernesto Zedillo, the relationship between the United States and Mexico deteriorated after NAFTA came into effect as members of the U.S. Congress insisted on radical changes in the way that Mexico should handle a host of issues, from drugs to immigration. Is Congress playing a more aggressive role toward Mexico? Has NAFTA changed the way Congress relates to Mexico?

The Presidential Focus and the Congressional Distraction

In both the United States and Mexico, the president has always been the center of politics. This is not just because it is simpler to focus on an individual than on an assembly, but mainly because the presidency is the fulcrum of political power in both countries. The U.S. president represents the most powerful country in the world, but he is constrained by a strong Congress and a decentralized federal system. In contrast, the Mexican president represents a weaker country, but he has had powers within his political system that would make his American counterpart swoon. Not knowing the U.S. system, many Mexicans have mistakenly believed that the U.S. Congress is as weak as their own and that the U.S. president is stronger than his Mexican counterpart. Therefore, they have dismissed the U.S. Congress and concentrated their attention and resources on influencing the president and the executive branch of the U.S. government.

In the area of foreign policy, most Americans have also given short shrift to Congress, and there have been fewer studies of Congress's role in foreign policy than of the president's. But those who have studied the subject have found the conventional wisdom about the lack of congressional influence to be inadequate, if not just wrong. In a study in the mid-1970s for a presidential-congressional commission, Robert A. Pastor found that Congress's role in the making of U.S. foreign policy toward Latin America was quite important—that, in brief, "Congress did make a difference." At that time he found that "the existence of Congress means that the United States sells less military equipment, leans harder on human rights issues, re-evaluates stagnant policies and bureaus more often, protects American citizens and corporations more actively and diligently, and is more dilatory and niggardly in giving aid and economic/trade concessions than if the president alone made foreign policy."[2]

In an essay on Congress and Mexico, Donald Wyman argued that the U.S.-Mexican relationship and the role of Congress changed as the distinction between domestic and foreign policy in bilateral affairs blurred: "The foreign-domestic dichotomy long ago ceased to make sense for U.S.-Mexican relations because U.S. policy toward Mexico, at least since the end of the Second World War, has been so much the product of decisions about domestic and economic issues."[3] Therefore, to explain U.S. behavior toward Mexico, Wyman concentrated on domestic policymaking, concluding that power in Congress was fragmented and dispersed among special interests. Subsequent studies have reviewed the attitudes and nodal points in the legislative process as it relates to Mexico.[4] In addition to Wyman's work, these studies have concluded that Congress plays a critical role in U.S.-Mexican relations, not in traditional foreign policy areas such as foreign aid, but in areas related to domestic issues, such as immigration, energy, and trade.

Two essays written by former Mexican diplomats stressed the parochial interests of the U.S. Congress.[5] Both authors confessed their surprise and indignation at the lack of diplomatic courtesy extended by

U.S. congressmen. One criticized the debates as often "offensive to the country of reference."[6] Nevertheless, these studies concluded that Congress is critical in bilateral affairs, and therefore the Mexican government must play an active role in congressional debates and present its positions persuasively. Comparing the 103d and 104th Congresses (1992–94 and 1994–96), Jorge Montaño, Mexico's ambassador to Washington, concluded that the latter, under Republican leadership, showed three worrisome tendencies: it was more isolationist, more conservative, and more confrontational than the former Congress vis-à-vis the executive branch.

Case Studies of U.S.-Mexican Relations

This chapter diverges from previous studies. Instead of seeking the decision points in congressional policymaking toward Mexico or explaining Congress's attitudes toward the United States's neighbor to the south, we examine trends or cycles in Congress's policies toward Mexico. Instead of accepting the conclusions in the literature as to whether Congress's role in policy toward Mexico changed or increased in importance after 1994, we decided to try to understand the nature of Congress's involvement in U.S.-Mexican issues over a period of 150 years—from the U.S.-Mexican War through NAFTA and contemporary drug and immigration issues.

We selected ten cases that range across the full gamut of issues in bilateral relations: classic security issues such as those raised by the U.S.-Mexican War and the French intervention in Mexico, issues related to the protection of the human and property rights of Americans in Mexico, diplomatic and resource issues such as the problem of the salinity of the Colorado River, immigration issues in the 1920s and in the 1980s and 1990s, and trade and financial issues such as those raised by NAFTA and the peso crisis.

Our purpose in examining these cases across time and issue areas is to discern Congress's impact. What difference did Congress make? Did it play a different role in security issues than in domestic issues? Has its role changed in the twentieth century, since the second world war, or since NAFTA? Is there a noticeable difference in Congress's foreign policy as it affects Mexico? We are asking these questions not for some abstract reason, but because Congress matters, and few understand the congressional policymaking process. In the current period, we want to learn what effect, if any, NAFTA has had on Congress and U.S.-Mexican relations. Can Congress accept the partnership implicit in NAFTA, or is there a bias in the process that guarantees congressional paternalism?

U.S. War and Peace with Mexico, 1846–48

The U.S. Constitution grants Congress the power to declare war and to approve treaties, but the president as commander in chief has the actual power to make war and negotiate treaties. President James Polk was a determined expansionist who was looking for an excuse to go to war when Mexican soldiers fired on U.S. soldiers on the Rio Grande, giving him a reason. Whigs in the House of Representatives, led by former president John Quincy Adams, led the opposition, but the declaration of war passed on May 13, 1846, by an overwhelming vote, 174 to 14. In the Senate John Calhoun called Polk the aggressor, not the Mexicans. Others tried to limit the southern march of the U.S. Army, but the declaration was approved by a vote of 40 to 2, with three abstentions, including Calhoun's.

The Whigs, the minority party in both houses of Congress, opposed the war either because they thought it was wrong to be imperialistic or because they feared the new territories would become slave states. They raised these concerns in the debates on appropriations bills, but in the end they helped pass the bills rather than harm the U.S. soldiers in the field. In 1846 the Whigs won control of the House of Representatives and strengthened their position in the Senate. Newly elected to the House, Abraham Lincoln denounced the war but then voted for supplies for the army.

The Mexican army was defeated, and Polk sent Nicholas Trist to negotiate with the Mexicans. He signed the Treaty of Guadalupe Hidalgo on February 2, 1848, taking more than a third of Mexico for the United States. Polk wanted more but realized that the Senate would barely approve of that. The vote on the treaty was 38 to 14. Of the dissenters, six wanted the United States to take more land, but eight believed the treaty gave the United States too much. In summary, Congress acquiesced to the president's decision to go to war, but the growing congressional opposition to the war and further annexations compelled Polk to accept a treaty and restrain his expansionism.

French Intervention in Mexico, 1861–66

Soon after Mexico defaulted on paying its debts to Europe in July 1861, Great Britain, France, and Spain sent troops to collect. The French decided to remain, and in alliance with Mexican monarchists they installed the French Emperor Maximillian on the throne. President Lincoln and the U.S. Congress protested the French intervention and provided some arms covertly to rebels led by Benito Juárez, but both wanted to avoid direct military involvement during the Civil War.

Matías Romero was Mexico's ambassador to Washington during this time, and he went to unusual lengths to secure U.S. help to liberate Mexico. In April 1862 he almost succeeded in getting Congress to lend Mexico $11 million to help it pay its debts. He persuaded Congress to pass resolutions condemning the French intervention. By 1864 he had become so desperate about his country's plight and President Lincoln's reluctance to intervene that he tried to organize a coalition of radical Republicans to replace Lincoln. A few days after Lincoln's death, Romero met with President Andrew Johnson. Having failed to persuade Johnson of the urgency of defeating the French, he met with General Ulysses S. Grant in July 1865. Grant subsequently announced that the Civil War would not be over until the French left Mexico. This was not Johnson's view, although the president dispatched troops to the Rio Grande, and the French left in 1866.[7] In sum, despite persistent interventionist efforts by Romero, Congress followed the president's lead, waiting for victory in the Civil War before bringing its force to bear on the issue.

The Mexican Revolution and American Property Holders, 1910–16

From 1877 until 1910, Mexico experienced the most dramatic period of economic modernization in its history. Under the authoritarian rule of Porfirio Diaz, Mexico welcomed capital and technology from all over the world. Railroads were built, connecting villages to cities. Oil was discovered, and old and new mines attracted investments. Rapid development widened the income gap between the small upper class and the masses of the poor.

Claiming that the 1910 election was a fraud, Francisco Madero (the popular candidate of the Anti Re-electionist Party that opposed Diaz's repeated manipulation of the electoral process) called for an insurrection. Diaz resigned in 1911 and Madero won election and took power, but his promise of reforms unsettled the oligarchs and foreign investors. In March 1912 9,000 U.S. citizens were advised to leave Mexican states that were considered dangerous. With the complicity of the U.S. ambassador and wealthy businessmen, the Mexican military overthrew and killed Madero in February 1913. This led to chaos and social revolution. Many U.S. citizens were killed, kidnapped, ransomed, or imprisoned, and the property of U.S. citizens—amounting to $1 billion—was raided, stolen, or looted. President Wilson recalled the U.S. ambassador, refused to recognize General Victoriano Huerta's coup, and called for a return to constitutional order.

Intensive research among public records has surprisingly revealed only a single reference of congressional involvement. In January 1915 Senator Morris Sheppard of Texas appealed to the State Department on behalf of three men sentenced to death by the Mexican president. Given the number of American citizens and investors affected by the social turmoil, one would expect Congress to have been much more involved. Perhaps one reason why Congress was not more involved was because the president himself was deeply engaged in the matter.

The massacre of fifteen people in New Mexico by Pancho Villa in January 1916 awoke Congress, and numerous legislators demanded that Wilson intervene militarily. Congress authorized sending the army and navy to Mexico and offered a $50,000 reward for the capture of Villa. After Wilson sent General John Pershing, the majority of the Senate asked for the troops to remain in Mexico until the murderers were punished.

Congress was outraged by the chaos in Mexico and its harm to U.S. citizens and property holders. Its role in this case was constituent-rooted, reminding the State Department of its responsibility to protect U.S. citizens abroad. President Wilson was also sensitive to the implications of increased tensions with Mexico in the context of war in Europe, and he acted quickly to settle the differences before bringing the United States into the war.

The U.S. Debates on Immigration Policy, 1921–30

"When the country was new, it might have been good policy to admit foreigners. But it is so no longer." These are the words of a congressman, and they have a contemporary ring, but they were uttered by

Representative Harrison G. Otis of Massachusetts on June 26, 1797, when the United States had but 4 million people.[8] Otis failed to persuade his colleagues, and since then more than 63 million people have immigrated to the United States.[9]

The first time Americans began seriously to consider quantitative limits on immigration was after the massive flow of immigrants at the turn of the century—more than 16 million from 1890 to 1914. In 1921 and 1924 Congress debated and passed two laws to restrict the numbers and origins of immigrants. Much of its effort was targeted at immigration from southern and eastern Europe, and racism permeated the debate.

As a positive gesture to Mexico, Congress spared it the "head tax" imposed on immigrants. In 1924, however, Georgia Senator William Harris argued for a quota to limit the numbers of Mexican immigrants. He feared the entry of as many as 100,000 Mexicans and said the Mexicans were "as undesirable as any people coming into this country," and he wanted to "get rid of them." This view had its adherents in Congress, but most were concerned that illegal European migrants could use Mexico as a back door to the United States. The majority in Congress voted to exempt Mexico and Latin America from any quotas to show that the United States wanted good relations and would accord the region special treatment. Also, there was no reason to fear migration from the region then. "Remember Mexico is not a populous country," said one senator. "There will no great influx if the border is left open."[10]

In fact, as immigration from Europe was restricted, the numbers from Mexico soon increased, and a debate ensued in 1930 as to whether to restrict Mexican immigrants. That debate divided those in Congress representing businesses or farms in the Southwest who wanted cheap Mexican labor, as well as those who opposed immigration from Mexico for racial reasons. That debate was stalemated in Washington, but neither argument was appreciated in Mexico.

Mexico's Expropriation of Foreign Oil Companies, 1938

After foreign oil companies rejected the Mexican Supreme Court's decision that they must compensate their workers, President Lazaro Cardenas expropriated all sixteen foreign oil companies. President Franklin Roosevelt acknowledged Mexico's right to expropriate foreign property but said that international law required it to offer prompt and effective compensation. The oil companies protested, calling the expropriation "robbery," and lobbied the foreign governments involved to impose sanctions on Mexico. Mexico's expropriation of U.S. silver companies also stirred concern in the United States.

Roosevelt took a moderate approach, influenced by his ambassador to Mexico and by the need to have good relations with Mexico as the second world war approached. The only reference to Congress's involvement in this issue that we have been able to find was a resolution introduced by Representative M. J. Kennedy asking for a report on the expropriation and the recall of U.S. Ambassador Josephus Daniels for questioning by Congress.

The Colorado River Salinity Treaty, 1973

The water of the Colorado River supplies the needs of numerous people in the southwestern part of the United States and the Mexicali Valley of northwestern Mexico. Over time, however, and particularly after the construction of the Wellton-Mohawk Project in Arizona in 1961, the water that reached Mexico had unacceptably high levels of salinity. In the 1960s an estimated 7,000 acres of Mexican farm land were destroyed, forcing some 500 farmers a year off their land.[11] Mexican protests were largely ignored.

The issue languished at the working levels of the U.S. and Mexican foreign ministries until Mexican legislators pressed their counterparts in the U.S. Congress in the annual meetings of the Mexico-U.S. Interparliamentary Group. The representatives to the group from the U.S. Congress, led by Senate Majority Leader Mike Mansfield, were convinced of the need to respond to Mexico's concerns, and they prompted President Richard Nixon to reach an agreement with Mexico in 1973.[12] The United States agreed to build a desalination plant near Yuma, Arizona, and a canal to carry off the brine.

Congress's role was not only critical in pressing the administration to negotiate a solution to the problem, but it also was central to approving the funding. In 1974 congressional leaders approved the State Department's request for $155 million and added $125 million for other salinity control projects. Both bills were approved in one-sided votes—a vote of 403 to 8 in the House and a voice vote in the Senate.

Drug Trafficking, 1969 to the Present

The penetrable 1,850-mile border between the United States and Mexico has long been an invitation to international drug traffickers. At times, such as in 1969 with Operation Intercept, the U.S. government has tried to stop the flow by choking the border. President Nixon's action grabbed the attention of the Mexican government but not its cooperation. By 1975, according to U.S. government estimates, Mexico had become the source of 80 to 90 percent of the heroin and 95 percent of the marijuana entering the United States. The Carter administration tried a more cooperative approach—providing aircraft for aerial spraying—and this proved more successful. By 1980 Mexico's share of the U.S. supply of heroin had declined to about 25 percent, and its share of the supply of marijuana was reduced to about 10 percent.[13]

America's drug problem worsened significantly in the mid-1980s with the spread of cocaine. Congress and the president competed with each other to see who could be tougher in the war on drugs, and the result was the Comprehensive Crime Control Act of 1984, constant congressional hearings, and a doubling of the drug program budget from 1981 to 1986. The Omnibus Act of 1986 doubled funding once again.

Mexico did not produce cocaine, but it provided the easiest route for shipment to the United States because of proximity, corruption, and reduced state capacity as a result of the Mexican debt crisis. In February 1985 Enrique Carmarena, an agent of the U.S. Drug Enforcement Administration in Guadalajara, was abducted and murdered. One year later, as Congress was drafting the Omnibus Act, a tape recording of Camarena's torture by a Mexican federal police official was made public. Senator Jesse Helms said the source of the drug problem was the same as that of Mexico's other problems—"a government dominated by corruption and fraud."[14]

The 1986 Omnibus Act was a drug law that contained a provision that required the president annually to certify to Congress whether countries involved in the drug trade were cooperating fully with the United States. If the president "decertified" a country, he would have to stop aid, vote against loans in the international development banks, and impose trade sanctions unless he declared it in the national interest not to do so. If the president certified a country, Congress had a thirty-day period to assess and reverse that decision by means of a joint resolution. This certification policy proved to be an annual source of tension in the relationship between the United States and Mexico.

No matter how much the U.S. and Mexican presidents try to put the best face on the relationship between their countries, most of Congress emphasizes the warts. In 1987, however, when the Senate reviewed the president's decision, Senator Richard Lugar helped defeat an amendment proposed by Helms, which would have decertified Mexico. "Mexico-bashing sometimes is popular," said Lugar, "but it is never a good idea."[15]

Each crisis or scandal in Mexico in the 1990s proved an occasion for individual members of Congress to demand that the Mexican government take additional steps to stop drug trafficking. During the peso crisis, for example, Senators Alfonse D'Amato and Dianne Feinstein insisted that Mexico should not get any loans until it took additional steps against drug trafficking.

On the eve of the certification decision in March 1997, General Gutierrez Rebollo, the head of the Mexican Institute for Combatting Drugs, was arrested and charged with protecting one of the most sought-after drug lords. Despite this report, President Clinton certified Mexico. Soon after the House of Representatives approved a measure that gave Mexico ninety days to show improvements. One week later the Senate voted for a five-month extension. The president made this a central issue in his talks with President Zedillo in May 1997 and reported to Congress in September.[16]

Congress, in brief, remains the principal engine and driver behind policy on the drug issue in U.S.-Mexican relations.

U.S. Trade Policy and the North America Free Trade Agreement, 1990 to the Present

In the spring of 1990 Mexican President Carlos Salinas reversed 150 years of Mexican policy and proposed a free trade agreement with the United States. He did so because Mexico had already reduced its trade barriers and he wanted to secure the U.S. market and promote more foreign investment.[17] Canada had already negotiated a free trade agreement with the United States, but it decided to make the agreement trilateral.

The U.S. Constitution gives Congress the preeminent role in making trade policy, but in 1934, after writing the disastrous Smoot-Hawley Tariff, Congress stopped making tariff policy. It delegated to the president the power to negotiate trade agreements, but it granted the authority for fixed periods and defined the parameters of the agreements—

how much to raise or reduce tariffs and with which countries. The United States negotiated twenty-two bilateral agreements from 1934 to 1945. After the war, it took the lead in establishing a multilateral General Agreement on Tariffs and Trade, which significantly reduced tariff barriers worldwide. By 1974 the agenda had shifted to nontariff barriers, and Congress approved a new instrument—fast-track negotiating authority—which permitted the president to negotiate wide-ranging agreements that would be submitted to Congress for votes without amendments.

Although Congress's role in trade policy had been reduced, it retained substantial power regarding the timing and the substance of NAFTA and whether it would be approved. The Salinas initiative had precipitated an unusual reversal of roles. Since the U.S.-Mexican War and especially since the Mexican Revolution, Mexico had tried to keep the United States at arm's length, fearing U.S. power and influence. It had built walls to keep out U.S. goods, capital, and ideas. But this had not inhibited or discouraged the U.S. government from trying to dismantle those walls.

When Salinas offered to take down the walls, the United States, as a nation, exchanged places with Mexico. Its former confidence was replaced with fear that a free trade area would harm U.S. jobs, the environment, and the quality of life. The executive branch of the U.S. government did not share those fears, but Congress exaggerated them. The debate within the nation and the Congress was between those who saw NAFTA as a great opportunity to develop Mexico and restructure U.S. industry and those who feared a loss of jobs and and a decline in living standards. In this debate the Republicans were mostly in the first group and the Democrats mostly in the second. That is why President George Bush pressed to complete negotiations before the Republican Convention in 1992 and why Bill Clinton, who was seeking the presidency, was hoping that national debate on the issue would be postponed until after the election.

In the end, Clinton favored the agreement. In an address in October 1992 in North Carolina, he said that he would support NAFTA, but only if the Mexicans would agree to negotiate side agreements on labor and the environment. In December 1992 Bush signed the agreement. After the inauguration of Clinton, his administration negotiated side agreements in an effort to accommodate the concerns of labor and the environmentalists, but the president waited until September 1993 to sign the agreements and send them to Capitol Hill for approval. The debate was intense and difficult, but on November 17 the House passed it by a vote of 234 to 200. The Senate approved it a few days later by a vote of 61 to 38.

Although NAFTA was approved without amendment, the president responded to a host of congressional concerns in order to win the necessary support. For example, to secure the vote of California Representative Esteban Torres, the administration accepted the idea of a North American Development Bank. The administration hoped that others in the House would follow Torres, but this proposal secured only one vote—or, as one leader said, "One man, one bank."[18] The original purpose of this bank was to make loans in geographical areas that were being left behind economically, much as the European Development Loan Fund does. By the time the bank opened, however, its appropriations were reduced, and its charter was narrowed to assist only environmental projects at the border.

To attract the support of legislators from sugar-producing states, the Clinton administration gained Mexico's agreement not to export sugar to the United States for the indefinite future. To secure the votes of legislators from Florida and California, similar understandings were reached about the imposition of tariffs on citrus and vegetables if imports surged.[19] Beyond addressing these specific issues, Congress's role was to slow the process and ensure that individual concerns were addressed and, when possible, accommodated. Labor issues and the environment were incorporated into side agreements. Other issues, including Mexico's authoritarian political system, were raised by both the opponents of NAFTA and those who favored NAFTA but wanted Mexico's political system to become more democratic. Three years later, Congress reviewed NAFTA. A few proposed abandoning the agreement, and some suggested changes, but all agreed that NAFTA should be closely monitored.

Although the agreement was supposed to be a watershed in relations between the U.S. and Mexico that would lead to a genuine partnership, in fact the agreement seemed to marshal ambivalent and uncertain feelings from each side. In the end, America's reluctance to associate too closely with a poor, authoritarian neighbor left many Mexicans feeling that they were badly treated.

Illegal Immigration, 1986–96

From the second world war until 1964, the United States and Mexico maintained a "bracero" program that permitted large numbers of Mexicans to undertake seasonal labor in the United States. In 1965 the U.S. Congress passed a new immigration law that repealed the quota system based on national origins and replaced it with one that allotted a quota to each country. Each country received a maximum quota of 20,000, but exceptions for family unification permitted Mexican immigration to be four to six times the "maximum" quota each year. With the passage of this law the source of immigration shifted from Europe to the third world, with the largest numbers of both legal and illegal migrants coming from Mexico.

Beginning in 1971, Congress began wrestling with the problem of how to stop illegal immigration. Presidents Ford, Carter, and Reagan all made proposals, as did a select commission established by Congress. Finally, in 1986 Congress approved the Immigration Reform and Control Act, which augmented the border control and imposed sanctions on businessmen who employed workers who were in the United States illegally. At the same time, reflecting the true ambivalence of the country on migration, Congress also legalized those who had been in the country illegally for many years (amounting to 3.1 million people, 75 percent of whom were Mexicans), and it provided for special agricultural workers to help growers in the Southwest.

Employer sanctions could work only if businesses could identify those who resided in the United States legally and those who did not. This was made more difficult because of the surfeit of illegal documents, and economic crises in Mexico increased the number of Mexicans going north. California passed its Proposition 187 to stop the provision of education or benefits to children of illegal immigrants in a one-sided vote, and the social tensions produced by high levels of immigration worsened. Signs of that unease could be viewed in the movement in many states to make English the official language, the racist comments on radio talk shows in the Southwest, and the presidential campaign of Pat Buchanan, who called for the use of a fence and the National Guard to keep out all Mexicans.

For all these reasons, the 104th Congress with its newly Republican majority revisited the issue and passed the Illegal Immigration Reform and Immigrant Responsibility Act (IIRIRA) of 1996. Along with the

Welfare Reform Act and the Anti-Terrorist Act, the IIRIRA removed benefits and judicial safeguards for immigrants who were in the United States illegally. IIRIRA also strengthened employer sanctions, barred people with fraudulent documents or no documents, and added funds for enforcement. Persons who overstayed their visas by more than six months would be barred from reentering the United States for three years. The Mexican Foreign Ministry estimated that 300,000 to 800,000 Mexicans could be affected by the various provisions, which caused an uproar in Mexico.

Although some in the 104th Congress were against Mexican immigrants, the dominant mood was against illegal immigrants. It is interesting that Congress did not reduce the very large numbers (averaging 1 million per year) of legal immigrants allowed. President Clinton approved all the laws after trying to blunt the impact of some of the more egregious provisions, such as barring education of children of illegal migrants and depriving legal residents of normal benefits.

The Peso Crisis, 1994–95

NAFTA came into effect in 1994, and trade soared as the proponents had promised, but two unanticipated events occurred at both ends of the year. On January 1 the Zapatista National Liberation Front launched a revolution in the southern Mexican state of Chiapas, decrying NAFTA for marginalizing Mexico's poor. This "revolution" unsettled foreign investors and others with no experience with or knowledge of Mexico, but the overall impact of the Zapatista uprising was negligible compared with the shock of the peso devaluation at year's end. When the government let the peso float, it sank by about 40 percent.

Meanwhile, on January 3, 1995, the Republicans took full control of the Congress for the first time in forty years. President Clinton proposed a $40 billion loan guarantee for Mexico, and Speaker of the House Newt Gingrich and Senate Majority Leader Bob Dole both endorsed the rescue package. However, the Republican leaders had misjudged the new crop of Republican representatives and senators, who were very critical of the bail-out and of Mexico. When the administration decided to provide guarantees by using the Exchange Stabilization Fund rather than seeking to pass a law, many in Congress protested, but the leadership sighed with relief.

Nonetheless, the package that was designed to help Mexico was greatly affected by congressional skepticism. It required a very rapid and severe adjustment by Mexico that would be fully monitored by U.S. government officials, including the U.S. Congress. In some ways the peso rescue package affected congressional and public attitudes toward Mexico more than NAFTA. This was regrettable, because NAFTA reflected a partnership based on reciprocal rules governing trade, and the peso rescue reflected the kind of donor-recipient paternalism that Mexico had hoped would be consigned to history.

Searching for Patterns

Even a cursory review of U.S.-Mexican relations confirms that Congress's influence is not a recent phenomenon. The U.S. Congress has played a consistently important role in U.S.-Mexican relations from the Mexican war through the drug and immigration crises of today. The particular role it has played has varied with the issue and the period. On security issues Congress has generally deferred to the president's prerogative, particularly when the United States has been at war, but it has alternately discouraged presidents from using force and encouraged them to use it. On economic and social issues, in response to constituent concerns, Congress has driven the president and the policy.

Congress was loath to deny President Polk a declaration of war, but for mixed motives it restrained Polk from annexing more of Mexico than Nicholas Trist had negotiated in the Treaty of Guadalupe Hidalgo. During the Civil War Congress was sympathetic to Mexico's desire to be liberated from French imperial rule from self-interest as well as because of the Mexican ambassador's persuasiveness. Nevertheless, the president and Congress understood that securing a Union victory in the Civil War took precedence over removing France from Mexico. Congress also seemed to defer to Presidents Taft, Wilson, and Roosevelt, letting the presidents choose how to protect U.S. interests affected by the Mexican Revolution.

Congress has always played a much more important role in domestic issues such as immigration, trade, drugs, and the environment. In the cases that we have reviewed, Congress was aware of the Mexican dimensions of these issues, but it was of two minds as to how to respond. It has been solicitous of Mexico, and it has been imperious.

Often it has been both at the same time, and occasionally a single member of Congress has spoken with both sentiments.

At the outset of the peso crisis on January 11, 1995, Senator Alfonse D'Amato rose to praise Mexico and urge President Clinton to spend more time on the issue and provide substantial assistance quickly: "Charity begins at home. Mexico and Canada are part of the American family. . . . Our national security and our economic well-being are inextricably linked to the health and stability of Mexican society and the Mexican economy. . . . We must help the Mexicans stabilize the peso, to renegotiate their debt, and to develop an economic strategy of long-term investment and growth."[20] Two months later, after conservative opposition emerged against the rescue package that he had recommended, D'Amato reversed his course and asked, "Why are we doing this?" His answer: Clinton had "ignored the will of the American people to bail out a mismanaged Mexican government." He called Mexico "a corrupt, dictatorial government" and said, "It is ironic that we spend as much time as we have with Mexico," although two months earlier he had called Mexico a friend and urged the president to spend more time on its problems.[21] By January 1996 D'Amato claimed he had called the "Clinton bail-out an ill-conceived disaster" from the beginning.[22]

D'Amato is unusual. More typically, some members of Congress have been respectful toward Mexico, and others have been arrogant. Interestingly, the Mexican press often magnifies the voices of the more insensitive Americans—typified by a headline that read, "U.S. Senators Lambast Mexico on Drugs"—and the more moderate voices are often harder to hear.[23] The U.S. press repeats this pattern in reverse, exaggerating the anti-American statements of Mexican politicians and ignoring the statesmen.

In its consideration of the immigration laws of 1921 and 1924, Congress exempted Mexico from the restrictions it imposed because of the "special relationship" between the two countries—and, frankly, because there were few emigrants from Mexico then. At the same time, however, individual members of Congress did not conceal their disdain of the idea of admitting more Mexicans. This schizophrenic approach to Mexico has also been evident in the way Congress has dealt with drug, trade, and financial issues. Responding to domestic concerns, Congress has attacked the problem and generally adopted or acquiesced to the correct approach, but some members have not been able to resist insulting Mexico. On drugs, Congress has not decertified Mexico; on trade, it approved NAFTA; on the peso rescue, it acquiesced to the package. But in each case, instead of using the policy to forge a respectful partnership, some members have remarked on our neighbor's unsuitability.

It needs to be said that when Congress makes foreign policy it does so with one eye on the foreign government and the other on the president and the U.S. State Department.[24] In December 1988 the House Select Committee on Narcotics Abuse and Control visited Mexico and received a blast of outrage over the certification policy from senior Mexican government officials. The congressional delegation became very defensive and explained that the certification process was "primarily directed toward the U.S. Administration" because it "was viewed by the U.S. Congress as not doing enough to address the drug crisis."[25] This explanation bewildered Mexicans: was Congress blaming Reagan or Mexico? The congressional leaders dodged the issue and instead extolled the virtues of cooperation.

On NAFTA, Congress requested that the president submit a report evaluating NAFTA's progress in three years—by July 1997—to ensure that the president would continue to pursue U.S. interests on trade. Similarly, Congress passed a resolution requiring periodic reports on the U.S. Treasury's monitoring of Mexico's repayment of the 1995 loan.

Although Congress sometimes delegates important authority to the president, it never grants unfettered authority. It always retains its oversight capacity by compelling the president to renew his authority after an interval and obtain approval for funds. And the number of reports the president is mandated by statute to give to Congress has proliferated over the years. Human rights reports must be submitted annually along with reports on the voting records of all countries in the United Nations. The House and Senate Foreign Affairs Committees often review these reports and rarely hesitate to identify their different views.

Although a few individuals have become experts on Mexico, such as Senator Charles Sumner in the 1860s, Senator Mike Mansfield in the 1970s, and Representatives Bill Richardson and Jim Kolbe in the 1990s, the vast majority of legislators view Mexico through the prism of their own constituencies' interests. The relationship between the U.S. and Mexican presidents and their cabinets has improved dramatically, especially since NAFTA. With few exceptions, executive branch personnel in the United States are very careful and judicious in their public statements about their Mexican counterparts. This, of course, contrasts with the comments made almost routinely by legislators.

In the United States the executive branch is sometimes able to use the negative comments of the legislators as the "bad cop" to their "good cop" to show how much worse a problem could get if Mexico were not cooperative. In that way Congress is a useful lever for the president, allowing him to turn congressional anger to his advantage in pressing Mexico for more "progress" on a particular issue.

As we review the ten cases we have presented, we see that Congress has played an important role throughout the entire history of U.S.-Mexican relations. In the broader sweep of history, perhaps the most interesting and disturbing conclusion is that NAFTA has not changed congressional attitudes toward Mexico—at least not in a positive way. The anticipated partnership has not occurred; if anything, Congress seems more insulting toward Mexico and more demanding in a public way than it was before.

Notes

1. *Situation in Mexico,* Hearings before the Senate Subcommittee on Western Hemisphere Affairs of the Foreign Relations Committee, 99 Cong. 2 sess. (Government Printing Office, 1986).

2. Robert A. Pastor, "Congress's Impact on Latin America: Is There a Madness in the Method?" in Abraham F. Lowenthal, ed., *The Conduct of Routine Economic Relations: U.S. Foreign Policy-Making to Latin America,* vol. 3, appendix 1 (Washington, D.C.: Commission on the Organization of the Government for the Conduct of Foreign Policy [Murphy Commission], June 1975), p. 269.

3. Donald L. Wyman, "The United States Congress and the Making of U.S. Policy toward Mexico," Working Paper in U.S.-Mexican Studies 13 (San Diego: University of California, 1981), pp. 2–3.

4. Rafael Fernandez de Castro, "La Importancia del Congreso de EUA en la Relacion Mexico-EUA," *Cuadernos Semestrales del CIDE,* no. 20, 1986; Guadalupe Gonzalez, "Banco de Datos para el Estudio de Mexico en el Congreso de Estados Unidos (1981–1982): Un primer Acercamiento," Documentos de Trabajo 6 Division de Estudios Internacionales (Mexico: Centro de Investigaciones y Docenia Economicas CIDE, 1993).

5. Jorge Montaño, "El Congreso de Estados Unidos y su Política hacia México," in Monica Verea Campos, Rafael Fernández de Castro, y Sidney Weintraub, eds., *Nueva Agenda Bilateral en la Relacion Mexico-Estados Unidos* (Mexico, D.F.: FCE, 1998), pp. 366–400; Herman Von Bertrab, *El Redescubrimiento de América* (México, D.F.: FCE, 1996).

6. Montaño, "El Congreso de Estados Unidos y su Política hacia México," p. 6.

7. For a full description of Matias Romero's lobbying, see Thomas D. Schoonover, trans. and ed., *Mexican Lobby: Matias Romero in Washington, 1861–67* (University of Kentucky Press, 1986).

8. Cited in Earl G. Harrison, *Immigration Policy of the United States* (Foreign Policy Reports of the Foreign Policy Association, April 1, 1947), p. 1.

9. U.S. Department of Justice, *1995 Statistical Yearbook of the Immigration and Naturalization Service* (Washington: Immigration and Naturalization Service, March 1997), p. 27.

10. For these citations and a general history of U.S. immigration policy with regard to Mexico and Latin America, see Robert A. Pastor, "U.S. Immigration Policy and Latin America: In Search of the 'Special Relationship,'" *Latin American Research Review*, vol. 19, no. 3 (1984).

11. See Sidney Weintraub, *A Marriage of Convenience: Relations between Mexico and the United States* (Oxford University Press, 1990), pp. 168–70.

12. See *Report* by Senator Mike Mansfield to the Senate Foreign Relations Committee on a Study Mission to Mexico, May 1973. For a discussion of the impact of the Inter-Parliamentary Committee, see Robert Pastor, "Congress's Impact on Latin America," pp. 208–09.

13. These are U.S. government estimates. For a summary of U.S.-Mexican cooperation on drug trafficking, see Robert A. Pastor and Jorge G. Castañeda, *Limits to Friendship: The United States and Mexico* (Vintage Books, 1989), pp. 265–77.

14. *Hearings on Mexico,* Hearings before the Senate Committee on Foreign Relations, 99 Cong. 2 sess. (Government Printing Office, 1986), p. 41.

15. Cited in Robert A. Pastor and Jorge G. Castañeda, *Limits to Friendship,* p. 272.

16. Executive Office of the President, *Report to Congress,* vol. 1, "U.S. and Mexico Counterdrug Cooperation" (Office of National Drug Control Policy, September 1997).

17. For a fuller description of NAFTA and its origins and consequences, see Robert A. Pastor, *Integration with Mexico: Options for U.S. Policy* (Twentieth Century Fund, 1993).

18. Cited in Dan Balz, "White House Intensifies NAFTA Push," *Washington Post*, November 1, 1993, pp. A1, A7.

19. David S. Cloud, "Bill Drafted; It's Down to the Wire," *Congressional Quarterly Weekly Report*, November 6, 1993, p. 3012.

20. Alfonse D'Amato, "Regarding the Economic Crisis in Mexico," *Congressional Record*, January 11, 1995, p. S812.

21. Alfonse D'Amato, "Mexican Peso Crisis and Bailout," *Congressional Record*, March 8, 1995, pp. S3664–66.

22. *Congressional Record,* January 30, 1996, p. S558.

23. Thomas Catan, "U.S. Senators Lambast Mexico on Drugs," *Mexico City Times,* March 29, 1996, p. 1. At the end of the article Catan refers to comments by Senator Christopher Dodd to his fellow senators asking them to hold up a mirror to themselves and ask how well the United States is doing against drugs before they condemn Mexico.

24. For a fuller development of this thesis, see Robert A. Pastor, *Congress and the Politics of U.S. Foreign Economic Policy* (Berkeley: University of California Press, 1980).

25. U.S. House of Representatives Select Committee on Narcotics Abuse and Control, *Report: Study Mission to Central America and the Caribbean,* 100 Cong. 2 sess., December 8–20, 1988, p. 8.

Chapter 3

Congress and Canada

Kim Richard Nossal

IN AUGUST AND SEPTEMBER 1988 and then again in November 1993, the two houses of the U.S. Congress approved two far-reaching trade agreements involving Canada that promised to radically transform the North American economy. In March and July 1996, the House of Representatives and the Senate passed two pieces of legislation designed to tighten American sanctions against Cuba, Libya, and Iran. The Cuban Liberty and Democratic Solidarity Act—colloquially known as the Helms-Burton Act after its sponsors, Senator Jesse Helms of North Carolina and Representative Dan Burton of Indiana—provides for the imposition of a range of punishments on non-Americans who choose to do business with Cuba. The Iran and Libya Sanctions Act of 1996, introduced by Senator Alfonse D'Amato of New York, permits the U.S. government to take punitive measures against anyone making substantial investments in the oil and gas sectors of the Iranian or Libyan economies; it was passed unanimously by Congress on July 23 and signed into law by President Bill Clinton on August 5, 1996.[1]

Juxtaposing the embrace of such farsighted legislation as the two free trade pacts and such parochial extraterritorial legislation as the Helms-Burton and D'Amato legislation vividly demonstrates the degree to which the Congress of the United States has been—and will no doubt continue to be—a North American political actor with essentially protean characteristics that pull it in opposing directions. Members of Congress have at times been careless, self-indulgent, shortsighted, and myopically parochial toward their northern neighbor. However, members of Congress have also proven to be farsighted, statesmanlike, and endowed with a regional vision.

Such an apparently inconsistent approach is similar to the "cry-and-sigh" syndrome identified by Robert Pastor in the case of trade policy. As he reminds us, cries of alarm at the protectionism of members of Congress are perennially followed by sighs of relief when Congress actually approves another part of a progressively more open trading regime.[2] This chapter identifies a comparable syndrome in Canada–United States relations: on the one hand, members of Congress tend to say and do things guaranteed to disturb the harmony of the Canada–United States relationship, either by causing offense to or injuring the interests of Canadians; on the other hand, Congress has persistently demonstrated over the history of the relationship that it is capable of acts of statesmanship that have far-reaching and generally positive effects on (and for) Canadians.

The influence of Congress on Canadian-American relations that can be so readily observed in the 1990s has deep historical roots, for Canada has always been affected by the changing moods of members of Congress and the fluctuating relationship between the legislative and executive branches of the American government. However, given the quotidian involvement of Congress in the hugely complex and multifaceted Canadian-American relationship, it would be impossible to provide a comprehensive survey of the impact of Congress on Canada in this chapter. Instead a series of vignettes drawn from the past 200 years is used to demonstrate the effects of Congress on Canada, both parochial and regional.

From American Independence to Canadian Confederation

The influence of Congress on the Canadian-American relationship can easily be traced back to the Continental Congress and the efforts of the delegates meeting in Philadelphia to convince those loyal to the British Crown in other parts of British North America to join in the republican experiment. Both persuasion and coercion were used. One of the Articles of Confederation held out the carrot: Canadians were promised all the benefits of the Union should they wish to join, and letters from the Continental Congress circulated in British North America urging them to do so. But at the same time, a stick was used: the same letters offering the benefits of the Union also threatened reprisals from American patriots if the Canadians maintained loyalty to Britain.[3]

Such involvement and interest of members of Congress in their neighbors to the north was evident throughout the 1800s, mostly through the exercise of powers granted to the upper house of the Congress under the Constitution of 1787 that were—and indeed remain—unique in the international system. The necessary involvement of the legislature in declarations of war and the approval of international treaties would involve the Senate and the House of Representatives in making decisions that would deeply affect the evolution of U.S. relations with Canada.

For example, the arrival of the "War Hawks" in the Congress that assembled in Washington in March 1812 had a powerful impact on President James Madison's decision in June of that year to seek a congressional declaration of war on Britain—with the idea of seizing Canada. Members of Congress such as Henry Clay and Richard Johnson of Kentucky, John Calhoun of South Carolina, and Felix Grundy of Tennessee clamored for a war of "national honor" against Britain. The vote in Congress on this issue reflected regional divisions and local interests. Although Madison cited the rights of American neutrality—freedom from British harassment of American shipping and the British propensity to impress American seamen—as the primary justification for declaring war, senators from the northeastern states, where maritime interests were concentrated, voted against war. The declaration was carried by votes from the South and the frontier states, where there was considerable bitterness over British attempts to create a separate Indian buffer state in the Midwest by supporting and inciting Indian subversion in the Indiana Territory and also over the protection that the British provided to Tecumseh, the Indian leader who had fled to Canada after the Battle of Tippecanoe in November 1811.

Just as the war-making powers of Congress had an impact on the willingness of Congress to embark on war in 1812, the treaty-making powers of the United States legislature were critical in the settlement that brought the War of 1812 to a close. The Treaty of Ghent of December 1814 had long-term effects on the evolution of relations between Canada and the United States. The agreement gave territorial gains to neither side, but did establish boundary commissions to settle the welter of territorial disputes that still plagued the northeastern border of the United States with Canada. The Senate embraced that treaty; it also approved the Rush-Bagot agreement of 1817, which provided a naval arms control regime for the Great Lakes and Lake Champlain, and it approved the Convention of 1818, which extended the Canadian-American border from Lake of the Woods west along the forty-ninth parallel to the crest of the Rocky Mountains. The enthusiasm for rapprochement with Britain that pervaded Congress was no doubt a reflection of the nationalism and the prosperity that had grown out of the War of 1812.

Other treaties approved by the Senate during the first half of the nineteenth century established the northern frontier of the United States more firmly and thus stabilized American relations with Britain and the British North American colonies. These included the Webster-Ashburton Treaty of 1842, which settled stretches of the Maine–New Brunswick border, the New Hampshire–Quebec border, and the Ontario-Minnesota border. The western boundary was settled four years later. One of the many consequences of the War of 1812 was that it channelled American expansion west rather than northwest. The last major area of disputed territory to the north was the Oregon Territory, which was administered by both the United States and Britain. The territory's northern boundary ran from the continental divide to the Pacific at 54° 40' north latitude. Responding to the demands of expansionists, James Polk had campaigned for the presidency using the slogan "Fifty-four forty or fight." Once elected, Polk asked Congress to endorse the American claim to all the Oregon Territory. Congress was divided on the issue, and it debated the Oregon claim. However, after Congress had approved a resolution of war against Mexico in May 1846, a compromise was quickly reached when it became clear that there was a possibility that the United States might have to fight Britain in the Northwest and Mexico in the Southwest at the same time. The Buchanan-Pakenham Treaty extending the treaty line of 1818 along the forty-ninth parallel was speedily ratified by the Senate on June 18, 1846, ensuring that the United States would have to fight on only one front.

The power of the Senate to advise and consent to international treaties played an equally important part in the stabilization of the evolving relationship between the United States and Canada in the middle of the century. In 1854 Congress approved the Reciprocity Treaty, opening the United States to a variety of Canadian goods and in the process boosting Canadian wealth. Freer trade enjoyed broad support in Canada but only sectional support in the United States. In Congress senators from the South backed the treaty in the belief that increased trade would be good insurance against the possibility that an impoverished British North America would apply for admission to the Union and thus upset the already precarious balance between North and South. The Civil War, however, brought reciprocity to an end: with the departure of the southern senators and the rise of a protectionist Republican Party, little support remained, and the treaty was denounced (that is, nullified) by Congress in 1865.

From the Civil War to the Great War

The other important treaty emerged in the wake of the Civil War. The conflict between the Union and the Confederacy spilled over into British North America—mainly in the form of Union raids across the border into Canada—and there were none-too-subtle hints by Abraham Lincoln's secretary of state, William Seward, that he favored a diversionary war with Britain as a means of reuniting North and South. As a result, the Civil War was one of the prime catalysts for federation— or Confederation, as it is known in Canada—among the British North American colonies; it resulted in the formation of the self-governing Dominion of Canada on July 1, 1867. But the war also left a residue of contentious issues involving Britain and British North America, including American claims against Britain over the damage done during the Civil War by the *Alabama,* a Confederate cruiser built in Britain; the issue of American access to Canadian inshore fisheries; a boundary dispute over the San Juan Islands on the west coast; Canadian compensation for raids into Canada by American-Irish Fenians; and trade concerns emerging from the denounced Reciprocity Treaty of 1854.

The negotiations were conducted by an Anglo-American joint high commission that convened in Washington in the spring of 1871. However, the commission almost foundered as a result of the staunch opposition of Senator Charles Sumner of Massachusetts, the chairman of the Senate Foreign Relations Committee, who proposed in all seriousness that there should be no settlement with Britain until there was a complete "withdrawal of the British flag" from North America. It was not until President Ulysses S. Grant's feud with Sumner over another matter resulted in the Massachusetts senator's being deposed as committee chair that the commission could begin its negotiations on British North American issues. The resulting Treaty of Washington was passed by Congress, formalizing a new post-Confederation North American relationship but demonstrating in the process how intervention by individual members of Congress could influence the direction of the relationship.[4]

The progressive settlement of the border and other matters between the expanding United States and the evolving British North America did not diminish the appeal of the idea articulated by a newspaper editor, John Louis O'Sullivan, in 1845 that the "manifest destiny" of the United States was "to overspread the continent allotted by Providence for the free development of our yearly multiplying millions." Many members of Congress, no less than other Americans, were seized with this idea, which had inexorable implications for the new Canadian federation. For example, in July 1866, on the eve of Confederation, Senator Zachariah Chandler of Michigan and Representative N. P. Banks sponsored a bill that repeated the offer of the Continental Congress nearly a century before: Canada could be admitted to the Union on request.[5] In 1870 Representative William Munger of Ohio expressed the view that with Britain declining in importance Canada would "fall into our lap like a ripe apple."[6] In the late 1880s Senate committees would hear comparably encouraging news: in 1890 the Senate Select Committee on Canada was told that Canada was coming under American control, "coming to us steadily, more rapidly than ever before."[7]

As late as 1911, members of Congress would still be expressing such views. Debating the Reciprocity Agreement that had been negotiated by President William Howard Taft and the Liberal government of Prime Minister Wilfrid Laurier, the speaker-designate of the House of Representatives, James Beauchamp ("Champ") Clark of Missouri, claimed that he was in favor of reciprocity because the United States was "preparing to annex Canada." He continued: "I hope to see the day when the American flag will float over every square foot of the British North-American possessions clear to the North Pole." George Prince, a representative from Illinois, was blunter yet: "I say to my neighbors to the north: be not deceived. When we go into a country and get control of it, we take it. It is our history and it is right we should take it if we want it."[8] Given such views, it was perhaps not surprising that the Reciprocity Agreement cleared both houses in Congress with both alacrity and large majorities.

Ironically, however, such enthusiasm by members of Congress for free trade helped contribute to the defeat of the Laurier government in the 1911 elections, in which seven Liberal ministers lost their seats. One of the persistent fears of Canadians in the years after Confederation in 1867 was that the United States would seek to annex Canada and bring the new country to an end. The views of members of Congress did little to alleviate such fears, and they were gleefully seized on by Canadian opponents of free trade and circulated as widely as possible in Canada as indications of what fate would befall Canadians if they voted to return Laurier. Although Laurier's defeat cannot be entirely attributed to the views of members of Congress—there were other domestic is-sues that galvanized opposition to the Liberals—there can be no doubt that had Clark, Prince, and others been more sensitive, defeat might not have been so easy. Moreover, there can be little doubt that the expres-sion of congressional enthusiasm for annexation in 1911 contributed to the resulting deep unpopularity in Canada of the idea of free trade with the United States for much of the rest of the twentieth century.

Yet although some members of Congress were behaving, in President Theodore Roosevelt's words, like "prize idiots,"[9] Congress had just finished ratifying a farsighted treaty with Canada, the Boundary Waters Treaty of 1909, which established a unique regime for the management of riparian relations in North America. The Boundary Waters Treaty established for both countries not only a mutual obligation not to cause environmental damage to downstream localities along the frontier, but also a binational institution, the International Joint Commission, for the resolution of disputes.[10] As I have argued elsewhere, the regime approved by Congress would prove both durable and effective in keep-ing potentially divisive riparian disputes off the Canadian-American agenda.[11]

The Interwar Years

The assertion of Congress's constitutional powers in the period be-tween the two world wars had a marked impact on Canada, although neither of the main legislative initiatives was necessarily directed at affecting the Canadian-American relationship. The first was the deci-sion of a majority of the members of the Senate to refuse to bend to President Woodrow Wilson's uncompromising stand on the Treaty of Versailles and the League of Nations that it established. The combina-tions of negative votes in 1919 and 1920 profoundly affected the course of global politics writ large in the aftermath of the Great War. Few might have been as blunt (or as rude) as Senator William E. Borah, who was wont to describe the league on the Senate floor as "the gathered scum of the nations,"[12] but American legislators were generally unwilling to involve the United States in this new experiment in international organization. This meant that the burgeoning power of the United States was not at all felt in the European theater during the interwar period, and that would have an inexorable effect on the course of great-power politics in Europe—and thereby on Canada.[13] By the late 1930s Canadians found themselves pulled back into the European vortex because of the isolationism in Congress that thwarted Wilson's grand designs.

Likewise, the protectionist propensities of Congress at the time of the great stock market crash in 1929 were not particularly aimed at Canada. After all, Senator Reed Smoot and Representative Willis Hawley—and their colleagues in both houses—were merely responding to President Herbert Hoover's invitation to be as parochial as they possibly could be. No one should be surprised that under the circumstances the bill signed into law by Hoover in June 1930 included tariff increases on more than 20,000 separate items.[14]

The Smoot-Hawley Act might not have been directed specifically at Canada, but because of the extent and importance of Canada's trade with the United States it ended up having more profound effects on Canada than on most other countries. The American measures prompted the Canadian governments of both William Lyon Mackenzie King and R. B. Bennett to engage in tit-for-tat retaliation, imposing countervailing Canadian duties on American goods. As a consequence, Canadian-American trade plunged, falling by fully half within two years. The collapse of this trade deepened and widened the impact of the Great Depression in Canada, leading, as elsewhere, to massive unemployment and economic dislocation.

A more parochial assertion of congressional power during this era that had an impact on Canadian-American relations should also be noted. A treaty was negotiated between Canada and the administration of President Herbert Hoover for the construction of a St. Lawrence deep waterway—a system of dams, canals, and locks that would open the Great Lakes to oceangoing vessels. The treaty was transmitted to the Senate in January 1933. Unfortunately for the treaty's prospects, by this time Hoover was a lame-duck president, Franklin Delano Roosevelt having won the 1932 elections. More important, however, regional interests along the American side rallied in opposition. Some hostility was entirely understandable: the Chicago Sanitary District, for example, objected to the treaty's provision that waters from Lake Michigan could no longer be freely diverted for sanitation purposes; likewise, those plumping for a link between the Great Lakes and the Mississippi were not in favor. But some opposition was somewhat less understandable: Senator J. Hamilton Lewis of Illinois, for example, objected to the treaty's provision giving Canada freedom of navigation on Lake Michigan. He claimed, apparently in all seriousness and certainly in blissful ignorance of changes that had occurred in great-power politics, that if the United States and Japan should ever be at war, allies of Japan such as Britain could slip a naval vessel into Lake Michigan and shell American towns.[15] Faced with an array of opponents, the Deep Waterway Treaty went down to defeat in March 1934.

The Post–World War II Era

Although the period between 1945 and 1970 was not marked by congressional assertiveness in foreign affairs, the U.S. legislature nonetheless periodically played a role in the evolution of the Canadian-American relationship. In some instances members of Congress played a positive role, such as when they supported key pieces of legislation that had powerful and marked effects on Canadian wealth. For example, Congress approved the construction of the St. Lawrence Seaway—although it did so only after President Dwight D. Eisenhower embraced it as a national security project, a justification that immediately trumped long-standing sectional opposition in Congress. Congress also agreed to a series of exemptions for Canada under "Buy American" legislation to allow the creation of de facto sectoral free trade in defense products. It passed the Columbia River Treaty in March 1961, embracing a massive power and flood-control project that involved sixty years of cooperative cross-border management and benefits on both sides of the border.[16] And, most important of all, in 1965 it approved an agreement concerning automotive products, the Canada–United States Auto Pact. Based on the success of the Defense Production Sharing Arrangements, the Auto Pact was a sectoral free trade agreement in autos and automotive products that within a few years dramatically boosted Canadian wealth.[17]

However, there were negative aspects to congressional activity during this period. The most profound negative impact that the Congress had on the Canadian-American relationship in the 1950s came as a result of the anti-Communist investigations of Senator Joseph McCarthy of Wisconsin. There was but one galvanizing case, that of E. Herbert Norman, a Canadian diplomat. Norman had been a Communist while at Cambridge University in the 1930s, had joined Canada's Department of External Affairs in 1939, and had occupied a number of sensitive positions in the 1940s. His name was provided to the Senate's Internal Security Subcommittee in August 1951 as that of someone with Communist connections. Although he was cleared by a Canadian government investigation, he was appointed to the relatively low-profile position of ambassador to New Zealand.

In March 1957 the Internal Security Subcommittee reopened its investigation of Norman, by this time ambassador to Egypt, and on March 14 published testimony implicating him as a Soviet agent. Formal diplomatic protests had little result: two weeks later more testimony on Norman was released. On April 4, 1957, Norman jumped off the roof of a Cairo apartment building to his death. The reaction in Canada to the suicide was heated and angry: politicians, the mainstream media, students, and others denounced the McCarthyite process by which Norman was hounded to his death, and the United States more generally. Although the issue did not play a prominent role in the Canadian general election later in 1957, there is general agreement that it dramatically fueled and deepened anti-Americanism in Canada and was in part responsible for the defeat of the Liberals.[18]

The Era of Congressional Assertiveness

Most students of Congress agree that after 1970 Congress began to exert its political power vis-à-vis the presidency, usually marked by the passage of the War Powers Act of 1973. One consequence of this legislative assertiveness was the increasing willingness of members of Congress to define the national interest of the United States in purely local terms; another was the tendency to resist the importunities of the executive branch, both the White House and the Department of State, to deal with those foreign states that were friendly to the United States in ways that would maintain strong ties of friendship. As a consequence, there were relatively few examples of the broader vision of Congress toward Canada that had been seen in some earlier periods. Indeed, the Canada–United States Free Trade Agreement and the North American Free Trade Agreement stand out as the only two exemplars. By contrast, this period saw a proliferation of disputes with close allies such as Canada. Of the many conflicts that touched the relationship since 1970, the issues of border broadcasting, East Coast fisheries, acid rain, and the Helms-Burton Act are surveyed here as illustrative.

The willingness of the Congress to defend American interests aggressively in the case of border broadcasting produced a sharp dispute with Canada in the 1970s. In July 1976, as part of the efforts of the Liberal government of Pierre Trudeau to promote Canadian culture, the House of Commons passed Bill C-58, an act to amend the Income Tax Act. The bill's purpose was to divert advertising revenue for magazines and television stations from American to Canadian sources: for example, under its provisions it would be impossible for a Canadian firm advertising on an American border-state television station to deduct those costs as business expenses for income tax purposes, even though the primary audience for the advertising was those Canadians who watched that station. American television station owners along the border saw their revenue from Canadian advertisers drop sharply, and not unnaturally, they were quick to press their representatives in Congress for relief.

An opportunity came in 1977, when the Senate was considering amendments to the United States Income Tax Act. One of the proposals was to disallow expenses incurred at foreign conventions. Because of the negative effects this would have had on the tourist industries in the Caribbean, Mexico, and Canada, an amendment was put forward to exempt these countries. But senators from the states affected by the border broadcasting legislation successfully argued for retaliatory action against Canada, with the result that convention expenses incurred in Canada by Americans could no longer be deducted as an income tax expense. Needless to say, Americans stopped coming to Canada for conventions, prompting the Canadians to plead for relief, which the administration of President Jimmy Carter eventually granted. In its place, the Carter administration proposed legislation that mirrored that of Canada—making expenses for advertising placed in Canada nondeductible for American firms—to mollify border-state senators. Between 1978 and 1980, when the convention amendment was withdrawn, it is estimated that the loss to Canada's tourist and convention industry was $200 million; the estimated value of advertising diverted from American border-state stations to Canadian networks was $20 million.[19]

The protection of American border broadcasters involved a relatively large number of senators from the states arrayed along the length of the Canadian-American border; the East Coast fisheries treaty dispute, by contrast, involved the determined efforts of a few senators from one region, including Senator Claiborne Pell of Rhode Island and Senator Edward Kennedy of Massachusetts. The dispute arose out of the need to establish new maritime coastal boundaries as a result of both countries' extending their coastal limits to the full 200-mile limit in 1977. Negotiators from both countries came to a complex agreement in March 1979 that involved two treaties for each coast and outlined management regimes for twenty-eight stocks, fixing joint access and catch shares for fishermen of both countries.

Although the negotiators could not agree on a boundary line in the Gulf of Maine, they did agree to submit their rival claims to the International Court of Justice (ICJ) for adjudication. The treaties were sent to the Senate for consideration in April 1979 by President Jimmy Carter. The result was an imbroglio: it turned out that the Carter administration had not secured the general approval of fisheries' interests in New England. As a result, the fisheries subcommittee in the House of Representatives advised against ratification, claiming that the management regimes were incompatible with existing American law. In the Senate Pell and Kennedy ensured that the treaty stalled. Indeed, Kennedy, responding to pressures from the scallop industry, went so far as to demand that Canada amend substantial portions of the treaty that had been signed by the American administration. Despite the deep anger that these tactics aroused in Canada, there was little that could be done.[20] Eventually, following the election of Ronald Reagan, the administration withdrew the treaties from consideration. The Gulf of Maine boundary issue was detached from the fisheries treaty and submitted to the ICJ, which in October 1984 recommended drawing the boundary between the two competing claims.[21]

The issue of acid rain produced a more sustained dispute with Canada.[22] Throughout the 1980s the Canadian government pressed its claims that sulfur dioxide and nitrogen oxide emitted into the atmosphere in the United States was being carried into Canada and deposited as acidic precipitation, killing lakes in the Canadian Shield, injuring the maple sugar industry, and even damaging public buildings. Ottawa proposed that the U.S. Clean Air Act be amended to deal with the problem, which would force old power plants burning local high-sulfur coal to embrace expensive strategies to reduce their emissions. Congress as persistently refused to consider such a course of action, siding with the administration of President Ronald Reagan, who took the position that more research was needed on the matter before decisive action should be taken. The dispute escalated and became an issue of national importance in Canada, prompting both the Liberal government of Pierre Trudeau and the Progressive Conservative government of Brian Mulroney to take an increasingly hard-edged line on the issue. Ministers and the Canadian ambassador to the United States, Allan Gotlieb, gave speeches that were highly critical of American policy, hapless American tourists in Canada were given anti–acid rain propaganda and asked to press their members of Congress on their return, and the issue was pressed in a variety of forums.

These efforts were all to no avail, for the reluctance in Congress to address Canadian complaints stemmed from the politics of the issue. Although there was some sympathy for the Canadian predicament in Congress—particularly in the New England states, where acid rain caused by emissions from the Ohio Valley and the Midwest was also doing damage—the correlation of forces overall was not favorable. The Senate majority leader was Robert Byrd of West Virginia, a prime coal state. The interests ranged against the environmentalist position were impressive: members of Congress from Illinois, Indiana, Ohio, western Pennsylvania, West Virginia, Kentucky, and Tennessee—mindful of the interests of the coal-mining industry, the electric utilities, and the automobile and other manufacturing industries, not to mention their unions—constituted a solid mechanism to block amendments to the Clean Air Act.[23] Some members of Congress gave as good as they were getting from Canada. Thomas Luken of Ohio got into a wrangling match with Allan Gotlieb, Canada's ambassador to Washington, decrying Gotlieb's "aggressive lobbying campaign," and calling on Secretary of State George Shultz to demand Gotlieb's recall.[24]

The dispute festered until the correlation of forces shifted in the late 1980s. First, Byrd was replaced by Senator George Mitchell of Maine, a state affected by acid rain and an open supporter of the Canadian lobbying efforts in Washington. Second, the indifference of many of the legislators from the southwestern states gave way to concern when a new copper smelter was built in Mexico in 1986, threatening air quality across the border. Not surprisingly, the Reagan administration deemed this problem to require very little further research: by early 1987 the administration had negotiated an air quality agreement with Mexico. Third, George Bush had embraced a "green" plank during the 1988 election campaign and actually sought to make good on those election promises: he appointed an environmentalist to head the Environmental Protection Agency and submitted acid rain proposals to Congress within six months of his inauguration. By March 1991 he signed an air quality agreement between Canada and the United States.[25]

The most recent dispute between Congress and Canada concerns the Cuban Liberty and Democratic Solidarity Act, cosponsored by Senator Jesse Helms of North Carolina, the chairman of the Senate Foreign Relations Committee, and Representative Dan Burton of Indiana. The bill was intended, in the words of a spokesman for the Senate committee, to create an "investment minefield" in Cuba. Its provisions included giving Cuban-born Americans the right to sue, in American courts, foreign companies alleged to be exploiting property expropriated by the regime of Fidel Castro Ruz. The legislation also required the federal government to bar executives from such companies and their families from entering the United States.

When the legislation was introduced a number of governments, including the government in Ottawa, went through the formalities of registering their objections to the extraterritorial provisions of the legislation. However, there was a widespread expectation that this bill would simply be allowed to die, like thousands of other bills that are introduced into Congress not with the expectation that they will pass, but simply for symbolic or electoral purposes. The Helms-Burton legislation received an unexpected reprieve when in February 1996 the Cuban air force shot down two unarmed Cessna aircraft belonging to Brothers to the Rescue, a Cuban group of exiles based in Miami. The political costs of opposing the legislation suddenly jumped; President Bill Clinton signed it into law (albeit with a certain reluctance), and the issue became another example of how the electoral cycle in the United States affects relations with other countries, including Canada.[26]

However, the Helms-Burton imbroglio in 1996 was a continuation of a conflict in Canadian-American relations, centered mainly in Congress, that has been of long standing.[27] Congress has traditionally shown little sensitivity about what William Graham, chairman of the House of Commons Standing Committee on Foreign Affairs and International Trade, has termed the "legal imperialism of extraterritoriality."[28] Even though the effects of extraterritorial legislation such as the Trading with the Enemy Act or the Helms-Burton or D'Amato legislation have traditionally been fairly minimal, the willingness of the U.S. Congress to behave in such a self-consciously imperial way, running roughshod over the sovereign rights of other states, has always been a sore point with Canadians. By the same token, the persistent Canadian refusal to take seriously thirty-five years of obsessive American efforts to unseat Castro mightily annoys many in the United States—even though the appearance of large numbers of Canadians on Cuban beaches hardly explains the durability of the Castro regime. However, in this dispute symbolism reigns: periodically the issue surfaces, creates a certain bitterness as both sides remind each other why they are so sore, and then slips into hibernation until the next time. Moreover, although the eventual death of Castro may remove Cuba from the Canadian-American agenda, the deep-seated willingness of Americans to act extraterritorially and the equally deep-seated sensitivity of Canadians to infringements on their sovereign rights by the U.S. Congress will surely transcend the life of any single individual.

Analysis

The brief survey presented in this chapter suggests the appropriateness of seeing Congress as having largely contradictory effects on Canadian-American relations. On the one hand, the account here suggests that members of Congress have historically had a relentless propensity to allow the parochialism of their institution to drive what they say and do about the relationship between the United States and Canada. On the other hand, however, Congress has also consistently shown its capacity for effective regional action.

No particular trend can be observed here: members of Congress in the late 1990s seem no more—or no less—likely to display both parochialism and statesmanlike behavior than their forebears in the past. Nor has the progressive integration of the North American economies in the 1990s had an impact on parochial and election-driven behavior in

Congress, as the cases of the Helms-Burton and D'Amato legislation clearly show.

To be sure, members of Congress are sometimes disposed to rise above the parochialism on which their institution is founded—and through which they are themselves sustained in office. At times of intense security threats to the United States, there is a willingness to subordinate sectional concerns to conceptions of the "national interest" as defined by the executive branch, as the cases of the 1846 war with Mexico and the St. Lawrence Seaway show. But at other times self-indulgence is the norm. Sometimes such self-indulgence takes the form of loose talk—a lack of care by members about what they put on the record; a willingness to speak as though others outside the United States were not listening, as exemplified by Clark's spouting the language of manifest destiny during a Canadian election in which the very future of the country was being debated; the isolationist Borah's dismissing foreigners as scum; or Lewis's worrying about British gunboats shelling the shores of Lake Michigan. Such self-indulgent, loose talk is not just an artifact of a historical past: consider the views of Representative Bill Barrett, the chair of the agriculture subcommittee, who suggested in May 1996 that a Canadian running wheat into the United States illegally should be shot.

More common than self-indulgent talk is self-indulgent action. Here, by contrast, the self-indulgence is entirely understandable. It takes the form of a careful calculation of the public interest that is unabashedly local in definition: "What benefit will be derived by—or harm inflicted on—the people in my own congressional district or my own state?" A closely related self-indulgence is the calculation of electoral self-interest: "What will this mean for my reelection prospects?" If there are no apparent implications, the question becomes part of the classic log-roller's calculus: "How can I turn my vote on this issue—one that doesn't affect my constituents and my electoral prospects—to good advantage? How can I pick up IOUs from other members of Congress on this issue for use when dealing with some issue in the future that may affect me and my constituents?"

Such dynamics, as Christopher Sands reminds us, reflect that overly quoted aphorism of Thomas P. ("Tip") O'Neill, long-time speaker of the House of Representatives, that "all politics is local."[29] Indeed, these local politics have persistently affected Canadian-American relations from the early period, when the pursuit of sectional interests actually led to war in 1812, to the present decade, when the Helms-Burton legislation of 1996 self-consciously sacrificed good American relations with a variety of friendly countries on the altar of votes.

Such dynamics, which have kept (and will keep) Congress so parochial, are perfectly natural given the structure of the U.S. Constitution and the evolution of American institutions of governance since the late 1700s. Moreover, how one sees the bifurcation of power over foreign affairs in Washington depends entirely on one's perspective. The autonomy of the U.S. legislature tends to annoy foreigners intensely,[30] particularly those from countries whose legislatures are designed to play a very different role in national politics. But from an American perspective the separation of powers is surely an advantage in dealing with foreigners. After all, it provides the American government with the structural power understood by every car dealership: the ubiquitous manager who must approve the deal negotiated and signed by the sales agent and the customer on the showroom floor.[31]

Conclusion

In this chapter I have sought to demonstrate how and why the Congress of the United States has always had an impact on the evolution of Canadian-American relations because of the crucial powers that the United States accords to the legislature. Members of the House of Representatives and the Senate do not often involve themselves in the minutiae of the day-to-day relations of Canada and the United States, but their power of appropriations, their control over economic issues, and above all their power to advise and consent on international treaties mean that members of Congress will periodically have opportunities to immerse themselves in the nitty-gritty of the relationship. And, as we have seen, occasionally the defense of parochial interests can have a negative impact on the overall course of the relationship.

But the long record of congressional parochialism that so annoys the northern neighbors of the United States must also be set against an equally compelling track record of congressional capacity for regional action and a persistent willingness to rise above the relentlessly local, to rein in self-indulgence, and to define American interests in more national terms. Therefore, along with the failed treaties, the punitive legislation, and the careless talk, we must consider all those treaties and agreements that Congress has passed that have deepened the complexity of the relationship between Canada and the United States, encouraged and fostered economic growth and wealth on both sides of the line, and contributed to the peaceful management of such a lopsided relationship.

Notes

1. On the Canada–United States Free Trade Agreement that went into force on January 1, 1989, and the North American Free Trade Agreement that went into effect five years later, see G. Bruce Doern and Brian W. Tomlin, *Faith and Fear: The Free Trade Story* (Toronto: Stoddart, 1991) and Charles F. Doran, "NAFTA, Uruguay, and Canada-U.S. Relations: Inside Looking Out," in Maureen Appel Molot and Harald von Riekhoff, eds., *Canada among Nations, 1994: A Part of the Peace* (Ottawa: Carleton University Press, 1994), pp. 195–209. On the Helms-Burton legislation, see Kim Richard Nossal, " 'Without Regard for the Interests of Others': Canada and American Unilateralism in the Post–Cold War Era," *American Review of Canadian Studies*, vol. 27 (Summer 1997), pp. 179–97.

2. For an elaboration of the argument that Congress has contributed to the development of a progressively more open international trading system, see Robert Pastor, "The Cry-and-Sigh Syndrome: Congress and Trade Policy," in Allen Schick, ed., *Making Economic Policy in Congress* (Washington: American Enterprise Institute, 1983), pp. 158–95.

3. John Herd Thompson and Stephen J. Randall, *Canada and the United States: Ambivalent Allies* (Montreal: McGill–Queen's University Press, 1994), p. 11.

4. C. P. Stacey, *Canada and the Age of Conflict: A History of Canadian External Policies*, vol. 1: *1867–1921* (Toronto: Macmillan of Canada, 1977), p. 29.

5. Mason Wade, "The Roots of the Relationship," in John Sloan Dickey, ed., *The United States and Canada* (Englewood Cliffs, N.J.: Prentice-Hall for the American Assembly, 1964), p. 43.

6. Thompson and Randall, *Ambivalent Allies*, p. 42.

7. J. L. Granatstein, *Yankee Go Home? Canadians and Anti-Americanism* (Toronto: HarperCollins, 1996), p. 47n.

8. Quoted in Granatstein, *Yankee Go Home?*, p. 61. See also J. L. Granatstein, "Free Trade between Canada and the United States: The Issue That Will Not Go Away," in Royal Commission on the Economic Union and Development Prospects of Canada (McDonald Commission), *Collected Research Studies*, vol. 29: *The Politics of Canada's Economic Relationship with the United States*, Denis Stairs and Gilbert R. Winham, eds. (University of Toronto Press, 1985), p. 24.

9. Quoted in Thompson and Randall, *Ambivalent Allies*, p. 91.

10. Robert Spencer, John Kirton, and Kim Richard Nossal, eds., *The International Joint Commission Seventy Years On* (Toronto: Centre for International Studies, University of Toronto, 1981); William R. Willoughby, *The Joint Organizations of Canada and the United States* (University of Toronto Press, 1979), chaps. 2–5.

11. Kim Richard Nossal, "Institutionalization and the Pacific Settlement of Interstate Conflict: The Case of Canada and the International Joint Commission," *Journal of Canadian Studies*, vol. 18 (Winter 1983–84), pp. 75–87.

12. Thomas N. Guinsburg, *The Pursuit of Isolationism in the United States Senate from Versailles to Pearl Harbor* (New York: Garland Publishing, 1982), p. 32.

13. See also Eric A. Nordlinger, *Isolationism Reconfigured* (Princeton University Press, 1995).

14. Robert A. Pastor, *Congress and the Politics of U.S. Foreign Economic Policy* (Berkeley: University of California Press, 1980), pp. 77–84.

15. C. P. Stacey, *Canada and the Age of Conflict*, vol. 2: *1921–1948* (University of Toronto Press, 1981), pp. 148–49.

16. Neil Swainson, "Harnessing the Columbia River, 1964," in Don Munton and John Kirton, eds., *Canadian Foreign Policy: Selected Cases* (Scarborough, Ont.: Prentice-Hall Canada, 1992), pp. 118–34. A more detailed account may be found in N. Swainson, *Conflict over the Columbia* (Montreal: McGill-Queen's University Press, 1979).

17. Charlotte S. M. Girard, *Canada in World Affairs*, vol. 13: *1963–1965* (Toronto: Canadian Institute of International Affairs, 1980), pp. 122–23.

18. Granatstein, *Yankee Go Home?*, pp. 112–18. There are two published accounts of the Norman affair, each coming to a radically different conclusion about whether Norman was in fact a Soviet agent of influence: Roger Bowen, *Innocence Is Not Enough: The Life and Death of Herbert Norman* (Vancouver: Douglas and McIntyre, 1986) and James Barros, *No Sense of Evil: Espionage: The Case of Herbert Norman* (Toronto: Deneau, 1986).

19. Donald K. Alper and Robert L. Monahan, "Bill C-58 and the American Congress: The Politics of Retaliation," *Canadian Public Policy*, vol. 4 (Spring 1979), pp. 184–95; Isaiah A. Litvak and Christopher J. Maule, "Bill C-58 and the Regulation of Periodicals in Canada," *International Journal*, vol. 36 (Winter 1980–81), p. 89.

20. Stephen Clarkson, *Canada and the Reagan Challenge: Crisis and Adjustment, 1981–85*, updated ed. (Toronto: Lorimer, 1985), pp. 209–11.

21. L. H. Legault, "A Line for All Uses: The Gulf of Maine Boundary Revisited," *International Journal*, vol. 40 (Summer 1985), pp. 461–77.

22. Charles F. Doran and Joel J. Sokolsky, *Canada and Congress: Lobbying in Washington* (Halifax, N.S.: Centre for Foreign Policy Studies, 1985), pp. 161–78; Clarkson, *Canada and the Reagan Challenge*, pp. 183–97.

23. See the map in Doran and Sokolsky, *Canada and Congress*, p. 174, repro-duced from the *Washington Post*, January 29, 1984, showing the "legislative geography" of acid rain controls.

24. Allan Gotlieb, *"I'll Be with You in a Minute, Mr. Ambassador": The Education of a Canadian Diplomat in Washington* (University of Toronto Press, 1991), pp. 67–68; see U.S. Congress, *Congressional Record*, April 20, 1983, p. E3389.

25. Don Munton and Geoffrey Castle, "Reducing Acid Rain, 1980s," in Munton and Kirton, eds., *Canadian Foreign Policy*, pp. 367–81.

26. Kim Richard Nossal, "Does the Electoral Cycle in the United States Affect Relations with Canada?" *International Journal*, vol. 36 (Winter 1980–81), pp. 208–27.

27. See, for example, the account of the attempts of Canadian and American legislators to discuss the matter of Cuba at their meeting in 1962: Matthew J. Abrams, *The Canada-United States Interparliamentary Group* (Ottawa: Parliamentary Centre for Foreign Affairs and Foreign Trade, 1973), p. 63.

28. William C. Graham, "Reflections on United States Legal Imperialism: Canadian Sovereignty in the Context of North American Economic Integration," *International Journal*, vol. 40 (Summer 1985), pp. 478–509.

29. Christopher Sands, "Canada: A Case of Local Foreign Policy," *Congress and the Americas Policy Paper*, vol. 6, study 1 (April 1996).

30. Kim Richard Nossal, "The Imperial Congress: The Separation of Powers and Canadian-American Relations," *International Journal*, vol. 44 (Autumn 1989), pp. 863–83.

31. Robert A. Pastor, "Congress and U.S. Foreign Policy: Comparative Advantage or Disadvantage?" *Washington Quarterly* (August 1991), pp. 101–14.

Chapter 4

Lobbying by Mexico and Canada

George W. Grayson

EXICAN AND CANADIAN LEADERS have often re-
sorted to cliches to vent their frustration over relations
with the United States. Dictator Porfirio Díaz lamented wryly, "Poor
Mexico: So far from God and so close to the United States." Almost as
memorably, Prime Minister Pierre Elliot Trudeau compared his nation's
proximity to the United States with "a mouse's sharing a bed with an
elephant."

Such complaints aside, neighboring a leading economy has ensured
both states a robust source of investments, ready access to technology,
and unparalleled trading opportunities. Moreover, sharing long fron-
tiers with a superpower has enhanced Mexican and Canadian security
while permitting both to maintain small militaries relative to their territories. However, both Canada and Mexico have pursued different
strategic courses.

Mexicans have kept their distance from the U.S. military, while Canadians have acceded to the integration of Canadian and American
defense structures. As a member of the British Commonwealth, Canada
entered World War II more than two years before Pearl Harbor sparked
the U.S. declaration of war. During that conflict the United States and
Canada coordinated their activities through a Permanent Joint Board on
Defense, created in 1940. After the war Canada and the United States
spearheaded the creation of a North Atlantic Treaty Organization

For extremely helpful comments on an earlier version of this chapter, I am
indebted to Christopher M. Sands of the Center for Strategic and International
Studies and Ramzi Nemo of the American University.

(NATO) in April 1949. As a complement to NATO, the Canadian and American militaries collaborated on a Distant Early Warning System and a North American Air Defense Command (NORAD) to protect them against missile and bomber strikes.

Trudeau, who held Canada's premiership for all but nine months between 1968 and 1984, actively asserted Canada's independence from the United States. In particular, he sought to establish Canada as a "middle power," providing economic and technical assistance to developing nations, participating more actively in the United Nations and other multilateral organizations, decreasing the number of Canadian bases in Europe, reducing its troop commitment to NATO, and reorganizing NORAD to focus on protecting Canadian territory. He also adopted an economic nationalism, especially in the sensitive petroleum sector.

Historically the degree of American cultural and economic penetration into Canada has caused more concern than the specter of Washington's political intrusion. In their vexing quest for cultural identity amid linguistic, geographic, and ethnic cleavages with Americans, Canadians have mainly defined themselves in contrast to Americans, enacting curbs on the influx of movies from Hollywood, television programs from Burbank, and magazines from New York.

With the Progressive Conservative Party's ascent to power in May 1984, U.S. President Ronald Reagan found a philosophical soul mate in new Prime Minister Brian Mulroney. The Canadian staged a vaunted "Shamrock Summit" with his political ally, negotiating a modest treaty on acid rain abatement. For his part, Mulroney eliminated the most contentious elements of Trudeau's nationalization program, which, in the view of one astute observer, "did more to improve [bilateral] relations than any [other] change in Canadian diplomacy."[1] In 1995, however, passage of the Helms-Burton Act by the U.S. Congress enacted criminal penalties against foreigners trafficking in properties expropriated in Cuba from Americans, vexing Canadians, Mexicans, and other U.S. allies.

Prickly issues notwithstanding, elite elements in the U.S. executive branch have traditionally managed bilateral relations with their counterparts in every country, practicing "quiet diplomacy" and preventing occasional flare-ups from exciting congressional or popular wrath. As Charles Doran and Joel Sokolsky have highlighted, four factors distinguished U.S. interests in Canada from its interests in other foreign countries, at least before the advent of the North American Free Trade Agreement (NAFTA).[2]

First, strong bilateral economic ties ensured continual communication between Canadian and American corporate allies, which were ready to decry policies deemed harmful to Canada or vice versa. Second, regional concerns—particularly on the environmental front— often found U.S. border states pursuing the same interests as neighboring Canadian provinces. Third, a dense network of policy links between Ottawa and Washington frequently alerted Canadian officials to proposed bilateral problems that they could resolve at the administrative level before the issues reached Capitol Hill. Finally, perceptions in Congress of Canadians as stable, friendly, democratic neighbors allowed for a focus on less contentious foreign policy matters that were considered on the Hill most critical to U.S. interests.

There are several other dynamics at work in the relationship between the United States and Canada. Canadian diplomats have become inured, if not sympathetic, to the majestic self-image held by certain representatives and senators, surrounded as they are by scores of staffers, lobbyists, and assorted sycophants. For instance, Ambassador Allan Gotlieb (1981–87) sought a senior U.S. senator's support for Canada's efforts to curb acid rain. Rather than address this subject, the elderly solon inquired about the possibility of naming for his deceased wife a lake in Quebec where the couple had honeymooned a half century earlier.[3]

Governments in Ottawa and Canada's Washington embassy have studiously monitored both the expansion of congressional initiative in foreign affairs vis-à-vis the executive branch and the fragmentation of influence over all policies as additional committees, subcommittees, select committees, and other ancillary bodies have sprouted like mushrooms in a dank cave under the Capitol rotunda. As the power of decisionmaking diffuses, all interests find new pressure points at which they can exert influence. An ambassador's effectiveness may depend on knowledge of what John Gaus has called "the political ecology" of the issues on the agenda.[4]

The shared heritage of English language, British common law, and preferences for bilateral problem solving form important linkages between most Canadian and American leaders. The advantage of familiarity can also prove disadvantageous when, for example, naive U.S.

policymakers conclude that the interests of the two similar countries must be identical.

Nevertheless, in the face of crisis pragmatism has generally prevailed over hyperbole in Mexico's and Canada's dealings with the United States. During World War I, for example, Mexico's government rejected a German-Mexican alliance proposed by the Kaiser's foreign secretary, Arthur Zimmermann, despite Berlin's offer to return Arizona, New Mexico, and Texas to Mexico if the Central Powers triumphed. Throughout the early years of the cold war, although Mexican governments did not overtly trumpet a pro-U.S. orientation, neither did they hesitate to ally with the United States on important security issues.

For their part, many Ottawa policymakers with a practical bent have taken great care to prevent teapot tempests from escalating into bilateral standoffs. A case in point involved Canadian protests against the testing of U.S. cruise missiles in northern Alberta and Saskatchewan. After Soviet fighters shot down Korean Airlines Flight 007 in September 1983, the Canadian public warmed toward the testing and Ottawa canceled Soviet flights over Canada and publicly reprimanded the Soviets.

Despite differences over Cuba, Central America, and immigration, among other issues, the U.S. government forged a tacit agreement with Mexico's Institutional Revolutionary Party (PRI), which has dominated Mexico autocratically during most of its seven decades of existence. American governments found it even easier to establish a modus vivendi with Canada, although America's neighbor to the north maintained diplomatic ties with Cuba. Highly favorable public perceptions of Canada in the United States fostered harmony in bilateral affairs.

The Evolution of Canadian Lobbying[5]

As recently as the 1970s, Canadian Embassy practices prevented most Canadian officials from traveling the seventeen blocks from their Massachusetts Avenue chancery near Dupont Circle to Capitol Hill. When problems arose a Canadian diplomat would register his country's viewpoint with the appropriate State Department desk and possibly with a White House official. The emergence of American protectionist pressures in response to a ballooning trade deficit and increased anti-Canadian lobbying of U.S. lawmakers by American businesses helped persuade the United States' largest commercial partner to dramatically change its diplomatic style in Washington. As Stephen Clarkson has noted, "While it was the administration more than Congress that was pressing Canada on the main economic grievances of energy and investment policy, it was the [American] legislature more than the executive that created most of Canada's economic grievances against the United States."[6]

In the 1950s then-Prime Minister Lester Pearson, himself a former envoy, recommended that newly accredited Ambassador Arnold Heeney pay more attention to Congress than Canadian envoys had done previously. Pearson suggested that Heeney develop a close rapport with a few key lawmakers rather than pursuing backbenchers. On one occasion Heeney inveigled Lyndon B. Johnson, then majority leader of the Senate, to block a proposal further diverting the waters of the Great Lakes at Chicago.[7]

Apart from such isolated interventions, a distinct change in Ottawa's diplomacy really began with Allan Gotlieb's arrival in Washington as ambassador in December 1981. Rather than tiptoeing around the capital or crafting discreet letters to State Department functionaries, Gotlieb, a bespectacled Harvard Law School graduate and former Rhodes Scholar, soon inserted himself into Washington's power game. As he explained his role to a U.S. journalist: "Your constitution works on the basis of deal making. The administration can't govern by itself. You need a 'treaty' to govern. I get caught in that. The administration can't move the Congress, so I've got to get my hands dirty and try to move Congress myself."[8] And move Congress he did. Thanks to an excellent flow of information from public opinion surveys and well-connected individuals he had befriended, Gotlieb's mastery of Washington's social life, his aggressive but suave lobbying techniques, and the assistance of his wife, Sondra—an iconoclastic novelist who contributed regularly to the *Washington Post*—the Canadian emissary became a bona fide Washington player.

Gotlieb insisted that the Canadian Embassy orchestrate its nation's efforts to achieve a bilateral Free Trade Agreement (FTA) congruent with Ottawa's interests. In an attempt to forestall any complications of the accord by Congress's asserting its constitutional right to review the agreement, the Reagan administration sought "fast-track" authority before starting negotiations. The quest for this expedited procedure for congressional consideration—in which legislators would be required to cast timely yea or nay votes without amendments or filibusters—began with the committees responsible for trade in the House (Ways and Means) and the Senate (Finance), respectively.

Not only did FTA advocates propose the bill in the face of a rising tide of protectionism in the United States, they also encountered legislators eager to punish the president for his alleged softness toward Japanese and European trading practices they considered unfair. As Gotlieb himself has recalled, "Other senators had other grievances. Some wanted to teach the Administration a lesson for reasons that had no connection with trade; others wanted to extract concessions on issues on their own agenda, such as appointments to the judiciary."[9]

Ultimately the Senate Finance Committee granted approval for fast-track authorization by a single vote—a result due in part to Canadian efforts, according to Gotlieb's analysis of events.[10] Through his consular staff, Ambassador Gotlieb convinced Hawaii's governor, John Waihee, to lobby Spark Matsunaga, then one of the state's U.S. senators and an FTA opponent. In Gotlieb's view, a vote by the senator against fast-track authorization would insult the many Canadians who regularly vacationed in Hawaii. Governor Waihee, the beneficiary of a major effort by President Reagan, prevailed on Senator Matsunaga, who eventually supported streamlined authorization. A parallel effort involved contacts between Ontario's provincial premier and then-Senator David Durenberger of Minnesota.

Once FTA deliberations began, Canadian diplomats adroitly courted U.S. officials. In cooperation with thirteen consulates around the United States, Gotlieb encouraged U.S. corporations that would be affected by the FTA to become involved through both existing advisory panels and direct contacts with legislators. Gotlieb and his staff recommended that Canada's business leaders consider hiring professional Washington lobbyists. As the vote on the treaty drew closer, the embassy seemingly had far better intelligence about the mood on Capitol Hill than did the White House—partly because of other demands on the executive branch, including the Iran-Contra hearings, arms control talks, and a summit meeting with Soviet leader Mikhail Gorbachev. Ottawa's hard work bore fruit when Congress approved the pact, which Reagan and Mulroney signed on January 2, 1988, eliminating most bilateral tariffs over a ten-year period beginning January 1, 1989.

The number of registered Canadian agents registered with the Justice Department under the Foreign Agents Registration Act tripled between

1978 and 1985, while the total for Mexico remained stable over the same period. A notably higher percentage of Canada's registered agents actually lobbied U.S. government entities compared with those registering on behalf of Mexican interests. Both government and business in Canada greatly expanded outlays for political (policy-related) and quasi-political (trade and countervailing duties) pursuits. Specifically, lobbyists for Canada endeavored to influence officials in the legislative and executive branches, whereas Mexican interests devoted fewer resources to these areas, concentrating on tourism promotion instead. Canadian clients consistently channeled 15 to 25 percent of total expenditures into attracting foreign commercial investment and fostering joint economic ventures between Canadian and U.S. firms. Both of these types of activities expanded an American constituency sensitive to the impact of Washington's policies concerning Canada.

Meanwhile, during the same time frame Mexican clients spent only a fraction of Canadian outlays on such endeavors—a fact that may stem from the harsh treatment that Mexico suffered at hearings conducted by Senate Foreign Relations Subcommittee Chairman Jesse Helms. Canadian clients' support for tourism efforts has declined steadily since the mid-1980s, even as their Mexican counterparts have continued to concentrate more than 90 percent of their disbursements on that sector. Despite this degree of focus, Mexican interests' total spending surpassed that of the Canadians for the first time since 1985.

Observing Gotlieb at that time, Senator Alan K. Simpson, the Republican Party's whip between 1981 and 1995, wrote, "No ambassador understands the jungle of our politics as well."[11] Eventually, however, the jungle's rigors caught up with Ottawa's peripatetic envoy. Soon after Michael K. Deaver, Reagan's deputy chief of staff, departed from the White House in 1985, the Canadians retained his services as a private-sector lobbyist on acid rain issues. Soon Gotlieb found himself embroiled in charges that Deaver had violated U.S. law, accepting the $105,000 assignment while still employed by the U.S. government. Gotlieb said that an unnamed Canadian official's quip to public servant Deaver about Canada's "need for a man of his talents" obviously was made in a "light-hearted, conversational" vein, "hardly [containing] the stuff of negotiations or offers or proposals, of which there were none."[12] The ambassador suffered another public-image setback when a distraught Mrs. Gotlieb slapped her social secretary before guests at a dinner party for Prime Minister Mulroney.[13]

Such faux pas did not prevent Canada's developing a superb reputation for effective influence in the United States. The opening of an imposing modern embassy on Pennsylvania Avenue just five blocks from the Capitol during Prime Minister Mulroney's tenure came to symbolize Canada's emerging profile in Washington, laying down a marker for other hemispheric neighbors to match.

Mexico's Jump into the Lobbying Game

Soon after taking office in December 1988, Mexican President Carlos Salinas de Gortari realized that an active, astute presence in the United States would prove crucial to advancing Mexico's interests, particularly with respect to economic issues. Although with far less intrusion, Salinas seemingly emulated Matías Romero, who had served in Washington first as secretary of Mexico's legation and later as chargé d'affaires during the 1860s. A protégé of liberal President Benito Juárez, Romero worked to convince U.S. politicians that the presence of the troops of Napoleon III in Mexico would harm the Union and provide aid and comfort to the Confederacy, claiming that an ideological affinity linked Paris to Richmond. The intrepid envoy used his contacts in Congress to publicize "Emperor" Maximilian's resurrection of slavery in Mexico, William Gwin's use of land grants to encourage Confederates to settle in northern Mexico, and the amicable ties between rebel leaders and their French counterparts across the Rio Grande. Romero convinced many Union military officers that they could not defeat the South until support for the Confederacy from the French and Maximilian ended, further disseminating his message by giving payoffs to newspapers, instigating favorable congressional resolutions, and socializing extensively with Washington's power brokers.

The young Mexican diplomat succeeded more with military leaders than civilian leaders. Therefore, Romero supported efforts to oust Secretary of State William H. Seward, who opposed aggressive action against France; he joined the radical Republican initiative to contest Lincoln's renomination in 1864; he threw his support behind efforts to impeach President Andrew Johnson; and he even attempted to influence appointments to the foreign relations committees of the House and the Senate.[14]

Since Romero's time most Mexican diplomats had moved quietly around Washington, like intruders in the night. While making pro forma visits to the State Department and graciously receiving visitors who solicited meetings, Mexican envoys seldom traveled the twenty blocks from their Hispanic-style mural-adorned embassy on Sixteenth Street to Capitol Hill. Only occasionally did the ambassador and his staff move to cultivate key members of Congress or luminaries in the press corps. A notable exception was Leonardo Ffrench, who served as the Mexican Embassy's first minister of press and public affairs for five years, beginning in 1984. Ffrench, a career public servant with a highly developed political acumen, went out of his way to promptly provide information to the voracious Washington media corps concerning bilateral differences over Central America, information from Mexico about the 1985 torture-murder of Drug Enforcement Administration agent Enrique Camarena, and U.S. congressional criticism of Mexico's handling of illegal immigration, drug traffic, and official corruption.

Ffrench's behavior aside, how can we account for the low-key approach pursued by the Mexicans as late as the mid-1980s, at a time when Canada, South Korea, Taiwan, Israel, and other middle-sized countries lobbied intensively, some of them even retaining high-priced, high-powered public relations, law, and lobbying firms? First and foremost, Mexicans saw lobbying as illegitimate intrusion into the affairs of another country. Lobbying flew in the face of Mexico's well-publicized commitment to nonintervention. A variation on this theme was seen in the Mexican government's antipathy toward justifying its policies to anyone, most especially to its powerful neighbor to the north, with which Mexico has traditionally manifested a love-hate relationship. Even more troubling to some Mexicans, assertiveness with Washington decisionmakers risked opening the door to even greater U.S. involvement in Mexico by way of reciprocation. John Gavin, U.S. ambassador to Mexico from 1981 to 1986, stepped on toes by speaking out on his host country's trade, investment, immigration, and Central American policies, and Mexico City did not want to offer a pretext for future repetition of these embarrassments.

In addition, any publicly discernible hint of kowtowing to Uncle Sam meant political suicide for Mexican officials. Close association between the United States and Mexico—deemed highly advantageous by U.S. politicians anxious to court the swelling ranks of Hispanic-American voters—proved more complicated for Mexican politicians. On the one hand an aspiring national leader in Mexico must exhibit knowledge of the United States and its impact at home, particularly in economic matters. At the same time he must avoid appearing to be an advocate or apologist for Washington's goals.

Limited resources and cautious envoys contributed to Mexico's unobtrusiveness in the pre-NAFTA period. A banker turned diplomat, Ambassador Jorge Espinosa de los Reyes (1983–88) politely acceded to requests for interviews but seldom took the initiative to meet with influential Americans, setting the tone for the Mexican Embassy's inertia. This posture met with approval in the career ranks of Mexico's Foreign Relations Ministry (Secretaría de Relaciones Exteriores, SRE), in which advocacy for third world causes, anti-U.S. nationalism, and suspicion toward politically appointed ambassadors to Washington throve. Besides, many Mexican policymakers took the fatalistic view that neither foreign nor domestic envoys could prevent the volcanic Mexico-bashing that periodically erupted in the United States. Further, Mexico signed one of its first lobbying contracts with Deaver: he received $62,500 in exchange for assisting Mexico in achieving certain economic objectives in Washington. The 1986 federal indictment of the former White House chief of staff on charges of lying to Congress on behalf of foreign clients (including Mexico and South Korea, as well as Canada) revealed the excesses of influence peddling by "superlobbyists" and reopened the intramural debate in Mexico City about how it should advance its cause in the United States.[15] To Ambassador Espinosa's credit, during his tenure the Mexican Embassy assigned a full-time staff member to monitor and analyze actions by the U.S. Congress. Modern systems date from 1985, when the embassy gained computer access to the *Congressional Quarterly*.

As recently as 1989, only 5.6 percent of pro-Mexican lobbying expenditures in the United States addressed political and quasi-political activities, compared with 86.8 percent directed to attracting American tourists. By contrast, the once-cautious Canadians devoted almost 43 percent of their lobbying funds to public affairs and legal representation and only 36.1 percent to tourism.[16] Although Mexico was still lavishing resources on drawing foreign vacationers, its spending on policy lobbying rose sharply because Salinas realized that the growing and complex "intermestic agenda"—namely, immigration, drugs, trade, and other matters salient at both the international and domestic levels—rendered his nation's "traditional diplomatic approach out of date."[17]

The inauguration of Salinas as president in December 1988 brought a sea change to Mexican diplomacy respecting the United States: a shift from a selective, unobtrusive focus on elites to grass-roots ventures coordinated with U.S. Latinos and friendly elements of America's corporate community.[18] As a first step, in early 1989 Salinas dispatched Gustavo Petricioli as Mexico's ambassador to the United States, where he served until replaced by Jorge Montaño in 1993. A Yale graduate and confidant of both Salinas and former president Miguel de la Madrid Hurtado (1982–88), Petricioli had succeeded the flamboyant Jesús Silva Herzog as finance secretary in de la Madrid's cabinet. Gregarious, avuncular, an entertainer even in office, "Gus" Petricioli became a familiar figure to the denizens of official Washington. The extroverted envoy made his mark early, moving beyond contacts inside the beltway. Indeed, as early as September 1990 Petricioli participated with House Agriculture Committee chairman Kika de la Garza of Texas in a West Coast forum on U.S.-Mexican relations that endorsed both NAFTA and a new era of bilateral cooperation.[19]

The new emissary selected Walter Astié Burgos, an adroit career diplomat, as his deputy chief of mission. Astié moved to Washington from assignment on the acutely nationalistic U.S. desk at the SRE, an agency whose policymaking role plummeted as Salinas and his economic cabinet rejected statism in favor of economic liberalization. Because SRE personnel march to their own ideologically charged institutional drumbeat, major tensions traditionally strain the relationship between the ministry and Mexico's ambassador to Washington, a presidential designee often lacking career staff members' enthusiasm for gringo baiting. In Astié Petricioli chose an SRE insider who could deal with the ministry's bureaucracy and thus free the ambassador to promote Salinas's broader goals in the United States.

To fill other senior posts Petricioli went outside the ministry to choose competent pragmatists who knew the United States well but exhibited little of the anti-Yankee sentiment associated with the home office. The embassy established a congressional liaison office, first headed by Joaquín González Casanova, a lawyer with extensive experience in the United States. Further demonstrating Mexico's change of attitude, the embassy's public affairs office grew from four to seven full-time employees to include three more diplomatic staff members. In 1986 the Mexican Embassy had fifty diplomats and support personnel; between late 1988 and early 1992 the number rose from sixty-five to eighty-five. Four additional agencies of the Mexican government established representation in Washington, raising the number to ten.[20] Not only did embassy personnel specialize to an unprecedented degree, but they benefited from more training than their predecessors had, as evidenced by a greater concentration of advanced academic degrees.

A new embassy, opened in late 1989 three blocks down Pennsylvania Avenue from the White House, epitomized Mexico's diplomatic about-face. The $16 million complex not only signaled a move toward Washington's center of power, but also enabled the Mexican government to place most of its presence under one roof, thus improving and harmonizing the flow of information.

In addition to changes in the physical setting or professional acumen of those responsible for Mexican diplomacy, Salinas directed his technocratic Commerce Ministry (Secretaría de Comercio y Fomento Industrial, SECOFI) to establish its own Washington office to coordinate support for NAFTA. Petricioli had no choice but to concur in this presidential decision, even though it relegated the embassy to an emphatically supportive role rather than a starring role in trade negotiations. The ambassador knew that Gotlieb, Canada's dynamic envoy during the early U.S.-Canada FTA negotiations, had alienated some U.S. officials by concentrating on the free trade pact to the detriment of other bilateral questions—a charge that Ottawa dismissed out of hand. Consequently, Petricioli focused on the overall Mexico-U.S. agenda, while SECOFI trade experts assumed the lead on free trade, just as when Mexican finance officials, accompanied by their own legal team, conducted negotiations in Washington on their country's mountainous debt with the U.S. Treasury and other creditors in 1988–89.

Foreign affairs professionals in the embassy did, however, contribute to the pro-NAFTA campaign. Ambassador Petricioli frequently appeared on Capitol Hill, delivered speeches all over the United States, and cultivated several key U.S. policymakers. In the Bush administration Petricioli earned the trust of Secretary of State James A. Baker III and National Security Adviser General Brent Scowcroft. In addition, Petricioli curried favor with border-state lawmakers such as Senate Finance Committee chairman Lloyd M. Bentsen, Jr., and Representative Bill Richardson.

Meanwhile, Javier Treviño, the embassy's adroit public affairs chief, took advantage of contacts arranged by hired media specialists. In addition to traveling to metropolitan areas, Treviño carried Mexico's message to the editorial boards of some forty newspapers in small- and medium-sized cities, often the home towns of important members of

Congress. This approach paid rich dividends in NAFTA endorsements by the *Cleveland Plain Dealer*, the *Milwaukee Sentinel*, the *Detroit News and Free Press*, and at least ten other newspapers in America's Rust Belt, imperiled by free trade in the eyes of the AFL-CIO and other enemies of the accord.

Despite the presence of several tested Washington veterans in the embassy, President Salinas's NAFTA point man, Commerce Undersecretary Herminio Blanco, chose one of his university professors to organize the D.C. office: Herman Von Bertrab arrived in Washington in December 1990. Von Bertrab hoped to assemble a platoon of talented NAFTA hands rather than building a cumbersome, hierarchical structure to confront Washington's bureaucratic chaos. To this end he recruited young U.S.-trained men, some of whom had worked for the International Monetary Fund, World Bank, Organization of American States, and other international organizations. In Von Bertrab's view this group's intelligence and resourcefulness overshadowed their paucity of experience in commercial affairs.

SECOFI's NAFTA office in Washington pursued its goal along several lines. The staff disseminated material on Mexico and proposals for the trade pact, supplied information to Mexico City about developments in the United States, provided speakers who could preach the gospel of continental free trade throughout the United States, took the pulse of Congress for Blanco and Commerce Secretary Jaime Serra Puche, helped to organize the visits of high-ranking SECOFI officials to Washington, and dispatched staff members to observe working groups on NAFTA.

Most important, SECOFI's Washington office helped recruit a "Who's Who" of political insiders adept at swaying the media and legislators, especially those in the Democratic majority. The Mexicans signed up two dozen prominent allies to help attract support for NAFTA.[21] They also hired Burson Marsteller, a public relations behemoth with clients ranging from the American Paper Institute to the U.S. Olympic Committee. B-M, as it is known in the "K Street canyon" inhabited by Washington lobbyists, spearheaded a campaign to take the message "directly to the people" by cultivating editorial writers, writing speeches for Mexican dignitaries, and preparing and publishing pro-NAFTA materials. In 1993 alone, Mexico's U.S. admen distributed some 100,000 brochures, fact sheets, and press kits.[22]

The SECOFI office also turned to Robert E. Herzstein, fondly known to colleagues as "Mr. Mexico" and "Mexico Central." A Democrat, Herzstein served as the first undersecretary for international trade in the Commerce Department during the Carter administration, subsequently advising Canada and Israel on their free-trade negotiations with the United States. A member of America's elite Council on Foreign Relations, Herzstein is also a partner in the Washington office of Shearman & Sterling, the only firm that conducted both legal work and lobbying on behalf of NAFTA.

An umbrella group for major U.S. corporations called USA*NAFTA began to play a more active role after two executives from chemicals conglomerate AlliedSignal—CEO Lawrence A. Bossidy and Kenneth W. Cole, vice president for government affairs—took charge of the organization in September 1993. The Bossidy-Cole team impelled a vigorous lobbying effort, complete with prime-time television commercials, prominent advertisements in major newspapers, deployment of lobbyists to Capitol Hill, and the designation of corporate captains in each state to generate local business support. In addition to maintaining its U.S. presence, SECOFI also opened an office in Ottawa, although on a much more modest scale. After all, despite low standing in public opinion polls, Prime Minister Mulroney's Progressive Conservatives still commanded a parliamentary majority that ensured NAFTA's ratification in Canada.

SECOFI involved several prominent Mexican Americans in its lobbying effort. Most important, as the moment of decision neared, Mexican officials enlisted Gabriel Guerra-Mondragón, a Democratic fund raiser long connected both personally and politically with Bill Clinton. Guerra-Mondragón wooed liberal Democrats and Hispanics in Congress.[23] In addition, Von Bertrab recruited several more Democrats, including Abelardo L. Valdes, President Carter's State Department protocol chief; Eduardo Hidalgo, a secretary of the navy under Carter; and two former New Mexico governors, Toney Anaya and Jerry Apodaca. Besides working on Capitol Hill, these men drummed up support for NAFTA among Hispanic Americans, especially in the South and the Southwest. SECOFI also hired regional Latino-owned firms to drum up backing for NAFTA in Texas and California.

Mexico's U.S. representatives appealed to Mexican Americans in several ways. First, in keeping with a broader effort to coordinate all his government's efforts in North America, Petricioli convened the first installment of what would become an annual meeting of Mexico's forty-two consuls in the United States, along with his country's attachés for trade and tourism.

Second, in March 1991 Von Bertrab and his team assembled 150 leaders of the Hispanic-American Alliance for Free Trade in Washington. This organization, founded earlier with the encouragement of SECOFI's NAFTA office, was composed largely of owners of small- and medium-sized businesses from El Paso, Chicago, Los Angeles, San Diego, and other cities with large Hispanic populations.

Third, Mexican diplomats disseminated information about NAFTA through their Presidential Program for Service to Overseas Mexican Communities. Salinas began this initiative after an October 1989 meeting in Washington with Mexican American leaders, seeking closer ties with Mexico. Lodged within the foreign ministry, the program cooperated closely with Mexican consulates in Chicago, Houston, Los Angeles, Miami, and San Diego.

Fourth, on the heels of their 1989 meeting with Salinas, leaders of organizations such as the National Council of La Raza Unida—an umbrella group of 134 Hispanic community affiliates—and the League of United Latin American Citizens began lobbying for NAFTA in the hope that they would advance their own agenda in exchange for their support for the agreement dear to the Bush administration's heart. La Raza, for example, sought a ban on guest workers and increased funding for border controls.

Meanwhile, Cuban-American activists, long critical of Mexico's unswerving friendship with the Castro regime, joined the effort "to mend fences and extend a gesture of good will." Puerto Rican Governor Rafael Hernandez Colón even dispatched a vaguely worded letter to congressional leaders declaiming the "benefits of open markets."[24]

Finally, in July 1992 Mexico's development bank, Nacional Financiera (NAFIN), and the Mexican Investment Board announced their readiness to promote joint ventures between Mexicans and Hispanic Americans. This program, in which NAFIN would furnish up to a fourth of the risk capital, would apply to investments in small businesses on both sides of the border.[25] Still, the combination of Mexican Americans' low incomes, modest educational levels, leadership conflicts, below-average voter registration, and ambivalence toward their homeland suggest that many years will pass before Chicanos play for Mexico the same role in influencing U.S. policy that Jews fill for Israel or Greek Americans do for Greece.

In the final analysis, Salinas himself proved Mexico's best lobbyist. He knew the United States better than any of his predecessors, having earned three advanced degrees from Harvard University. A month before taking office, Salinas met with President-elect Bush in Houston. Their initially good rapport only improved as the two chief executives joined forces to wage the free trade "battle." By late 1993 Salinas had met eight times with Presidents Bush and Clinton, more often than any previous Mexican chief executive.[26] Invariably the presidents used the sessions to extol—often exaggerate—the virtues of NAFTA.

Mexico's heightened activity in Washington even came to the fore in the statements of State Department officials. As one reporter put it, "One observed that the Mexicans used to be invisible here. Now they're all over the place."[27] A writer for the *Wall Street Journal* even claimed that Mexico had "suddenly upstaged Japan as the foreign government with the most visible lobbying muscle in the U.S."[28] A Mexican official summarized his government's new-found activism by saying, "When in Rome do as the Romans do. When in Washington, do as people inside the beltway do."[29]

By the end of the campaign, Mexico's estimated expenditures on NAFTA promotion reached $45 million,[30] with upward of $15 million paid in 1993 alone.[31] Such substantial outlays, although a normal part of shaping political outcomes in Washington, handed a sword to critics of foreign influence peddling and NAFTA's opponents that they could wield with a vengeance. Charles Lewis, executive director of the Center for Public Integrity, an organization established as a watchdog over initiatives to affect government policies, suggested that Mexico's foreign lobbying campaign may have been the biggest in history. "With Mexico hiring a large number of officials," he said, "it can look like they're trying to buy ratification of the treaty."[32] H. Ross Perot, an independent presidential candidate in 1992 and 1996, went even further to condemn efforts to pressure Washington decisionmakers: "Mexico is a good neighbor and friend of the United States," he wrote, "but the U.S. should not be subjected to foreign political campaigns and foreign lobbying."[33]

Did Mexico get its money's worth in the NAFTA struggle? The answer depends on Mexican policymakers' expected payoff. Undoubtedly Salinas and his colleagues benefited during negotiations from the legal advice rendered by Shearman & Sterling, as well as other law firms. Admittedly enormous amount of intelligence about the U.S. political process gathered and analyzed by Mexico's NAFTA advisers gave the Mexican government a clearer picture of the prospects for ratification. Nonetheless, these advisers fell short by failing to alert Mexico City to the possibility that Bush, with whom the Salinas regime had identified closely, might lose the 1992 presidential election. Indeed Bill Clinton's victory persuaded Petricioli, whose nonlegislative contacts included mostly Republicans, to return home so that a new envoy could start afresh with the Democratic administration. His replacement, Montaño, enjoyed a cordial relationship with the new administration, at least partially because during his service as Mexico's United Nations ambassador Montaño had hosted a cocktail party for Clinton during the Democratic convention in New York.

In terms of lobbying, however, Mexico City officials quickly learned that U.S. lawmakers respond most briskly to contacts from constituents, not to entreaties from foreign governments and their professional agents. In the final analysis, NAFTA passed in 1993 because the president of the United States, albeit belatedly, committed the enormous prestige and resources of his office to ratification. In this effort USA*NAFTA's activities, as an extension of American corporations' interests, proved more effective than the several dozen K Street firms that SECOFI had mobilized to represent Mexican concerns. But even as Mexican policymakers saw domestic interests make the difference for NAFTA ratification, the experience also gave them a crash course in the operation of the U.S. political system while developing and honing their congressional lobbying skills for future use. Ironically, the Mexican government's Herculean labors on Capitol Hill served to legitimate efforts by Mexican and international human rights groups, religious bodies, dissident trade unions, and international nongovernmental organizations to take their quarrels with the obdurate PRI-run government to Washington.

A Comparison between Canadian and Mexican Lobbying

There were many similarities between the negotiations for the Canada-U.S. FTA and those for NAFTA. In summary, however, this chapter highlights the differences of Canadian and Mexican lobbying efforts, respectively between approaches to the U.S. Congress in each political culture.

First, although Gotlieb recruited law firms and lobbying groups in pursuit of his goals, Canada's Department of External Affairs, currently known as DFAIT,[34] took charge of free trade negotiations through its Washington embassy. This responsibility generated relatively few problems of coordination. DFAIT consulted Industry Canada, Energy Canada, Investment Canada, and other agencies with a major stake in the outcome. Even more important, Parliament had integrated the Trade Commissioner Service into the foreign ministry in 1981. By contrast, President Salinas had given rein over his pro-NAFTA efforts to SECOFI and left SRE in a supporting role.

Second, although Canadian consulates occasionally became actively involved in FTA deliberations, Canada's Washington embassy operated as the nerve center for in-country FTA initiatives—a division of labor that prevails even today in Canada's diplomacy. Almost a decade after the period in question, Canadian consulate staffs typically concentrate on the traditional functions of issuing visas, assisting Canadians in the United States, supplying economic information to American businessmen, and submitting their analyses of local developments to Ottawa. Distinctively, Mexico City affirmatively engaged its many consulates in mobilizing support for NAFTA, and in the late 1990s it has assigned an even greater priority to senior consular officers for courting U.S. congressmen.

Third, neither before, during, nor after the passage of the FTA did the Canadian government ask private U.S. citizens of Canadian origin to contact their representatives in Washington on behalf of Ottawa's agenda. By comparison, U.S.-posted Mexican diplomats attempted to mobilize Americans of Mexican descent, although for the various reasons already described their success turned out to be, at best, limited.

Fourth, Canadians have only recently begun taking advantage of the policy networks that suffuse Capitol Hill. Early in the first Clinton administration, for example, the embassy staff enjoyed some assistance from the Northeast Midwest Institute, which assists 36 senators and 120 representatives in gathering information and coordinating legislative initiatives on behalf of their regions. The Canada-led action succeeded in killing a projected tax of $1.50 on each visitor crossing from Canada and Mexico into the United States. In late 1997 the Canadian government spearheaded a move to allow Canadians to enter the United States without the I-94 credential, a privilege apparently lost to sloppy drafting in the Immigration Reform and Control Act of 1986. With respect to issues that might adversely affect cross-frontier commerce, the embassy has worked closely with organizations such as the Canadian-American Border Trade Alliance; the International Bridge, Tunnel, and Turnpike Association; and the Eastern Border Transport Coalition.

More often, however, Canadian diplomats prefer to rely on the good offices of individual legislators. For instance, Canada's current ambassador, Raymond Chrétien, has made it his goal to visit personally a select list of legislators, with particular emphasis focused on the men and women who chair the key subcommittees of the committees regarded as most important to Canadian interests.[35] In addition, before accepting a speaking engagement outside Washington, Chrétien tries to meet with the senators and possibly the House members from the state he plans to visit.

Of course delegations of U.S. and Canadian lawmakers participate in the U.S.-Canadian Interparliamentary Group, whose annual meetings take place alternatively in Canada and the United States. Even though missteps have occasionally beset these encounters, they do attract such powerful U.S. legislators as Senator Frank H. Murkowski of Alaska, who maintains an active interest in the salmon-fishing disputes that soured U.S.-Canadian affairs in mid-1997.

Mexico has also built individual relationships with senators and representatives. In recent memory Mexico's strongest advocates have included Representatives Kika de la Garza of Texas, Bill Richardson of New Mexico, Xavier Becerra and David Dreier of California, and James Kolbe of Arizona and Senators Christopher S. Dodd of Connecticut, Bill Bradley of New Jersey, Lloyd Bentsen and Phil Gramm of Texas, and Jon Kyl and John McCain of Arizona.

In the Senate Bentsen (1971–93), harbored an especially warm spot in his heart for Texas's neighbor to the south. During later service as Clinton's Treasury secretary (1993–95) he may have single-handedly achieved Mexico's admission to the Organization for Economic Cooperation and Development (OECD). Bentsen traveled to the body's Paris headquarters in early 1994 to meet with his counterparts and other high-level officials. To his dismay, the U.S. delegation was prepared to present a pro forma speech, cobbled together by an interagency committee and devoid of substantive proposals. Reaching beyond insipid generalities, Bentsen seized on urging Mexico's OECD membership—an idea contained in a speech delivered by Commerce Secretary Ron Brown. The proposal surprised the Europeans in attendance, many of whom believed Mexico's corruption and authoritarianism should bar affiliation. A number of OECD members were "frosted"—in the words of one observer—and wasted no time voicing their concern to U.S. colleagues in the OECD secretariat. They quickly learned that even the Americans did not know in advance of Senator Bentsen's decision to go to bat for Mexico. Nonetheless, in a move that indicated President Clinton's high regard for the widely experienced Texan, the White House threw its full weight behind the proposal, and Mexico proudly became the OECD's twenty-fifth member in May 1994.[36] To his credit, President Salinas had his ducks in a row, so Mexico could take full advantage of the U.S. backing.

Like their Canadian colleagues, Mexican legislators also meet their U.S. counterparts through annual interparliamentary sessions. Since their inception, three factors have sapped the utility of these meetings. First, during his tenure de la Garza treated the interparliamentary conclave as his personal project, discouraging active involvement by other legislators.[37] Second, the constitutional prohibition on Mexican legislators' serving consecutive terms in their posts impedes the continuity of the Mexican delegation, posing a striking contrast to the policy expertise and institutional memory of senior members of Congress. And third, Mexican congressmen have earned such nicknames as *levantadedos* ("yes men"), *mandaderos de presidentes* ("presidential messenger boys"), and *cajas de resonancia presidencial* ("presidential echo chambers"), for their erstwhile deference to the executive branch.

The PRI's mid-1997 loss of its majority in the 500-member Chamber of Deputies will assuredly change the composition of Mexico's delegation to future binational parleys. The presence of 261 opposition members in the lower house, including opposition-party chairs of thirty-two of the body's fifty-nine committees, may lead more nongovernmental organizations and other groups with grievances against the Mexican government to air them before Mexico's Congress rather than taking their cases to Capitol Hill. Nevertheless, key members of the U.S. Congress will remain hospitable to Zedillo's detractors, especially Minority Leader Richard A. Gephardt, who seeks to discredit NAFTA en route to wresting the Democratic nomination for the year 2000 from Vice President Al Gore, an enthusiastic advocate of the trade pact.

Quite apart from individual contacts, Mexican interests often enjoy backing from the U.S.-based Congressional Hispanic Caucus (CHC), a seventeen-member body created in 1976 to highlight the concerns and advance the agenda of Hispanic American legislators and their constituents. The caucus, boasting eleven members of Mexican descent, most closely shadows Mexico City's line respecting questions of immigration, human rights, and drug enforcement sanctions. Despite their representation of different and dispersed constituencies affected differently by trade, nine of the then-fifteen CHC members voted for the NAFTA legislation.

Assistance from the caucus helps partly offset a tradition of Mexico-bashing on Capitol Hill, most fervently performed by Senator Jesse Helms of North Carolina since the mid-1980s. Although extremely hostile to the 1995 Helms-Burton Act, the Mexican government kept quiet its interest in Canadian suggestions that the NAFTA partners invoke the treaty to defang or dilute the anti-Castro legislation. Wary of incurring the wrath of Helms and other detractors, Mexico's embassy, in compliance with President Zedillo's unwavering commitment to economic liberalization, bent over backward to avoid "contaminating" NAFTA with the Helms-Burton legislation or other controversial measures. Similarly, despite extensive front-page coverage of the process back home, Mexican diplomats assiduously avoided public involvement in President Clinton's star-crossed nomination of Massachusetts' former governor William F. Weld as ambassador to Mexico—an appointment killed by Senator Helms in September 1997.

Since the December 1994 collapse of the peso followed by the Salinas family tragicomedy (involving allegations of drug trafficking, sex crimes, and murder), criticism of Mexican policy has arisen in Mexico City as often as in Washington. For example, nationalist elements within both the ruling PRI and the left-center Democratic Revolutionary Party (Partido de la Revolución Democrática, PRD) have reviled Ivy League–educated technocrats for championing U.S.-favored economic liberalization at the expense of the Mexican masses. In this vein some firebrands have unfairly labeled former foreign secretary, later finance secretary, José Angel Gurría Treviño the Angel of Dependence in contrast to the striking bronze statue of the Angel of Independence that adorns Paseo de la Reforma, one block from the American Embassy.

Although seldom the focus of extensive mean-spirited campaigns, Canadian policymakers can sympathize with Mexico over strident rhetoric by U.S. lawmakers, who since the end of the cold war have evidenced even less concern than before over the quality of relations with neighbors. Canadians stoically endured a tongue-in-cheek barb offered by Senator Kent Conrad of North Dakota during hearings decrying the competition suffered by Midwest producers of durum wheat at the hands of Canadian farmers. Conrad stated, "We have a lot of strategic missiles in North Dakota pointed at Russia. Perhaps we should aim them at Canada." Like Queen Victoria, Ottawa was not amused by the senator's mordant humor.

As recently as July 23, 1997, Senator Murkowski of Alaska and Representative Don Young of Arkansas successfully presented a resolution condemning the Canadian government for "its failure to accept responsibility for the illegal blockade of a U.S. vessel and calling on the President to take appropriate action." These nonbinding congressional acts sprang from actions by Canadian fishermen to protest U.S. curbs on salmon fishing in the North Pacific.[38]

U.S. lawmakers showed uncharacteristic restraint, however, when Prime Minister Jean Chrétien sharply criticized President Clinton and American elected officials in comments he unknowingly made into open microphones to Belgian and Luxembourg colleagues attending a NATO meeting. Chrétien attributed the White House's eagerness to expand the alliance to its courtship of "ethnic voting blocs in the United States." For instance, admission of the Baltic states "has nothing to do with world security," the Canadian leader averred. "It's because in Chicago, Mayor Daley controls lots of votes for the [Democratic] nomination." In addition, he said that U.S. politicians are so brazen in buying votes that they "would be in jail" in other countries. Finally, Chrétien boasted that his standing up to the United States proved "popular" at home.[39]

A fifth way in which Canadian and Mexican lobbying differ is with respect to the roles of ambassadorial spouses. Mrs. Gotlieb and Mrs. Chrétien, for instance, have made a determined effort to include lawmakers' wives in activities held in and sponsored by the embassy. Although gracious hostesses, the spouses of Mexican ambassadors have generally paid less attention to congressional wives. Several explanations underlie this attitude. Mexican congressmen boast few of the substantive prerogatives taken for granted by North American legislators. Besides, Mexico's lawmakers enjoy relatively low social status compared with that of senior diplomats and their wives. And lack of fluency in English may restrict some Mexican envoys' wives to socializing principally with peers from Spanish-speaking countries.

Finally, Mexican diplomats are quick to identify a major difference in their Washington lobbying capability vis-à-vis Canada. As a senior official in the Mexican Embassy exclaimed, "They've got a helluva lot more money to spend!" All told, five professionals and an administrative assistant comprised the Congress and Legal Affairs section of the Canadian Embassy in mid-1998. In contrast, the Mexicans could count only four professionals and two secretaries. Mexico's Washington presence, which went from underrepresentation to overkill in less than five years, now essentially follows the Canadian model, to the extent that the ambassador and government professionals shoulder most of the burden of lobbying the U.S. Congress.

As I have shown, both historic proximity and modern commercial demands have led to intensified and changed trade diplomacy between Mexico, Canada, and the United States. Despite the nightmare of commingling commerce and foreign policy evoked by John Huang's fundraising/influence-peddling surrounding the 1996 American presidential campaign, observations of the earlier North American free trade deliberations only underscore the current convergence and evolution of trade politics. Washington's NAFTA partners have adopted many similar means to influence policymaking in the United States, and they have chosen the same focus for their lobbying, devoting about half their time and resources to Congress and half to administrative agencies. In the final analysis, though, American lawmakers respond more readily to domestic interest groups, organized constituents, and the executive branch of government than they do to representatives of other countries. The late 1997 congressional probe of offshore fund-raising by Clinton and Gore will only serve to sharpen this tendency.

Notes

1. Christopher M. Sands, *Canada: A Case of Local Foreign Policy* (Washington, D.C.: Center for Strategic and International Studies, Americas Program, April 15, 1996), p. 2.

2. Charles Doran and Joel Sokolsky, *Canada and Congress: Lobbying in Washington* (Centre for Foreign Policy Studies, Dalhousie University, 1985) and referred to in Sands, *Canada: A Case of Local Foreign Policy*, pp. 3–4.

3. Allan Gotlieb, *"I'll Be with You in a Minute, Mr. Ambassador": The Education of a Canadian Diplomat in Washington* (University of Toronto Press, 1991), p. 29.

4. Überpolitician Bob Strauss summed up the changes buffeting Capitol Hill with crudity: "Gotlieb," he said, "the difference between Congress now and fifteen years ago is the difference between chicken-salad and chicken-shit." See Gotlieb, *"I'll Be with You in a Minute, Mr. Ambassador,"* p. 29.

5. This section draws on George W. Grayson's *Oil and Mexican Foreign Policy* (University of Pittsburgh Press, 1988), pp. 83–106, and Grayson's *The North American Free Trade Agreement: Regional Community and the New World Order* (Lanham, Md.: University Press of America, 1995), pp. 75–81.

6. Stephen Clarkson, *Canada and the Reagan Challenge: Crisis and Adjustment 1981–1985* (Toronto: James Lorimer & Co., 1985), cited in Sands, *Canada: A Case of Local Foreign Policy*, p. 3.

7. Arnold D. P. Heeney, *The Things That Are Caesar's: Memoirs of a Canadian Public Servant* (University of Toronto Press, 1972), p. 127.

8. *Wall Street Journal*, July 29, 1985, p. 1.

9. Gotlieb, *"I'll Be with You in a Minute, Mr. Ambassador,"* pp. 105–06.

10. Ibid.

11. Quoted in the *Wall Street Journal*, July 29, 1985, p. 1.

12. As it turned out, Deaver began discussing a "possible contract" with Canada on May 16, 1985, six days after he left government service. See the *Wall Street Journal*, May 12, 1986, p. 12.

13. *Washington Post*, May 12, 1987, pp. B–1, B–4.

14. Thomas D. Schoonover, ed. and trans., *Mexico Lobby: Matías Romero in Washington, 1861–1867* (University of Kentucky Press, 1986), pp. xii–xiii.

15. Eisenstadt, "The Rise of the Mexico Lobby in Washington," p. 97.

16. Based on lobbying reports filed under the Foreign Agents Registration Act, U.S. Department of Justice, Washington, D.C., outlays on trade and countervailing duties are considered "quasi-political."

17. Eisenstadt, "The Rise of the Mexico Lobby in Washington," p. 95.

18. Ibid., p. 92.

19. *Proceso*, September 24, 1990, p. 8.

20. The additional agencies were the Office of the Attorney General, the Office for the Negotiation of Free Trade Treaty, and the Ministries of Fisheries and Finance and Public Credit. Already present were the Ministries of Commerce and Industrial Development, Agriculture and Hydraulic Resources, National Defense, Navy, and Tourism, as well as the Nacional Financiera development bank. Data supplied by the Office of Press and Public Affairs, the Mexican Embassy, Washington, D.C., April 10, 1992.

21. For copious information on pro-NAFTA lobbying through 1992 with emphasis on former U.S. government officials, see *The Trading Game: Inside Lobbying for the North American Free Trade Agreement* (Washington, D.C.: Center for Public Integrity, n.d.).

22. *Washington Post,* September 28, 1993, p. A21.

23. Ibid.

24. Jorge Mas Canosa, the head of the Cuban-American National Foundation, quoted in the *Washington Post,* May 23, 1991, p. A21.

25. Among the Hispanic organizations invited to take part in the program are the National Council of La Raza, the U.S. Hispanic Chamber of Commerce in Texas, and the California Hispanic Chamber of Commerce; Press Office of the President of Mexico, *Mexico: On the Record,* 1, no. 8 (August/September 1992): 3.

26. The two leaders met in Paris (July 1989), Washington (October 1989 and June 1990), Monterrey (November 1990), San Antonio (February 1991), Houston (April 1991), Camp David, Maryland (December 1991), and San Antonio (October 1992). Salinas's predecessors, López Portillo (1976–82) and de la Madrid (1982–88), held six meetings apiece with their U.S. counterparts.

27. *New York Times,* December 30, 1991, p. A4.

28. *Wall Street Journal,* April 25, 1991, p. A16.

29. Ibid.

30. *Wall Street Journal,* May 20, 1993, p. A18.

31. Ibid.

32. Ibid.; Charles Lewis and Margaret Ebrahim, "Can Mexico and Big Business USA Buy NAFTA?" *The Nation,* June 14, 1993, pp. 826–39.

33. Ross Perot (with Pat Choate), *Save Your Job, Save Our Country: Why NAFTA Must Be Stopped—Now!* (New York: Hyperion, 1993), p. 63.

34. The current name of Canada's foreign ministry is the Department of Foreign Affairs and International Trade (DFAIT).

35. Among the Senate committees are Foreign Relations, Finance, and Environment; those in the House include International Relations, Ways and Means, and Environment.

36. Telephone communication from Senator Bentsen, August 19, 1997.

37. The replacement of de la Garza, who retired in 1996, by Arizona's Kolbe has reenergized these bilateral meetings. In addition, the PRI's losing its majority in the 500-member Chamber of Deputies in mid-1997 should spark a more diverse and feisty Mexican delegation at upcoming sessions.

38. S. Res. 109, *Congressional Record,* July 23, 1997, p. S7965.

39. John F. Harris, "Tape Catches Choice Words about Clinton," *Washington Post,* July 10, 1997, p. A24, and "First U.S. Leader to Visit since Fall of Communism Is Hailed Despite Stalling NATO Bid," July 12, 1997, p. A16.

PART TWO

The New Context

Chapter 5

The New Congress

Norman Ornstein

IN LATE JULY and early August 1997, the nation's capital was captivated by the struggle between Senate Foreign Relations Committee Chairman Jesse Helms and Massachusetts Governor William Weld. Weld, a Republican, had been picked by President Clinton as his nominee to be American ambassador to Mexico. When he first heard of the choice, Helms made it clear that he would refuse to allow a hearing on the nomination, much less a vote in the Foreign Relations Committee or on the floor of the Senate. Helms offered no public statement or grounds for his opposition to his fellow Republican; speculation on his motives included unease with Weld's positions on medical uses of marijuana and gay rights (he favors both), Weld's general position as a social moderate or liberal, and Weld's response when he was running for the Senate in 1996 and asked during a debate if he would support Helms as Foreign Relations chair if he were in the Senate (he said no).

Weld did not try quiet diplomacy or obeisance to the powerful Helms. He called a press conference to blast Helms in which he said that his confirmation was a fight for the soul of the Republican Party and vowed to fight either a land war or an air war, whichever was required, to win the confirmation battle in the Senate. When the White House and Foreign Relations Committee aides privately suggested that he seek to become ambassador to India, Weld angrily refused, challenging the president to back him for the post he had originally accepted. The president offered backing, but Weld's bravado did not allow him to prevail. Eventually, with the rules of the Senate and the majority leader against him, Weld withdrew his candidacy.

The Helms-Weld brouhaha captured a lot of attention because it was a fight between two Republicans over a Democratic president's nomination—and because it exploded during the summer doldrums when there was little other news to occupy journalists and pundits. The episode, however, underscored a basic reality about Congress and foreign policy: in the absence of a big knockdown, drag-out fight, the public and the press pay little attention to Congress as a maker of American foreign policy—and even less attention generally to Congress and hemispheric relations. If the press focuses attention on anything, it is on the political wrangling, not on the policy concerns.

If the inattention is motivated by a belief that Congress is insignificant in foreign policy toward our neighbors, the public and the press are misguided; every chapter in this book emphasizes the important—even critical—role that Congress plays in American relationships with Canada and Mexico. These chapters make it clear that the role of Congress has been significant not just in recent episodes such as the forging of the North American Free Trade Agreement (NAFTA) but in important areas of policy throughout U.S. history. But if the role of Congress has been significant, it has not always been the same. The role of Congress depends on the times, the personalities, the politics, and the issues. In all these ways, the role of Congress has changed and continues to evolve in important and not necessarily salutary ways.

Among the most important changes are partisan ones, especially those involving control of the various houses and branches of government. Since the end of World War II, America has experienced divided government nearly two-thirds of the time—usually with a Republican president facing a Democratic Congress. The first six Reagan years brought a variation of that alignment, with the Republican president and a Republican-majority Senate taking on a Democratic-majority House of Representatives. For Reagan's final two years and George Bush's four years as president, the more typical pattern of Republican president and fully Democratic Congress prevailed.

Bill Clinton's election in 1992, fueled by a clear-cut voter desire for change after twelve years of Republican presidents, brought back the second most typical post–World War II pattern, with Democrats in charge of both ends of Pennsylvania Avenue. But the 1994 election ushered in an unusual alignment, one America had not seen since the Truman years, 1947–48—a Democratic president and a Republican Congress. The 1994 election signaled dramatic change in American politics, change triggered by anger, cynicism, and frustration across the electorate. The 104th Congress (1995–97) that it shaped was an extraordinary one, more active and assertive in policy terms than any Congress in modern times, with a boisterous and belligerent freshman class that promised to have a long-lasting impact on American politics, much like the Democrats' post-Watergate class of 1974.

The 1974 election had been a landmark election, driven by the Watergate scandal and the subsequent pardon of former president Richard Nixon by his successor, Gerald Ford. With Republican turnout dampened by demoralization and Democratic turnout heightened by outrage, the Democrats picked up forty-eight seats in the House of Representatives and five seats in the Senate, creating supersize majorities in both houses. Seventy-four freshman Democrats stormed the House of Representatives, nearly all aggressive proponents of activist government and sweeping governmental reform.

The 1974 class included members such as Tom Downey of New York; Henry Waxman, George Miller, and Norm Mineta of California; Christopher Dodd of Connecticut; Paul Simon of Illinois; and Tim Wirth of Colorado—savvy politicians who stayed in Washington for two decades and more after their first election, shaping policy in areas such as welfare, education, health care, and the environment. That class was also instrumental in implementing reforms that transformed the seniority system and the internal dynamics of Congress and in underscoring a new entrepreneurial style in Washington that was described by political scientist Burdette Loomis in his book *The New American Politician*. Loomis quoted class member Tim Wirth as saying, "We were the children of Vietnam, not children of World War II. We were products of television, not print. We were products of computer politics, not courthouse politics. And we were the reflections of JFK as president, not FDR. We were the first class that was like that, and now the whole place is."[1]

Like the 1974 election, the 1994 election had been fueled by anger, in this case aroused by policy failures in areas such as health care. A mirror image of the 1974 election, the 1994 election saw a dampened Democratic turnout and a heightened Republican one, a Republican gain of fifty-two seats in the House and eight in the Senate, with seventy-four freshman majority members coming to the House. Like their 1974 counterparts, they were products of television and computers. But in contrast with their predecessors, the new Republican members of Congress were children of the cold war, not Vietnam, and reflections of Ronald Reagan, not George Bush or Richard Nixon.

There were two other significant differences between the class of 1974 and the class of 1994. Loomis referred to the earlier group as "new American politicians." Most members of the 1994 group viewed the term *politician* as an epithet; they viewed themselves as antipoliticians who were in Washington for a short time to clean up a mess, but then would return home to resume their previous jobs or careers. Most said they would limit their own terms to three or six years total. Second, the members of the class of 1974 were generally internationalist and oriented toward free trade.[2] Most had traveled extensively in the world in college or after. The members of the class of 1994 were more insular and introspective in their views, and they were both less well traveled and less interested in travel abroad.

Still, both groups brought a revolutionary ardor to Washington, along with a determination to turn the existing order upside down and to shake up the leadership ranks. For many of the Democrats in the class of 1974, the ideology remained for many years, but the revolutionary spirit was subsumed by a desire to build power inside Congress—and by success at doing so. For the Republicans in the class of 1994, the shock of voter reaction against their revolutionary rhetoric, combined with their desire to retain their slim majority in the next election, caused the rhetoric and behavior to tone down by the spring of 1996. Indeed the revolutionary atmosphere and attitude that characterized the class of 1994 was absent by the end of the 104th Congress. By the time of the 1996 election anger had changed to complacency, albeit with little change in voter cynicism, but a higher level of voter contentment led to an election not of change but of stability, bringing back both Democrat Bill Clinton as president and the Republican majorities in both houses of Congress.

The changing alignments over the past decades have shaped the policy agenda and often policy outcomes as well, but not always in predictable ways. In some respects the more pronounced impact has come from the overall changes, particularly the striking turnover in Congress among both Democrats and Republicans—turnover that has created a clearly post–cold war Congress.

The 1992 Election and the 103d Congress

By the fall of 1992 a prediction of election victory for Democratic challenger Bill Clinton was commonplace among political prognosticators. But eighteen months earlier such a prediction would have been met with universal ridicule. In mid-1991, in the aftermath of the overwhelming U.S. victory in the Gulf War, George Bush peaked at 91 percent approval of the electorate, the highest level ever recorded for a president in the history of national surveys. But no president in the six decades since systematic polling began has suffered the sustained drop in popularity and approval that Bush subsequently experienced, going from that high of 91 percent to 38 percent at the polls in November 1992.

If the absence of voter loyalty was a hallmark of American politics in 1992, the sharp drop in approval for Bush did not translate into a huge jump in approval for his Democratic rival. Arkansas Governor Bill Clinton struggled in the spring and early summer of 1992 to win the Democratic party nomination, stung in particular by his draft history and allegations of sexual impropriety. However, he recovered early enough to emerge with a clear-cut victory at the Democratic convention in New York and to run a strong campaign in the fall. But he ended up with only 43 percent of the votes in November.

Clinton could end far short of a majority of voter support and still win the presidency handily because of the performance in the election of a third candidate, H. Ross Perot. Perot's campaign was an erratic one, marked by his abrupt withdrawal in July and subsequent reentry in the fall, but he nevertheless ended up with 19 percent of the votes, the strongest showing by a third-party or independent contender since former president Theodore Roosevelt's Bull Moose Party candidacy in 1912. Perot's support underscored both the weakness of the two major parties and the power of a reformist, populist message delivered by a credible outsider, and Perot emerged as a major figure in American politics in 1993.

Bill Clinton's victory was accompanied by continuing Democratic control of both houses of Congress, but for the first time in the twentieth century an incumbent president, Bush, lost even as his party, the Republicans, gained seats in the House of Representatives. The ten-seat gain in the House by the Grand Old Party (GOP), coupled with no net change in the Senate, left the Democrats with comfortable majorities in both houses, 259 to 176 in the House and 57 to 43 in the Senate. But the unified government that followed did not find easy and comfortable majorities in policy. The first nine months of 1993 were dominated by the struggle over Clinton's economic plan; a major part, an economic stimulus package, had to be dropped, and the compromised plan eventually passed by one vote in each house of Congress, without a single Republican vote.

Soon after that struggle, in September 1993, President Clinton began the battle over NAFTA. Clinton had inherited the treaty from his predecessor; when he began his major effort, votes for NAFTA clearly were not there in either house of Congress. But a full-scale campaign by the White House, punctuated by a unique television debate on the Cable News Network between Vice President Al Gore and NAFTA opponent Ross Perot, ultimately prevailed. In mid-November NAFTA was supported in the House 234 to 200 and then in the Senate 61 to 38. Unlike the battle over the economic plan, NAFTA was a bipartisan effort that passed with the support of more Republicans than Democrats. Indeed in the House Republicans voted by a three-to-one margin for the treaty, 132 to 43, whereas a majority of the Democrats, 157, voted no compared with only 102 in favor.

Democratic Party opposition to NAFTA was led by House Majority Leader Dick Gephardt of Missouri and Majority Whip David Bonior of Michigan, bolstered by vociferous opposition from the AFL-CIO and from Ross Perot, who in turn was joined in opposition by conservative Pat Buchanan, who had challenged George Bush for the Republican presidential nomination in 1992, and by liberal Ralph Nader. After the vote Perot said, "There will be three votes on this agreement. This is the first one. The second vote will be in '94, and the third one will be in '96."[3] And the AFL-CIO announced that it would single out Democrats who defied labor's wishes and voted for NAFTA and punish them at the polls.

Clinton's success on NAFTA did not provide sufficient momentum to give him unbridled policy success in the second year of the 103d Congress. As a result of a series of defeats on Clinton's top priority, comprehensive health care reform, no health package made it through Congress. The humiliating nature of that defeat underscored for many voters a belief that the system was not producing; that view, in turn, played into the 1994 elections.

The 1994 Election and the New Republican Congress

Despite the signs in public opinion surveys of public anger and disillusionment with politics and politicians, few political professionals predicted that the Republicans would actually capture Congress in 1994. In the final preelection prediction roundup published by the *Washington*

Post the Sunday before the election, only three of fourteen political analysts picked the Republicans to win both houses of Congress.[4]

Win the Republicans did, by stunning margins and across the board. Republicans gained a net of fifty-two seats in the House and eight in the Senate. In the South they won a majority of the seats in both houses for the first time since the Reconstruction. They gained seventeen seats in the Midwest, sixteen in the South, and ten on the West Coast. The only gains the Democrats made in the House were four open GOP seats; not a single Republican incumbent lost.

In the Senate Republicans swept all nine open-seat races and defeated two Democratic incumbents while not losing a single one of their own incumbents. The Senate freshman class consisted of eleven Republicans and no Democrats in the first shutout for a party since 1914. After the election the Republicans got a huge bonus when two Democratic senators, Alabama's Richard Shelby and Colorado's Ben Nighthorse Campbell, defected to the Republican side.

When the 104th House convened in January 1995, there was not one Republican among the 230 representatives who had ever been in the majority before that time. A full 52 percent of all the members of the House had come there for the first time in the 1990s. The freshman class of seventy-three Republicans entered the body as a majority and ballyhooed political force, likened by journalists and their colleagues to the fabled Watergate class of seventy-four freshman Democrats in 1974 who had helped transform the institution through reform and activism.

Most of the freshmen had run for Congress on a common agenda, including hostility to Washington and Congress, term limits, a balanced budget amendment to the Constitution, cutting government, welfare reform, the line item veto, and tax cuts. Foreign policy had not been a significant part of that agenda or of the dialogue in their campaigns; if trade came up, it tended to be in a domestic or job-related context. A majority of the freshman Republicans were young (under forty-five years of age) and inexperienced (only 53 percent had previously held elective office, about two-thirds the level of previous classes).

The freshman Republicans were uniformly grateful to Representative Newt Gingrich, the new Speaker of the House, for his election help and strategy, and they made it clear that they viewed him as their top leader. But the election was not one in which candidates ran by pledging to subjugate their own views to those of their party leaders. A comment made in April 1995 by freshman Linda Smith of Washington state reflected the feisty and independent attitude of many of the junior GOP lawmakers: "We are here on a mission, and I will remain loyal to Gingrich only as long as he doesn't lose sight of what the people of Washington want us to accomplish." Smith went on to note: "My base is more populist than Republican."[5]

The freshmen remained almost uniformly loyal to the Speaker through the first hundred days of the 104th Congress. The agenda was the Contract with America, ten policy and procedural objectives that Republican candidates had pledged during the campaign to support and bring up at the beginning of the new Congress if they were given the majority. To fulfill that promise, the new majority moved the House on a crash course, resulting in the most active legislative agenda for a new House since the 73d Congress under newly elected president Franklin Delano Roosevelt.

The House had a string of legislative successes in the first hundred days, but few of the bills, including a constitutional amendment to balance the budget, the line item veto, crime legislation, welfare reform, a national security reform bill, tax cuts, and product liability and tort reform, passed the Senate or were even brought up for votes. Virtually all the bills passed in the House did so on nearly pure party lines, more reminiscent of a parliamentary system than the typical congressional one—a development even more remarkable because the Republican majority, with 230 of 435 seats, was the smallest partisan majority in four decades.

As the Congress moved to its second and third hundred days in 1995, the agenda shifted increasingly to the budget, supplanting the specifics of the Contract with America agenda. With a mix of substantial tax cuts and major program cutbacks, including $270 billion to be taken out of projected Medicare and Medicaid budgets over five years, congressional Republicans pointed toward a year-end confrontation with the president over priorities. The confrontation began when the new fiscal year started, at the end of September 1995, and continued, with two extensive periods when substantial portions of the federal government shut down due to lack of money, into January 1996.

The public reaction to government shutdown and gridlock was strongly negative—and aimed squarely at the Republican Congress and Speaker Gingrich. Congress eventually retreated, and through the remainder of 1996 it took a more circumspect and less confrontational attitude toward the policy process and the White House. As a consequence, the final six months of the 104th Congress resulted in a spate of bipartisan legislative achievements, including small-scale health reform, welfare reform, and some environmental reform.

The 1996 Election and the 105th Congress

The combination of good economic times and an aura of bipartisan cooperation and accomplishment helped to bring about a status quo election resulting in the reelection of both the Democratic president and the Republican Congress. The 105th Congress (1997–98) had two more Republicans in the Senate, making their margin fifty-five to forty-five, and ten fewer Republicans in the House, reducing their majority to ten seats. The class of 1996 was different in many respects from its predecessor, less revolutionary and more experienced in politics; the majority of the newcomers had previously served in elective office, most in state legislatures.

The 1996 campaign was itself different from the preceding 1994 campaign, with more of a focus on the accomplishments of the previous two years than on the failures. But the 105th Congress started with a lurch, not a smooth landing, into policy deliberations. Pending allegations of ethics violations against Speaker Newt Gingrich erupted into weeks of turmoil, with Democrats charging Republicans with malfeasance and cover-up and Republicans charging Democrats with leaks and treachery. The Speaker barely held onto his position on the first day of the new House, as nearly a dozen of his Republican colleagues abstained or voted against him on the traditionally party-line vote that opened the Congress. Two weeks later a tense and sometimes divided ethics committee voted nearly unanimously to recommend that the House impose harsh penalties—including a formal reprimand and a $300,000 "assessment"—on Gingrich in an unprecedented rebuke of a Speaker, a recommendation ultimately accepted by the House. Speaker Gingrich kept his position but had to cope with division in his own party and harsh partisan divisions between the majority Republicans and the minority Democrats.

In March the House convened a "civility" retreat in Hershey, Pennsylvania, for members and families to try to "bond" and find ways to reduce the corrosive atmosphere and rhetoric. Two weeks later, while the House Rules Committee was holding a hearing on how to implement recommendations to create a more civil environment in the House, a fistfight nearly broke out on the House floor between Republican Whip Tom DeLay and Democrat Dave Obey over campaign reform, causing the "civility" hearing to be cut short.

The 105th Congress started out addressing a divisive and contentious issue, a proposed constitutional amendment to balance the budget, which had failed by one vote in the Senate in 1995. Now, with two more Republicans in the body, the Republicans felt more confident. But after weeks of intensive efforts Senate Majority Leader Trent Lott, who had replaced Bob Dole during 1996, fell one vote short yet again.

In the spring congressional Republicans stumbled in a fashion eerily reminiscent of the abortive government shutdown in 1995–96. This time the Republicans forced a confrontation over relief aid for flood disasters that had rocked the Midwest, trying to tie passage of the aid legislation to a GOP proposal to prevent any future shutdown while giving them bargaining advantage over the president. The president accused the Republicans of holding desperate flood victims hostage to their policy whims, a charge that a clear majority of voters agreed with in surveys; ultimately the Republicans were forced to back down amid harsh public criticism.

Still, despite the early stumbles and partisan tensions, the 105th Congress had several early accomplishments. Despite harsh criticism from his right and the vigorous opposition of Senate Foreign Relations Committee Chairman Jesse Helms, Trent Lott supported American ratification of the Chemical Weapons Convention and helped to shepherd it through the Senate. And President Clinton's team of negotiators, led by Chief of Staff Erskine Bowles, worked with House and Senate Republican leaders, Senate Democratic leader Tom Daschle, and a House Democratic contingent that excluded the top House party leaders, to craft a fiscal compromise to balance the budget by 2002 that passed muster against long odds in both houses of Congress. Congress also approved President Clinton's plan to extend most favored nation trade status to China despite vigorous opposition from House Democratic leader Dick Gephardt and Whip David Bonior, along with prominent Republican conservatives like Rules Committee Chairman Gerald Solomon. Gephardt and Bonior opposed the president's request for fast-track authority to negotiate trade agreements, and they eventually prevailed in November 1997.

By July 1997, as negotiations on the specifics of the tax and appropriations components of the budget plan were moving forward, the House was rocked by an abortive effort by several Republican Party leaders and rank-and-file conservatives to depose Speaker Gingrich, making it clear that any future accomplishments would have to occur in an atmosphere of upheaval and uncertainty in the majority leadership. The president had to cope as well with at best a cool relationship with his party's top House leader, who had signaled his interest in pursuing the Democratic presidential nomination in 2000.

By the end of 1997 the most significant news coming out of the 105th Congress was that the economy's remarkable, sustained robustness had resulted in the likelihood of a balanced budget, even a surplus, in the 1998 fiscal year—years ahead of schedule—prompting President Clinton to propose a balanced budget for the next fiscal year for the first time in three decades and generating a debate in Washington on what to do with the coming budget surpluses.

The good feeling generated by surpluses and economic growth did not eliminate all the political or policy problems that had surfaced in congressional-presidential dynamics. In mid-January 1998, just before the president's State of the Union message, a new scandal erupted over the possibility that the president had had a sexual relationship with a young intern and encouraged her to cover it up during the discovery process of the Paula Jones civil suit against the president for alleged sexual harassment.

This scandal brought an array of additional allegations against the president and dominated politics and the media for months. As it unfolded, however, public support for the president rose to the highest levels of his presidency, averaging about 65 percent—an extraordinarily high mark for a second-term president. At the same time public expressions of personal satisfaction and optimism about the future rose sharply, as did approval of most other institutions, including Congress.

Kenneth Starr, the independent counsel initially appointed to investigate Whitewater and then a host of other allegations including the Lewinsky affair, continued his long investigation of the president. The government constantly faced the possibility of impeachment hearings in the early spring. That prospect, in turn, raised questions about what Congress would do during the remainder of the 105th Congress and how its actions or inactions would affect the November elections—elections in which the slender Republican majority in the House would be at stake.

The Republican leaders had scheduled only eighty-nine days in session for the second year of the 105th Congress—the smallest number of days in session in modern times—underscoring their belief that satisfied and comfortable voters did not want a lot of action from Washington. But that desire conflicted with a substantial agenda, including completion of the budget, a major tobacco deal whose revenues were necessary to finance both Republican tax cuts and Democratic social programs, reform of the Internal Revenue Service, and dealing with a host of foreign policy issues, including expansion of the North Atlantic Treaty Organization, troop commitments in Bosnia, and funding for the International Monetary Fund (IMF) and the United Nations. Despite Republican leadership agreement with the President on IMF funding, a small group of conservative activists in the House blocked it in late 1997 and again in early 1998, not wanting funds to be spent on abortion. Their power showed both the indifference of many rank-and-file members from the post–cold war era to international affairs or institutions—and their leverage in a period of closely divided Congresses.

The New Congress and Foreign Policy

When the Senate passed the Chemical Weapons Convention (CWC) in 1997 with votes to spare, despite a lot of yelling, threats, posturing, and maneuvering, it indicated a fairly typical treaty ratification—not, as it appeared for a time, another Treaty of Versailles. The reversion to normalcy led many observers of American politics to breathe a sigh of relief; they thought maybe the contemporary Congress would end up boringly conventional in its treatment of international affairs, deferring on most matters to the executive branch of government.

However, the ultimate ease of passage of the CWC was deceptive. If the Clinton administration managed to dodge an embarrassing setback, thanks in major part to the spadework of Secretary of State Madeleine Albright, the acumen and efforts of National Security Advisor Sandy Berger, and the savvy and backbone of Senate Majority Leader Trent Lott, that model did not appear to be transferable to other foreign policy battles, including Bosnia, the Middle East, trade, or funding for diplomacy and foreign aid. Actually at least one part of the model appeared transferable to a host of foreign policy matters large and trivial—the enormous effort required to get Congress to go along.

A more cautious or pessimistic view of Congress and foreign policy stems from several characteristics, starting with one overarching reality: the 105th Congress is firmly, officially, irrevocably a post–cold war Congress in membership, experience, and outlook. That means it is a Congress that will rarely have the world outside American borders on its radar screen unless events put it there—events such as crises or scandals. That reality is especially true for most rank-and-file lawmakers. But the change is not just from the bottom up. The 105th is also a Congress without the raft of strong internationalist opinion leaders in the party or committee ranks that characterized many earlier Congresses.

To start with the membership, the status quo nature of the 1996 election masked a continuing underlying sea change in the makeup of Congress. There were 74 freshmen sworn into the House in January 1997, joining 15 new senators. There were 87 freshmen sworn in at the beginning of the 104th Congress and 110 at the start of the 103d. Putting the numbers together, they mean that over 62 percent of the 105th House had come in new since the nineties began—in other words, since the Berlin Wall had fallen—whereas 42 of the 100 members of the Senate were serving their first six-year term.

This is a striking turnover. Both the numbers and the time frame matter. Lawmakers' policy frameworks and worldviews are set in large part through their first election experiences—what motivates them to run in the first place, what rhetoric and issues dominate the campaigns—what they say, over and over, during the campaign. The class of 1946, which included John F. Kennedy, Richard M. Nixon, and Carl Albert, among others, was filled with newly returned World War II veterans who had been shaped and motivated by their efforts overseas to fight for American values against the evils of fascism. That class and its immediate successors created a post–World War II Congress, soon expanded to a cold war Congress, that was motivated by the struggle against international communism and the Soviet threat.

Every class, to be sure, has its own personality, based on the conditions at the time of its election. The freshman class of the 104th Congress was an angry and revolutionary one, the 105th a more complacent and evolutionary group. But these two classes, along with their immediate predecessors, have a larger framework in common. It is one in which members were motivated to run by their desire to fix problems or change policies inside the borders of the United States—or by their own personal ambitions outside of any ideological or partisan motivation. For few if any was the world outside the main or even a major factor.

Still, it would be overstatement to characterize the last few congressional classes, combined, as largely isolationist—although they surely are not internationalist. Terms such as *isolationist* and *internationalist* tend not to apply to people for whom the world is barely on their radar screens. However, sizable numbers of junior members of Congress could more readily be characterized as protectionist to one degree or another, influenced as they were by 1994–96 campaign rhetoric on trade that was dominated by populists Pat Buchanan, Ralph Nader, and Ross Perot.

The following table, showing the number of veterans in recent Congresses, underscores the generation change in Congress:

Congress	House	Senate
101st (1989–90)	217 (50%)	68
102d (1991–92)	212 (49%)	70
103d (1993–94)	180 (41%)	62
104th (1995–96)	159 (37%)	54
105th (1997–98)	141 (32%)	49

Less than 22 percent of the 105th House freshman class had served in the armed forces, along with a more robust 40 percent of the new senators. But "more robust" in this case is in comparison with an earlier period in which three-fourths or more of the new members were veterans. Of course veteran status does not in and of itself shape political ideology or partisan outlook, not to mention knowledge of or views about America's role in the world. But it does mean something in terms of sensitivity to America's interests abroad and an inclination to support an assertive role for the superpower in protecting and promoting those interests.

More generally, the striking decline in the number and proportion of veterans does underscore the change from the post–World War II and cold war outlook in the Capitol to that of the post–cold war Congress. The change also underscores another reality about this Congress—its lower level of travel and international experience. To be sure, we have only anecdotal evidence to support this assertion. But many lawmakers would agree with the observation that Representative Tony Hall of Ohio made at a Rules Committee hearing in mid-1997 that many new members do not have passports and are proud of their lack of travel and of their commitment not to engage in travel during their tenure in Congress. Indeed the National Security Caucus Foundation in Washington has reported that a third of the members of the current Congress do not have passports.[6]

Lack of interest in international affairs, lack of military experience, lack of travel—these are not unique to this generation of lawmakers. The fact is that few previous generations of newer members of Congress included swarms of J. William Fulbrights, Jacob Javitses, Arthur Vandenbergs, or their equivalents. But in previous generations newer members deferred to the expertise of their seniors and to the prerogatives of the president and delegated the congressional responsibility for foreign affairs to their party or committee leaders. Not this generation. Deference to leaders is the antithesis of what they are about.

In any event, there are fewer forceful and engaged congressional opinion leaders in the international arena to influence the new class or the broader agenda. If one defines *opinion leader* as one who takes to the House or Senate floor and causes members to stop talking and listen, while drawing colleagues in from the cloakrooms to hear something significant, by that standard recent Congresses have had examples such as Les Aspin, Sam Nunn, Bill Bradley, Dick Cheney, Bob Dole, and several others, following earlier models such as Fulbright, Richard Russell, and Jacob Javits.

The 105th Congress commanded a few opinion leaders in this area, starting with Richard Lugar and Daniel Patrick Moynihan. But the top committee leaders on the National Security and International Affairs Committees and most of the top party leaders did not readily meet the definition of opinion leader just given. Of the four top party leaders—Gingrich, Gephardt, Lott, and Daschle—only Gingrich had devoted a lot of time and energy to the issues of America and the world, and only Gingrich could be characterized as a full-fledged, enthusiastic internationalist. Gingrich, of course, was also unique among the top four for being embattled and distracted. At the same time, Gephardt in the 105th Congress had hardened his populist trade stance, adopting an even tougher line on fast-track trade authority for the president, China's status, and free trade zone expansion to Chile.

The party leaders' challenges were made greater by another characteristic of the modern Congress—the sharper ideological divisions between the parties. Throughout the 1990s the nature of retirements, election defeats, and the recruitment of new members meant that each party lost proportionately more of its members who were in the middle of the political spectrum and saw greater shares occupy ground closer to their ideological wings. This meant, in other words, more strongly liberal members of the Democratic caucus and more staunchly conservative members on the Republican side. The narrow partisan majorities in both houses, particularly the House of Representatives, meant that finding a purely partisan majority on a given issue would be difficult or impossible. Majorities would more often than not have to be bipartisan, which in turn would mean compromise toward the middle of the spectrum. But with more lawmakers clustered toward each end of the ideological continuum and fewer in the middle, the challenge to leaders trying to build coalitions has been progressively greater.

If one takes the nearly two-thirds of Congress that comprises new members and combines their largely noninternationalist outlook with their unwillingness to defer to leaders, then adds to the mix the paucity of real opinion leaders, the results are unsurprising. Research on the 104th Congress by Jeremy Rosner shows that the junior members are less willing to support the president on foreign affairs, more willing to cut foreign affairs budgets, and sharply less willing to support trade agreements and free trade generally than are the more senior members.[7] There was no reason from rhetoric or early votes to believe that the new members of the 105th class would be any different. The challenge for leaders was great and growing. Moreover, China seemed to be the only major international issue on the congressional foreign policy radar screen in the 105th Congress, but only as a villain in either campaign finance abuses or human rights violations—making internationalism an even tougher sell.

The New Congress, Canada, and Mexico

Congress has gone through tumultuous change over the past three decades, with few respites. The change has been especially pronounced in the 1990s, with the most significant development being the shift to a Republican majority for the first time in forty years. But the GOP majority is not the only major change. Washington has gone from a Republican president and a Democratic Congress (1991–92) to a Democratic president and a Democratic Congress (1993–94) to a Democratic president and a Republican Congress (1995–   ). The House of Representatives has gone from Tom Foley as Speaker to Newt Gingrich and from a nearly omnipotent Speaker Gingrich to an embattled one. The Republican majority has gone from a highly centralized power structure in the first Gingrich Congress to a more diffused power structure with an enhanced role for committee chairmen in the second. Diffusion has been accompanied by democratization, with junior members increasingly vocal and willing to raise their voices and flex their muscles.

The Senate has gone from Majority Leader George Mitchell to Majority Leader Bob Dole and on to Majority Leader Trent Lott. All three could be characterized as assertive and confident leaders, but each discovered to his chagrin that the Senate, consisting of 100 well-staffed and independent egos, does not react well to leaders' trying to impose their preferences on the rank and file—and that in the Senate minority leaders can have as much or more leverage as majority leaders.

Through all this change, both houses have undergone substantial turnover, becoming more junior, and have seen major changes in collective outlook as they have completed the transition to the post–cold war period. Both the shift in majority status and the turnover have meant huge changes in the leadership of many major committees and subcommittees. The result has been fluidity and uncertainty across a range of policy areas, with strong implications for the issues that affect U.S.-Canadian and U.S.-Mexican relationships. In many or most of these issues, from trade to immigration, the president, the Speaker of the House, and the Senate majority leader have been in accord, often forming an informal alliance to make their internationalist policies work. Often, however, they have been at odds with congressional Democratic leaders, especially House leaders Dick Gephardt and David Bonior. Just as often the Clinton-Gingrich-Dole or Clinton-Gingrich-Lott axis has found itself embattled and having to fight hard to prevail—and not always with success.

Trade and Economic Policy

The modern history of trade policy in America is that presidents wrangle regularly with Congress but end up prevailing both on proposed trade agreements and on vehicles to enhance presidential bargaining authority. That pattern prevailed both in the NAFTA battle in 1993 and in the battle over the General Agreement on Tariff and Trade later in the same Congress. Nevertheless, trade policy and trade authority are increasingly contentious issues in Congress, with evolving coalitions. As Rosner's findings (cited above) indicate, junior members of Congress in both parties are less oriented toward free trade than their predecessors or their senior colleagues; anti–free trade members include both liberal, union-oriented Democrats and populist, conservative Republicans. That observation was bolstered by comments made to me by a range of lawmakers lobbying their colleagues in late 1997 on fast-track trade authority for the president. A similar coalition exists in favor of applying trade sanctions against countries on human rights or trade retaliation grounds, including votes against continuing most favored nation status for China. The combination of strong labor opposition to expanded hemispheric trade, ardent opposition from activist conservatives such as Pat Buchanan and well-financed populists such as Ross Perot and Ralph Nader, and the inside role of congressional leaders such as Gephardt and Bonior created a formidable political force, enhanced as well by the willingness of the AFL-CIO to back up its opposition with tens of millions of dollars in "issue" attack ads against lawmakers who support expanded free trade agreements and zones.

Many members of this coalition seized on the reports of political corruption in Mexico and the economic upheaval that followed devaluation of the peso to decry the lack of political and economic freedom in Mexico, call for reevaluation of NAFTA, and put together enough votes to derail the bipartisan leadership loan plan to bail out Mexico's faltering economy in 1995. President Clinton was able to cobble together an alternative plan that did not require congressional approval, and the plan worked without any Washington expense or American burden—and on a faster timetable than promised. Still, the experience was a difficult one for the president, Speaker Gingrich, and Majority Leader Dole, and the aftermath did not appear to win any converts should comparable decisions have to be made in the future.

A pro-Mexico, pro-Canada, and pro–free trade president, combined with like-minded allies in Speaker Gingrich and Majority Leader Dole, consistently found ways to counter that anticoalition—or to uncover alternate avenues where it could not prevail on the House or the Senate floor. But the shaky situation of Gingrich in the 105th Congress, along with the even shakier status of his majority leader, Dick Armey, along with the less enthusiastically internationalist orientation of Dole's successor, Trent Lott, made their alliance less certain to prevail in the trade battles that loomed ahead.

Drugs

The simmering anti-Mexico sentiment that surfaced with NAFTA in 1993 and reemerged with the economic bail-out in 1995 boiled over again in 1997 over the issue of drugs. When President Clinton certified Mexico as an ally in the war against drugs, a range of members of Congress objected vociferously. In the House of Representatives an acrimonious debate resulted in a 251 to 175 vote to give Mexico ninety days to dramatically upgrade its cooperation with the United States on drug control or face decertification.

The Senate acted in a different fashion a few weeks later, voting 94 to 5 for an amendment that required the president to report to Congress within several months whether Mexico had made real progress in areas such as dismantling drug cartels and reforming money-laundering laws, while upgrading the United States' own border patrol capabilities but dropping any ultimatums, including a provision requiring a congressional vote on the president's findings. When asked why the Senate's action had been so much more dispassionate and moderate than that of the House, Republican Senator John McCain said, "Look, over half the Republicans over there have been there for four years or less."[8]

The drug issue arose again later in 1997 when the president made known his intention to nominate Republican Massachusetts Governor William Weld to be U.S. ambassador to Mexico. Senate Foreign Relations Committee Chairman Jesse Helms quickly made his opposition known, focusing on his doubts about Weld's willingness or ability to challenge Mexico on the drug issue because Weld had supported legalizing medical usage of marijuana. He made it clear that as chairman he was not inclined to hold a hearing on such a nomination. Weld challenged Helms publicly, saying that Helms's opposition came from larger objections to Weld's brand of Republicanism and that he would fight vigorously for the post. In late July 1997 Weld was formally nominated, increasing the prospects for a visible battle with Helms, in which drug policy toward Mexico would be a major issue.

Conclusion

So what is new here? On issues such as trade and drugs, congressional criticism or demagoguery about Mexico or Canada has been commonplace for decades. In similar ways conflicts over difficult border issues such as immigration or acid rain have often arisen, and often delicate diplomacy by the State Department or the White House has been required to smooth over problems raised by influential border-state lawmakers, whether they come from New York and Washington state or from Texas and California. In past decades, just as in the current one, the bark of Congress on these issues has usually been more menacing than its ultimate bite; trade agreements have ultimately passed; warnings about severed relations over trade or economic policy have been balanced and resolved; and confrontations over fishing rights, territorial waters, or cross-border pollution have been worked out.

It might also be said that Congress has never been over-represented by foreign policy gurus or loads of members conversant with the geography or economy of our huge and important neighbors. Today, after the enormous visibility given to the NAFTA debate, I would wager that no more than 10 percent of the members of the 105th Congress could tell you the size of Mexico's gross domestic product in relation to America's (roughly a twentieth) or answer correctly when asked to name America's largest trading partner (Canada). The numbers would have been little different for comparable questions asked in 1940, 1950, 1960, 1970, or 1980.

The post–cold war period is different from other postwar periods in one key respect: except by indirection, the cold war was not a war in the traditional sense, with battles and battlefield casualties. Still, if we compare, say, the post–World War I 66th Congress (1919–20), the post–World War II 80th Congress (1947–48), and the post–cold war 104th Congress (1995–96), we see some fascinating parallels. Each of these postwar congresses was characterized by divided government. In each case a Republican Congress swept in to confront a Democratic president. Each had a preoccupation with reform. Changing the budget and appropriations process was a mainstay of the 66th Congress, ultimately resulting in the Budget and Accounting Act of 1921. The post–World War II Congress resulted in national security reform, including the creation of the National Security Council in 1947, which followed by a year the Employment Act of 1946, creating the Council of Economic

Advisors among other things. The 104th Congress had congressional reform and broader governmental restructuring, including a line item veto and a constitutional amendment to balance the budget, as mainstays of the Contract with America.

Each of these postwar Congresses resulted in a swing toward domestic concerns. After a war, that is no surprise; the process of demobilization, including reintegrating veterans into society and turning to neglected domestic needs, is a given. It was not quite the same after the cold war, but the focus on domestic needs, including tax reform, deficit reduction, product liability reform, and health care reform, dominated the concerns of the 104th Congress. Another characteristic of these Congresses was pressure to adopt protectionism. After World War I protectionist pressures ultimately resulted in a bill to raise tariff rates that passed Congress in 1921 and was vetoed by President Woodrow Wilson. As Robert Pastor notes, "The next year, the Fordney-McCumber bill, to which the Senate alone added twenty-four hundred amendments raising duties on as many products, became law."[9] The movement toward multilateral trade agreements after World War II mitigated against enactment of any serious protectionist laws, but the 80th House still found ways to make President Truman's life difficult on the trade front, especially on the issue of "peril points," but the Senate managed to preserve presidential discretion. The 105th Congress opened with controversy over the extension of fast-track trade authority for the president, an issue on which he ultimately could not prevail.

Each Congress also saw a search for new foreign enemies and an occasional wave of intolerance for domestic minorities. There was a spate of lynchings following World War I, the "red scare" after World War II (not to mention the cold war itself). There were antiimmigration trends during each of the periods, and an anti–affirmative action move in the post–cold war period. At the same time, there is an important distinction to be made between the post–World War I period on the one hand and the post–World War II and post–cold war periods on the other. If one event involving Congress and foreign policy after World War I still resonates, it is the Senate's rejection of the Treaty of Versailles, the collapse of the League of Nations, and a new era of international cooperation. But the end of the second world war saw the birth of the United Nations and the rise of multilateralism in trade, aid, monetary affairs, and diplomacy. The post–cold war period, to be sure, saw a surge in anti–United Nations and anti–World Bank/IMF sentiment, including congressional refusal to pay United Nations dues, but the ingrained nature of multilateral institutions still created a backwater against isolationist and protectionist sentiments.

More specifically, there are significant differences between the contemporary Congress and the legislature in past periods that are relevant and troubling for the future of U.S.-Canadian-Mexican relationships. The lack of deeply knowledgeable and sophisticated followers does not matter so much when there are knowledgeable, sophisticated, and balanced leaders. There are a few such leaders today. But they are fewer in number and less well placed than in the past; they are less powerful and persuasive; and there are many fewer lawmakers who would even consider themselves followers on anything. Today's typical rank-and-file lawmaker is junior, is much more concerned about domestic affairs than about foreign policy, starts with no deep-seated attachment to free trade or to an expansive internationalist role for America in the world, starts with no particular attachment to Canada or Mexico as critical allies, and has between eighteen and twenty-two staff members to promote his or her views and interests and maintain independence from party and institutional leaders or the president.

There is another important difference between now and the past: today there are powerful and significant congressional leaders who take views on international issues that are the opposite of those of the usually dominant internationalists, and they are joined by well-heeled, well-positioned, and articulate leaders of populist movements outside the body, including Ralph Nader, Ross Perot, and Pat Buchanan. They contribute to making the external environment notably inhospitable to a free trade, internationalist consensus. None of this means that policies will be reversed, relations allowed to deteriorate, or chaos to ensue. But the challenge to leaders to maintain some level of stability and consensus will be that much greater in the years ahead.

Can anything be done about this? Structural changes are not the answer. Indeed some popular structural suggestions, such as term limits, could make things much worse; as junior members of Congress gain experience and educate themselves about economic policy, they tend to become more sensitive to the implications of free trade. But beyond structural reform there are things that could be done to change the climate. First, internationalist, free trade–oriented political figures need to be more assertive year round to recapture some control over an agenda that has been dominated by the populists of the left, right, and center and by the AFL-CIO. They need help as well from persuasive academics and especially from a business community that has curiously grown more complacent even as its stake in a vibrant global economy has increased. An assertive business community can make a concrete case about how free trade protects and expands jobs, providing evidence congressional district by congressional district.

Another area for sustained attention is the press. The economics of journalism has changed, resulting in curtailments of foreign bureaus and a culture of journalism that no longer regards a tour abroad as a prerequisite to service as a White House correspondent or anchor. Therefore, when President Clinton traveled to South America in October 1997 to promote North American free trade, the reporters who accompanied him were not deeply knowledgeable about either South America or the trade issue. Their coverage focus and questions to the president were aimed far more at the allegations of campaign finance abuses than at trade and its political and economic implications. Groups such as the Freedom Forum and the Council on Foreign Relations need to put some resources into considering ways to educate and sensitize journalists about the world around them—and especially to sensitize the editors and producers who make assignment decisions and lay out evening news broadcasts and front pages.

These suggestions underscore the fact that there is no magic solution to a deeper post–cold war dilemma shaped by the global economic revolution. Rather we need hard work—and a little luck.

Notes

1. Burdette Loomis, *The New American Politician* (Basic Books, 1988), pp. 9–10.

2. Ibid., pp. 95–100.

3. Mark Z. Barabak, "Perot, Prophet of Pique, Won't Go Away; It's That Simple," *San Diego Union-Tribune*, November 19, 1993, p. A30.

4. David S. Broder, "National Punditry," *Washington Post*, November 1, 1997, p. C1.

5. Hanna Rosin, "Invasion of the Church Ladies," *The New Republic*, April 24, 1995.

6. Reported in David Gergen, "Bring Back the Junkets!" *U.S. News & World Report*, October 20, 1997.

7. Jeremy D. Rosner, *The New Tug-of-War: Congress, The Executive Branch and National Security* (Washington, D.C.: Carnegie Endowment for International Peace, 1995).

8. *Congressional Quarterly Weekly Report*, March 22, 1997.

9. Robert A. Pastor, *Congress and the Politics of Foreign Economic Policy 1929– 1976* (University of California Press, 1981), p. 76.

Chapter 6

Congress and Foreign Trade

I. M. Destler

THIS CHAPTER ANALYZES U.S. trade policymaking in the 1990s in the light of two intertwined patterns. The first is the ongoing trade policy "game" between the executive and legislative branches: the broad pattern of executive-congressional dealings variously labeled "protection for Congress" or the "cry-and-sigh syndrome."[1] This pattern features highly visible (and, at the margin, influential) congressional participation in trade policy, joined with substantial de facto delegation of power to the executive branch, which generally employs the power to promote trade liberalization.

This trade policy game has clearly persisted in the 1990s. At the same time it has been complicated by an emerging political pattern centered on the North American Free Trade Agreement (NAFTA) and featuring greater public controversy and the intertwining of trade with related issues, especially worker rights and the environment.

In part this NAFTA-centered pattern reflects the growing importance of North American trade to the United States. In 1980 merchandise trade (exports plus imports) with Canada and Mexico comprised 22 percent of U.S. trade worldwide. By 1996 this share had risen to 30 percent. Trade with Mexico grew particularly fast, from 5.8 to 9.2 percent of overall U.S. trade. And North American trade was a growing share of a growing total, for over this same period overall trade rose from 10 to 12 percent of the U.S. gross domestic product (GDP).[2] For the three countries of North America as a whole, commerce with one another grew from a third of the total trade in 1980 to nearly a half in 1996.

I thank Raymond Ahearn and the three Brookings Institution readers for their helpful critical comments on earlier drafts of this chapter.

The numbers show a substantial increase in U.S. trade dependence on North America. They also show a lesser dependence than that of Canada and Mexico. Their logic suggests higher priority to North America in U.S. trade policy and asymmetric U.S. bargaining leverage with its northern and southern neighbors. In fact, U.S. priority to regional trade has increased. And the political importance of that trade has skyrocketed, with the focus almost entirely on the Mexico connection. But rather than reflecting the powerful U.S. leverage (and hence, bargaining opportunities) inherent in the asymmetry, the politics of NAFTA in the United States have highlighted the downside: negative developments in trade and the broader Mexico relationship to which NAFTA can be plausibly connected.

Anxiety over NAFTA and its effects was a prominent feature of the heated congressional trade policy debate in the fall of 1997, when the House of Representatives failed to approve President Bill Clinton's request for fast-track trade negotiating authority.[3] Republican efforts to revive the issue in summer 1998 faced uncertain prospects. This chapter explores the roots of the fast-track failure. First, it spells out the interbranch game as it existed through 1990, before NAFTA came to Congress. Second, it discusses how Congress reinforced this pattern through its action on NAFTA and the multilateral Uruguay Round agreement concluded in 1994. Third, it sets forth how NAFTA and the broader evolution of U.S.-Mexican relations have complicated the trade game, bringing heightened prominence to related issues such as labor and environmental standards. Fourth, it reviews the experience since December 1994, with particular emphasis on the long executive-congressional stalemate over new fast-track authority for trade negotiations. Finally, it explores the consequences of the fast-track stalemate and the broadening of the substantive agenda for the future of U.S. trade politics and the congressional role therein.

The Basic Pattern through 1990

The Constitution gives Congress original authority over trade policy. Since 1934 Congress has delegated this authority, at least for product-specific trade action, to executive branch and regulatory institutions.[4] Tariff rates for particular products, once set by Congress in comprehensive trade legislation, are now proclaimed by the president based on the results of international negotiations. Industries facing special trade pressures seek and obtain relief not (in the main) from Congress directly, but by pursuing quasi-judicial procedures in which they must prove injury to the U.S. International Trade Commission or foreign unfairness (dumping or government subsidies), or both, to the Department of Commerce. Private sector interests are encouraged to lobby the executive branch directly through participation in three tiers of advisory committees established by statute for major negotiations. Last but not least, Congress has established, protected, and regularly strengthened an agency in the president's executive office tasked with governmentwide trade policy leadership, the Office of the United States Trade Representative (USTR).

These devices have enabled trade-minded members of Congress to play prominent roles while eschewing final responsibility. They have given some of them the freedom to advocate trade restrictions for producers within their districts without the worry that comprehensive trade protection might actually come about. And when existing delegations of authority have seemed to reach their limits, Congress has proved willing to move in new directions. After tariffs receded as the prime governmental barrier to trade, Congress granted "fast-track authority" in 1974 for agreements on reducing nontariff barriers. When multilateral initiatives looked stalemated, Congress extended this authority to bilateral free trade agreements in 1984.

Of course Congress has certainly not abdicated all influence over U.S. trade policy. It has regularly set statutory limits on what USTR can negotiate. It has strengthened the trade hawks within the executive branch by buttressing USTR and through the enactment and progressive strengthening of Section 301 of the Trade Act of 1974, which mandates action against "unreasonable and unjustifiable" foreign barriers affecting U.S. trade. And Congress has periodically amended the quasi-judicial trade remedy statutes to make relief easier for firms to obtain, particularly the antidumping law. But legislators have allowed executive officials substantial leeway in practice on most issues: witness Carla Hills's permissive reading of the Super 301 legislation vis-à-vis Japan.[5] And Congress approved, by one-sided margins, every multilateral and bilateral trade liberalization agreement brought to it under the fast-track procedures.

This pattern was essentially unaffected by a major departure in U.S. trade policy, the U.S.-Canada Free Trade Agreement (FTA). A preferential agreement with the biggest U.S. trading partner was, in form at least, a sharp break with the post–World War II U.S. insistence on multilateralism and nondiscrimination. And the Canada negotiation had a rocky beginning. According to the 1984 legislation, negotiations on a bilateral free trade agreement under the fast-track procedures could proceed only if the Senate Finance and House Ways and Means Committees (which hold primary responsibility for trade policy in their respective chambers) were notified in advance and neither vetoed the agreement by majority vote within sixty days. The notification of the FTA with Canada reached the Senate Finance Committee in early 1986, a time of strong bipartisan frustration with overall Reagan administration trade policies. With members determined to send a strong message to the White House and lacking other means of doing so, the committee came within one vote of blocking the negotiations.

But in the words of one who was directly involved, the incident "had very little to do with U.S.-Canada trade relations."[6] And once this crisis was surmounted the agreement was easily absorbed within the established political pattern. The main concern and resistance came from product-specific interests—grain farmers and the lumber industry. The rest of the United States did not know the negotiations were proceeding—nor did most of Washington in any detail.[7] When the U.S.-Canada FTA came up for congressional approval in 1988, it won by lopsided majorities of 366 to 40 in the House and 83 to 9 in the Senate. And it was far less prominent than the 1988 trade act and certainly less important to members of the House and Senate who cared about trade.

The larger test for the interbranch trade game was that omnibus legislation. Conceived in the white heat of unheard-of twelve-digit U.S. trade deficits and initiated by Congress over administration objections, the law ended up reinforcing the long-standing pattern. Congress maintained its practice of limiting its actual engagement in trade policy. It delegated product-specific trade action to the executive branch and quasi-judicial institutions. It exerted its policy impact at the margins, through the wording of legislation that the administration had leeway in interpreting. And it regularly ratified the results of major trade negotiations.

NAFTA and the Uruguay Round: The Pattern Reinforced

NAFTA posed a particularly severe test for the interbranch trade game. First of all, Congress never consciously authorized a free trade agreement with Mexico prior to the onset of negotiations in the sense that it had the Tokyo and Uruguay Rounds and the free trade agreements with Israel and Canada. When fast-track authority was renewed in 1988, neither executive nor congressional leaders saw free trade with Mexico as conceivable during the period covered by the legislation. It was believed to be at least a decade away. By contrast, the Tokyo and Uruguay Rounds were the known targets of the 1974 and 1988 laws, and free trade with Canada was seen as a strong possibility when the 1984 amendments were enacted (though the relevant title of the bill was labeled Trade with Israel).[8] When Presidents Salinas and Bush suddenly agreed to proceed in 1990 under the existing fast-track law, this raised real questions about the legitimacy and appropriateness of the procedure.

Second and more important, NAFTA involved deepening integration with a semideveloped, semidemocratic neighbor toward which U.S. citizens harbored ambivalent feelings. Members of Congress reflected these feelings.[9] With the U.S. economy just emerging from recession and with workers entering their third decade of stagnant wages, NAFTA triggered a firestorm of anxiety about the broader fate of U.S. workers in international competition. Its "symbolic politics" generated a new broadly protectionist coalition, a veritable crusade by a range of labor, environmental, and other grass-roots organizations (including Ross Perot's United We Stand and the Public Citizen organization led by Ralph Nader and Lori Wallach).[10] Finally, the political route taken by candidate, then President Bill Clinton to endorsement of the agreement negotiated by his predecessor, George Bush, was to condition it on the negotiation of side agreements on labor and the environment. These took half of 1993 to conclude, effectively immobilizing the White House politically for a crucial period as opponents lined up congressman after congressman.

Still, Congress acted twice in support of NAFTA. First came the vote in May 1991 to extend the deadline for negotiations under the fast-track procedures. Congress had inserted the requirement for this extension into the 1988 law as a means to ensure that USTR consulted it regularly on the substance of the Uruguay Round. But it applied to NAFTA as well, and in fact the vote on extending the fast-track deadline was widely treated as a referendum on NAFTA. After multinational business rallied in support, and the Bush administration made some modest promises on labor and environmental issues, victory came with relative ease; the vote was 231 to 192 in the House and 59 to 36 in the Senate. Significant was the support of House Majority Leader Richard Gephardt, a frequent critic of U.S. trade policy who had growing ties with labor and environmental groups.

The struggle on the actual NAFTA agreement was far harder. As noted earlier, the Clinton administration had failed to provide clear and unambiguous support prior to completion of the labor and environment side agreements in August 1993, and the conventional Washington wisdom through most of the year was that NAFTA would meet defeat in the House of Representatives. Through the summer and fall the agreement became a battleground for alternative American visions of the future, with the tone of the debate vastly exaggerating NAFTA's impact on the United States.

The NAFTA battle also involved features typical of post–World War II trade policy and politics: the micropolitics of special benefits for key U.S. producers of items such as autos, textiles, and sugar and the macro-ideology stressing the perils of protectionism. Free trade ideology was featured in the debate televised in early November between Vice President Al Gore and third-party presidential candidate Ross Perot, when the former presented the latter with a portrait of Reed Smoot and Willis Hawley, co-sponsors of the high-tariff Smoot-Hawley Act of 1930, which is believed to have deepened the Great Depression. But, in its prominence as a national issue and the broad range of causes to which it was linked, NAFTA was a notable departure from standard American post–World War II trade politics. And it gave rise to exaggerated rhetoric on both sides, including forecasts of future trade surpluses with Mexico that NAFTA supporters would later regret.[11]

Yet once the Clinton administration got its act together, it won going away. The fight resembled, in some respects, the Panama Canal ratification battle of 1977–78 more than postwar trade policy fights, with swing members looking to the administration to help them rationalize support for a controversial agreement. There were deals on sugar and citrus and on the establishment of a North American Development Bank. As in the case of the Panama Canal, these were widely reported as a desperate administration's "buying votes." But although that characterization was not entirely wrong, it was misleading: what members of Congress were seeking in both instances was political protection so they could do what they had come to regard as the right thing. And the result was the same: enough votes for passage (234 to 200 in the House), with a larger majority available if Congress could only have figured out how to act by secret ballot.

The Uruguay Round vote in 1994 was a return to the standard trade pattern. There was general support among the minority of legislators who paid attention to trade. The public was largely inattentive. The administration used consultations on drafting of the implementing legislation (nonmarkups) to buttress congressional support. And once major interests were addressed in that legislation, solid bipartisan majorities were available (2 to 1 in the House, 3 to 1 in the Senate), although a combination of partisan sparring and Senator Ernest Hollings's exploitation of a never-before-invoked provision of the fast-track legislation forced the vote into a postelection "lame-duck" session.[12]

By the end of 1994, therefore, Congress had approved, within twelve and a half months, first the most controversial and then the most comprehensive trade agreement of the postwar period. And the Clinton administration, without much vocal congressional protest, signed declarations in November and December promising free trade among the members of the Asia-Pacific Economic Cooperation (APEC) forum by the year 2010 (2020 for the least developed) and a Free Trade Area of the Americas (FTAA) by 2005. At the Miami Hemispheric Summit that endorsed the FTAA, Clinton posed with the leaders of Canada, Mexico, and Chile, highlighting that South American nation's "next-in-line" position for a free trade agreement. So the bottom line for trade liberalization was strikingly positive. Congress had once again shown its readiness to approve trade-liberalizing agreements. And the president was forging ahead to negotiate new ones.

NAFTA's Aftermath: The Broadening of Trade Politics

Typically in American trade politics, success in trade liberalization is followed by a protectionist reaction. After the Kennedy Round agreements of 1967 came a powerful campaign for new textile quotas and a broader labor-based drive for trade protection. After the Tokyo Round accords of 1979 came more: not just textiles and steel, but, most important, pressure for protection of the embattled automobile industry.

This time this dog has not barked: there has been amazingly little new protectionism of the traditional (industry-based) sort in the United States since the end of 1994.[13] There have been no major new industry campaigns, relatively few new antidumping cases, and so on. The reasons are not entirely clear, but contributors to this situation have surely included the robust economic recovery, the relatively modest change in the U.S. trade balance, and the internationalization of a number of key industries, including those producing textiles, autos, and steel. (The trade deficit accelerated sharply, however, in early 1998.)

Another positive development for trade has been the generally faithful implementation of NAFTA by the three member nations and the resulting upsurge in regional trade summarized at the outset of this chapter. Responding to congressional and interest group pressure, however, the agreement allowed each nation to maintain its trade remedy procedures against the others, and specific cases continued to be filed. Prominent were disputes over the safety of Mexican trucks (the United States suspended implementation of a NAFTA provision expanding truckers' access to one another's national territory in December 1995) and a seemingly endless U.S.-Canadian controversy over subsidies of softwood lumber by Canadian states (in April 1996, the two nations signed an agreement regulating Canadian sales for five years). All prominent U.S.-Mexican cases involved access to the U.S. market.[14] U.S. economic disputes with Canada were somewhat more numerous and involved both markets: U.S. imports of Canadian wheat and wool suits as well as lumber, and Canadian tariffs on U.S. exports of poultry and dairy products and restrictions on "cultural" products, including magazines and country music cable television programs.

The procedures for settling NAFTA disputes contained an innovative provision, originated in the U.S.-Canada FTA, which gave firms the option of having antidumping and countervailing duty determinations reviewed by binational panels of experts in lieu of appealing to national courts. This "Chapter 19" provision was controversial in Congress; in August 1995 Senate Majority Leader Bob Dole and a bipartisan group of senators urged that it be amended or abandoned, and in any case not extended to any future FTA partners. Nonetheless, twenty-four dispute settlement panels had been established under this provision by the end of 1996.[15]

These were standard, garden-variety commercial disputes: trade policy and politics as long practiced in the United States. During the same period, however, NAFTA was fueling a different sort of reaction, one centered not on specific economic interests, but on trade's broader impact. The congressional battle over the NAFTA had raised consciousness about trade policy among a broad range of politically active groups: labor and environmental organizations in particular, but also those concerned with democratization and human rights in Mexico. These groups are at the heart of the cause-related activism generally associated with the Democratic Party. In 1993 these groups had either opposed NAFTA or used it to further their causes. Thereafter they would watch it carefully.

These groups now constituted a potential antiliberalization bloc, a coalition capable of being mobilized for a NAFTA-like cause. It could not be just any trade cause: the Uruguay Round, with arguably greater impact on their interests, never caught fire for them, notwithstanding the vocal opposition of Pat Buchanan, Ralph Nader, and Ross Perot. And had U.S.-Mexico trade and the Mexican economy and polity moved along the tracks projected by pro-NAFTA optimists the bloc might have gradually eroded, its components shifting their energy to more promising causes.

Unfortunately the positive scenario was not fulfilled. Within six months of NAFTA's approval by the U.S. Congress came first the Chiapas rebellion and then the assassination of the ruling party's candidate to succeed Carlos Salinas de Gortari as president of Mexico. Both these events were prominently reported in the United States. Both highlighted Mexican political instability. But the August presidential election that followed was judged by outside observers to be less tainted than previous elections, particularly that of 1988. Had economic progress continued in its wake, the political events of early 1994 might have receded in North American consciousness.

But that was not to be. In late December 1994 Mexico suffered a catastrophic currency crisis, with markets pushing the peso down to half of its former value. The crisis would drive the nation into deep recession, reversing much of the economic progress of the previous decade. In January 1995 President Clinton—supported by leaders of the new Republican majorities in Congress, Bob Dole in the Senate and Speaker Newt Gingrich in the House—asked Congress to enact loan guarantees to help Mexico's new president, Ernesto Zedillo, cope with the crisis. Rank-and-file members of both parties rebelled. Within a month the president withdrew his proposal, substituting a smaller rescue package cobbled together under his own executive authority.

The collapse of the peso took the bloom off Mexico's economic rose. The resulting devaluation and recession transformed the U.S. merchandise trade balance with Mexico from a modest surplus of $1.4 billion in 1994 to a substantial deficit of $15.4 billion in 1995. In the NAFTA debate supporters had unwisely pointed to the U.S. trade surplus with Mexico, asserting that it would grow if the agreement were approved. The reversal undercut their credibility; they were reduced to arguing (accurately) that U.S. exports would have suffered even more had NAFTA not prevented Mexico from raising import barriers against U.S. products as she had in the debt crisis of 1982.[16]

From 1995 forward Mexico and NAFTA were burdens for U.S. (and particularly congressional) free traders to carry. Capitol Hill sentiment turned negative, and opinion surveys found the American public split down the middle on whether NAFTA had been good for the United States.[17] Nor were matters helped by the increased role of Mexican drug lords in the marketing of narcotics to the United States or by the early 1997 arrest of Mexico's chief antidrug official for accepting bribes to protect one of those drug lords. The timing of the arrest—just prior to the administration's required decision on whether to certify that Mexico was cooperating on narcotics enforcement—ensured maximum congressional attention and predictable expressions of outrage when Clinton decided to so certify.

The rise of congressional activity on issues such as drugs and human rights was accompanied by a declining interest and expertise in trade and Mexico. By 1997 stalwarts like Lloyd Bentsen, Bill Bradley, and John Danforth had left the Senate. Counterparts like Dan Rostenkowski, Bill Frenzel, Sam Gibbons, and Bill Richardson were no longer in the House. And if the protectionist pressures of the 1980s had contributed a generation of congressional trade leaders, controversy over NAFTA had not done the same for the 1990s. House Ways and Means Committee Chairman Bill Archer was committed on trade but still untested. House Democratic leader Dick Gephardt retained his strong trade interest, but he had voted against NAFTA in 1993 and had become a strident critic of the agreement in practice. Bob Matsui, ranking Democrat on the Ways and Means trade subcommittee, retained strong interest and potential influence as leader of the free trade Democrats, but their numbers were dwindling. Energetic Republican Jim Kolbe showed strong interest in both trade and Mexico, but his influence was limited by his committee assignments.

The result of all this was a Congress in which traditional (manufacturing-based) protectionism was remarkably weak, but in which trade policy leadership was weak as well. It was a Congress with limited interest and diminished expertise in trade per se or in Mexico per se, but one in which passionate advocacy on ancillary issues—labor standards, the environment, and human rights—was very much on the rise, complicating the debate and impeding movement on trade expansion. Another important source of ambivalence, however, was the Clinton administration.

From 1995 Onward: The Policy Stalemate

Within the Uruguay Round success there had been one important failure—the administration's inability to obtain fast-track authority for future trade negotiations. U.S. Trade Representative Mickey Kantor had highlighted trade-related labor and environmental issues in the administration's proposed draft; Republicans and business leaders had rebelled. They had swallowed the NAFTA side agreements reluctantly, and they feared that further emphasis on these issues would reduce the administration's leverage on foreign trade barriers even if labor-environment negotiations did not bring about onerous new regulations. For the administration, however, the emphasis was good substance and good politics: the issues themselves were important, and the administration needed to mend political fences with important components of the Democratic coalition that NAFTA had alienated. And emphasis on trade-related labor and environment issues offered the hope, over time, of broadening support for trade liberalization.

There was an eleventh-hour effort to bridge these differences in the summer of 1994. Kantor put forward tentative compromise language, which Ways and Means Republicans found promising. But he later backed off, and in any case the Senate Finance Committee opposed inclusion of fast-track language in the Uruguay Round implementing legislation, fearing (among other things) that it would endanger final passage of the bill. So the matter was put off until 1995. Bill Clinton became the first president to go more than eight months without fast-track authority since its initial enactment on January 3, 1975.

Even before the Uruguay Round was approved, the American public had ensured that 1995–96 would be different. In a remarkable and sweeping repudiation of the president and his party, voters had opted for Republican majorities in the Senate and the House—in the latter for the first time in forty years. International trade had not been a prominent issue, despite efforts by militants such as Ralph Nader during the election campaign to target the Uruguay Round and the new World Trade Organization (WTO) it established. But the seventy-plus Republican freshmen were thought to be more populist and less responsive to big business than their previously elected brethren.

Facing an uphill fight for reelection, the president sought first to secure his Democratic Party base, of which organized labor was a key component. Trade policy was subordinated to this objective. Kantor had always been up-front about giving top priority to winning Clinton a second term, and he would be one of the few substantive officials who took part in the weekly White House campaign planning sessions. Nor were the administration's prospects for gaining fast-track authority exactly enhanced by the peso crisis and the virulent congressional response to the proposal of a loan guarantee. So, in the words of former administration Latin America policy official Richard Feinberg, there was a "retreat from NAFTA expansion."[18] Notwithstanding its APEC and FTAA commitments, the Clinton administration did not submit a proposal for fast-track renewal to the 104th Congress. Indeed, by the end of 1995 Kantor had "turned [his] attention to slowing NAFTA implementation in the face of labor opposition" by postponing access of Mexican truckers to U.S. roads.[19]

Not for the first time in the history of the republic, executive inaction spawned Capitol Hill initiative. The new chairman of the House Ways and Means Committee, Bill Archer, moved first to hold hearings jointly with the House Rules Committee and then to mark up a fast-track bill. In a departure from committee tradition on trade, the proposal was developed on a partisan basis, as Democrats stayed to one side. Nor were there any indications that the Senate Committee on Finance was ready to consider a proposal if it was passed by the House. But there were intermittent negotiations between Archer and his staff and Kantor and his deputy, Charlene Barshefsky, and senior Ways and Means Democrats like Gibbons and Matsui were sometimes involved in these.

The Ways and Means proposal was quite restrictive on the labor-environment question. It did not rule out all negotiations on these issues, however, and the congressmen were willing to bargain on the matter—more so, it appears, than Kantor. Negotiations intensified in the early fall, with USTR responding to committee proposals in some detail, and one important participant recalled "95 percent agreement" on outstanding issues. Shortly thereafter, however, "it fell apart," perhaps because Kantor did not want agreement and the consequent cost to labor relations.[20] By this time, in any case, trust between him and House Republicans had become badly frayed. Shortly thereafter Bob Dole jumped on the go-slow bandwagon with a floor statement in the Senate. Stating rather implausibly that "the administration seem[ed] to be in a great hurry to pile on not just one, but many more trade agreements," he set forth a cautionary view: after "the largest restructuring of our trading relations ever" with the Uruguay Round and NAFTA, "We need time to assess the impact . . . a cooling-off period." Therefore, "it would be a mistake to extend new fast-track authority" at that time.[21] And there the matter rested until 1997.

Trade's main prominence in 1996 came early in the presidential primaries. Republican front-runner Dole faced an unexpectedly formidable opponent, Patrick Buchanan, who was campaigning on an avowedly protectionist platform, championing the cause of American workers victimized by multinational business. Buchanan won the prized New Hampshire primary but faded rapidly thereafter, and exit polls suggested that trade played only a minor role in his success. Several months later Ross Perot highlighted trade by naming as vice presidential candidate on his ticket the protectionist coauthor of his book on NAFTA, Pat Choate.[22] But Perot came nowhere near matching his 1992 electoral performance. The main contest was between two experienced politicians, two major party candidates who had consistently supported trade liberalization when push came to shove and saw no net electoral advantage in advertising that fact. Both managed to answer the one trade question in the 1996 presidential debates without making protectionist noises but also without clear endorsement of economic openness.

As 1996 ended, however, the stage appeared to be set for prompt action on fast-track by the 105th Congress.[23] Clinton had won a strong victory, with no constraining trade policy commitments. The Republicans had retained control of Congress, albeit with a thinner House majority. The electorate's message to both seemed to be that they should reason together. The administration was solidly behind fast-track renewal, with economic, foreign, and trade policymakers in agreement. The costs of inaction were mounting, particularly in Latin America, as nations continued to strike deals without and around the United States. The issue's divisiveness within the Democratic Party, particularly in the

House, made it logical to move sooner rather than later, to have any bloodletting as far removed as possible from November 1998 or November 2000. Acting U.S. Trade Representative Charlene Barshefsky, whom the president had just nominated to fill the position on a permanent basis, was "viewed as far more of a free-trader and far less of a pol than Kantor."[24] And Chairman Archer and his Ways and Means Committee Republicans were more than ready to resume the effort. In fact, they showed a willingness to compromise further on trade-related labor and environmental issues.

Administration policy leaders were also ready to move. So were the Republican leaders of the House and Senate and, as it turned out, the leaders of the Senate Finance Commitee. But the president and vice president were not. Trade and foreign policy specialists urged them to quick action: get fast-track through the House by April or May, to coincide with scheduled presidential travel to Latin America and to advance the legislation as far as possible before the administration had to submit a comprehensive congressionally mandated report on NAFTA at midyear. But Clinton and Gore worried about the labor-environment connection, about balancing fast-track with other administration priorities such as the budget and the Chemical Weapons Convention and (when June came) the House vote on renewal of most favored nation (MFN) treatment for China, and about how the issue would affect Gore's presidential prospects in 2000.

Clinton encouraged fast-track supporters by giving the issue some prominence (four paragraphs) in his February 4 State of the Union address, calling for "authority now to conclude new trade agreements" in Asia and Latin America so Americans could "prosper in the global economy." But the vice president received a chilly reception at the February meeting of the executive council of the AFL-CIO in Los Angeles, in contrast to the cheers that greeted his potential rival, House Minority Leader Gephardt.[25] On February 19 the council issued a statement opposing any "grant of fast track negotiating authority . . . that does not include provisions and enforcement mechanisms for addressing worker rights, labor standards and environmental protection [as] part of the core agreement." Gephardt followed a week later with a twelve-page "Dear Democratic Colleague" letter denouncing the "failure" of NAFTA, particularly in the area of industrial relations, and declaring, "We should limit any grant of fast track authority . . . to bilateral negotiations with Chile or to remedy the flaws in the NAFTA." Labor and environmental measures should be an integral part of the Chilean agreement, the letter argued. And, as if trying to push as many hot Democratic policy buttons as possible, the minority leader further declared that new trade agreements should also address such issues as "capital flight and currency stability," "human rights—rule of law," "trade in narcotics," and "foreign corrupt practices."

To the frustration of congressional fast-track supporters, the White House did not respond with equal vigor or specificity. Barshefsky, confirmed in February as Kantor's successor at USTR, plugged away, pushing for progress within the administration and holding useful face-to-face meetings with 170 members of Congress, most of them Democrats. But the president seemed determined to avoid or postpone the hard decisions. After waiting four months for an administration proposal, Ways and Means Republicans were ready to push matters on their own, but the administration did not want that either. Ways and Means Chairman Archer then went public with his frustrations, declaring in a May 15 letter to the president his deep disappointment "that the Administration is unable to give what should be a major trade priority—early renewal of fast-track negotiating authority—the attention it deserves."[26] Six days later the president met with his top advisers and decided to delay the administration's fast-track proposal for four more months, until September. The reason stated was the need for time to mobilize: the White House—and the president personally—could not give the matter adequate attention until after the votes on the budget and renewing China's MFN status were taken. Barshefsky added that this would give them time to mount a broad campaign for the legislation and that delay in submitting the administration proposal would deprive opponents of a concrete target.

This delay had the unintended effect of energizing the hitherto lethargic Senate Committee on Finance. Driven also by jurisdictional conflict with the Commerce Committee, Finance held a hearing on June 3. When USTR's Barshefsky testified she "came under repeated attack by Senate Finance Committee chairman Bill Roth (R-Del.), ranking member Patrick Moynihan (D-N.Y.) and other committee members" for the administration's delay. Said Moynihan, "If this is being held up because of the politics of the New Hampshire primary in the year 2000, that is an intolerable act."[27]

Delay also meant that the administration had to weather the publicity about NAFTA generated by its congressionally mandated mid-year report.[28]. The administration sought to minimize its impact by making a solid but modest case and releasing the report rather quietly (and, as it turned out, more than a week late). USTR attributed most of the negative trade and economic developments to the peso crisis and found that NAFTA itself was having a moderate positive impact on U.S. net exports and income, "controlling for other factors." The administration found that U.S. exports to Mexico did far better after 1994 than after Mexico's previous financial crisis in 1982 because NAFTA prevented Mexico from raising barriers to U.S. exports as it did then. The report also emphasized the mercantilistic asymmetry of NAFTA that favored the United States: the fact that Mexico's tariff reductions had been much sharper than those of the United States. Under NAFTA up to mid-1997, the United States had reduced tariffs on Mexican products from 2.07 to 0.65 percent. Mexico had reduced tariffs on U.S. products from 10 to 2.9 percent.[29]

The U.S. Trade Representative's assessment was countered by a critique entitled "The Failed Experiment: NAFTA at Three Years," published under the leadership of Public Citizen's Global Trade Watch project, with substantial ties to organized labor.[30] Although making only an intermittent effort to separate the impact of NAFTA from other forces at play, the report highlighted the increase in the U.S. trade deficit with Canada and particularly with Mexico between 1993 and 1996. This fed a broader argument, that "NAFTA and globalization generally have changed the composition of employment in America" toward "lower paying services industries." The report linked "imports from low-wage countries" to "increasing wage inequality," cited use of "the threat of moving to Mexico as a weapon against wage increases and union organization," declared that "the unregulated expansion of North American trade has made an already heavily polluted border region much dirtier," and found NAFTA's labor and environmental institutions "utterly inadequate." Given this indictment, the conclusion was modest indeed: "Before it can be expanded, NAFTA should be revised to include enforceable labor and environmental standards, effective adjustment assistance, financial market regulation, and protection of national safety nets for those left out of the benefits of trade."

The U.S. Trade Representative's report and the Public Citizen critique foreshadowed the congressional debate that followed in the fall. The summer campaign promised by the White House largely failed to materialize, and the president returned from vacation after Labor Day still not committed to a specific legislative text. After a frenetic eleventh-hour review, Clinton submitted his fast-track proposal on September 16. The bill followed the lines long anticipated and recommended by the trade policy community. With labor firmly in opposition and exerting strong pressure on liberal and moderate Democrats, Clinton needed strong Republican support if his bill was to win congressional approval. So the draft he submitted resembled the Archer proposal on the key issue of labor and environmental issues. Agreements on these topics could be implemented in a fast-track bill only if "directly related to trade." Legislation reported out by the Senate Finance Committee (by consensus, October 1) and by the House Ways and Means Committee (by a vote of 24 to 14, October 8) followed the same basic approach. The president would have liked a bill less restrictive on these issues, and he included in his proposal a mandate to press labor and environment issues within the WTO and (for labor) the International Labor Organization. But previous administration efforts to advance these issues in trade negotiations had not borne much fruit, particularly on labor vis-à-vis the WTO.

The White House then launched an intense campaign for congressional approval, climaxing in early November when Clinton met with numerous undecided House members. Of his personal commitment to the cause there could no longer be any doubt. But he paid a price for the eight-month delay in submitting his proposal. Administration hopes notwithstanding, the lack of a proposal to shoot at did not hamper opponents in their campaign. Its main impact was on business supporters. Contrary to the myth that trade policy is driven by multinational business lobbying, protrade companies are never "ahead of the curve" in pushing trade-expansion legislation. In this instance, however, organized business was substantially behind the curve, in part because it was wary of what Clinton would finally seek on labor and the environment. So it was the supporters who waited until they saw precise language before moving to political action.

Opponents felt no such hesitation. Organized labor made fast-track authority a "litmus test" issue, responding to (and playing upon) workers' anxieties about factories' moving south of the border. Environmental groups were less active, but they were overwhelmingly negative—unlike on NAFTA, which the larger-membership groups had supported. The opposition campaign was energized by Public Citizen, which had learned from its rather shrill efforts against NAFTA and the Uruguay Round. Instead of using attention-getting arguments that mobilized the faithful but tended to alienate the undecided, the organization centered its attack on perceived problems with NAFTA (if you liked NAFTA, you'll love fast-track), the alleged diminution of legislative power ("Congress loses the authority and the ability to shape [trade] issues"),[31] and the exclusion of most trade-related labor and environmental issues from coverage under the legislation. It was particularly effective with the argument that if the United States could negotiate trade-related issues such as intellectual property rights, it was wrong to exclude workers' rights and trade-related environmental issues.

Arguments like this did not dominate the debate, but they ate into the advantage that free traders had enjoyed in prior legislative rounds: the idea that they were promoting the general interest against narrow protectionist forces. Thus White House and congressional leaders lost a key asset that had been very much present in the NAFTA fight four years earlier: the general recognition of the rightness of their cause even among many who were driven to vote otherwise. The worker-environment argument joined with Democratic House members' increased dependence on labor for campaign funding (now that Democrats were in the minority, business gave them less, Republicans more). Therefore, through October and into November, Democrat after House Democrat came out against fast-track.

Things went better for the administration in the Senate, where the Finance Committee, led by William Roth and Daniel Patrick Moynihan, proved surprisingly successful in putting together a consensus package. With the hope of providing some cover for House members, this was brought to the Senate floor in early November, and it passed a preliminary procedural hurdle by a one-sided 68 to 31 vote, with majority backing from Democrats as well as Republicans. But as the month began counts of firm House Democratic supporters of fast-track were stuck in the twenties.[32]

In an effort to force the issue with uncommitted representatives, House Speaker Gingrich, working with the White House, set a specific date for the vote, November 7. The administration made an intensive push—a typical eleventh-hour Clinton all-nighter—employing both argument and inducement to sway the undecided. But this time the formula failed: the pressure brought the hard count of House Democrats supporting fast-track to only about 43; this was just 21 percent of their total, compared with the 40 percent that had backed NAFTA. A softer count had the number of Republican supporters at about 160, 70 percent of their total, with others perhaps available. Unfortunately for the president, the minimum needed in the House was 218, and when that proved lacking he asked Gingrich to postpone the vote. When the weekend that followed produced no breakthrough, he decided it was better to let Congress adjourn than to lose on a recorded vote. In the end, neither house voted on fast-track in 1997.

Prognosis and Conclusions

The system faltered in 1997. For the first time since the Roosevelt administration, when the United States had launched its trade liberalization policy, Congress failed to approve major presidential trade legislation. And though the president initially spoke of resubmitting the bill in 1998, by spring this had become highly unlikely: the votes were still lacking, and the White House had other battles to fight. On the international economic front fast-track lost priority to legislation replenishing the resources of the International Monetary Fund, the world's instrument for managing and containing the east Asian financial crisis. Republican and business leaders sought to revive fast-tract in mid-1998, presidential reluctance notwithstanding, but prospects were uncertain at best.

Would this prove a fundamental turning point, the end of the American drive for trade liberalization? Would future Congresses refuse to delegate trade-negotiating power? Or would the stalemate confirmed in 1997 prove temporary, resembling other periods (1967–74, for example) between completion of an old trade-negotiating agenda and congressional readiness to authorize a new one? The latter seems more likely, for the legislators who fought fast-track had no alternative trade policy. Instead they had, in the words of one Democratic opponent, "taken a hostage."[33] In his view the need was to bargain with a budget-balancing Clinton for new programs to help Americans hurt by trade and globalization. Moreover, the 1997 fast-track campaign was damaged by its advocates' reluctance to defend the trade liberalization record of the past—NAFTA in particular—and the administration's difficulty in establishing the urgency of its near-term negotiating agenda. With the passage of years if not months, that agenda is likely to become better defined. And the costs of not proceeding with it are likely to become clearer.

One could imagine a significant victory by either party in the November 1998 House elections making fast-track enactment easier to attain. If Republicans increase their majority, more votes should be available for the proposal that failed in 1997. If Democrats regain the majority, it could open the way for a bargain providing greater coverage of labor-environment issues, or more promising programs to help those Americans hurt by globalization, or both.

But even if the interbranch game of delegated authority is replayed by Congress one more time, it is an open question whether this approach will remain viable very far into the twenty-first century. It targets a political problem that appears to be receding; it does not deal well with the new, NAFTA-accelerated emergence of ancillary issues. It is based on bipartisan consensus, yet these new issues are making it harder for Democrats to play their assigned role.

The political problem that the interbranch game addresses admirably is that of industry-specific constituency interests' seeking trade restrictions. These have not disappeared; the protectionist tilt of current U.S. antidumping laws is evidence enough of that.[34] What does not seem in the cards, however, is a serious protectionist backlash such as those that threatened in the early 1970s and the middle 1980s. The product-specific protectionism that would fuel such a backlash is near an all-time low, in part because globalization is a reality and recognized as such. What is rising instead is pressure to link trade policy to some-times-related issues that have traditionally been outside its domain.

This pressure has multiplied as the United States has sought to supplement global trade liberalization with the negotiation of free trade agreements. Once the proposal is to develop a special economic relationship with a specific country or group of countries, many members of Congress—and of the broader society—will not limit their concerns to the commercial arena. They will raise other issues. Is the country a democracy? Does it respect human rights? Is it promoting or undermining world peace? Congress has had no problems with Canada on these matters. It has had, as previously noted in this and other chapters, plenty of problems with Mexico.

We see such issue linkage, of course, in the annual ritual over China's MFN status.[35] We see it, in extreme form, in Gephardt's "Dear Democratic Colleague" letter of February 1997, with its oft-peremptory

tone in stating that other nations should shape up if they want to negotiate trade deals with the United States. Many U.S. citizens may deplore
it; U.S. partner nations see it as intrusive and perhaps insulting. But it is
unlikely to disappear. As long as Congress is being asked to vote on
whether to grant something to and enter a special relationship with a
particular country or countries, a broad range of country-specific matters will seem relevant as potential objects of U.S. leverage. The case
becomes stronger if trading partners' policies on, say, labor relations or
environmental regulation directly affect policies or situations within
our borders. In a case like that of NAFTA, where people can visit en-
vironmentally depressed border areas or feel low-wage competition
nearby, the case grows stronger still.

Linkage also comes with broader globalization. Trade affects tropical
rain forests or workers' leverage in bargaining over wages and working
conditions. Some of the impacts are not positive,[36] just as the effect of
economic nationalization on U.S. states and communities was enor-
mously disruptive a century ago. Some impacts may be grossly exaggerated. But many are relevant targets of government policy. If national
policy levers are of diminishing use to advance values that important
groups of Americans favor, it is logical to reach for international levers.

How much should these matters be addressed through trade negotiations? Many free trade supporters would say as little as possible: the
global and regional trade regimes work best when focused on direct
governmental regulation of commercial transactions. Advocates of
trade expansion in the United States typically seek to limit their arguments to the commercial sphere, to the economic gains Americans will
reap from trade in general and from exports in particular.[37] But trade
policy has been a victim of its relative success. If trade policy insiders
see a fragile system that is ever vulnerable to political reversal, advocates of the environment or other causes see expanding global commerce, trade agreement after trade agreement, and a new central institution (the WTO) to cap it all. There is no equivalent international
institution or process to protect the environment or human rights, nor is
one available in practice for labor (today the International Labor Organization is hardly a potent force for advancing labor standards). No
wonder that advocates of these causes seek to connect with the live
international policy process that trade negotiations have become.

And trade does affect the plight of workers. Trade does affect the
environment. If means are not available to address the effects, advo-

cates of these causes will oppose trade liberalization, as many now do. Thus the trade regime needs to be sensitive to them if it is to maintain and expand its political base, particularly in Congress. Moreover, it is self-contradictory to argue simultaneously how important trade has become to people's lives and then to declare it illegitimate to deal with trade's impact on a wide range of values.

Yet the trade-negotiating agenda can easily become overloaded with related issues for which there is no domestic or international consensus, no established mode or legitimacy of international negotiation, and hence little prospect of meaningful agreement. President Clinton, who certainly wants to advance the workers' rights agenda, has found his ability to do so undercut not just by a Republican Congress and business interests, but by lack of receptivity internationally.

Moreover, the key institutions for managing the old trade policy game—the Office of the United States Trade Representative and the congressional trade committees—are not well suited to balancing commercial interests with labor or environmental interests. They have built up admirable credibility and effectiveness vis-à-vis traditional protectionism; they lack credibility with the unions, with the environmental organizations, and with the cause-driven Democrats who are responsive to both.

Hence, even as nations seek cautiously to expand the scope of trade negotiations, they should also develop parallel channels for addressing human rights, international labor standards, global warming, narcotics trafficking, or promotion of democracy. They need to develop these in North America. They need to envision them for the Western Hemisphere. And, to an increasing degree, they need to build such channels worldwide. The more that ancillary issues can be pursued along separate, viable negotiating tracks, the less will be the pressure on the trade track. But since progress on the other tracks will be slow, the pressure on trade policy will remain.

The executive-congressional power-sharing game on trade is likely to continue for some time. It meets important policy and political needs in both branches; it is backed by an increasingly internationalized business constituency. But the stronger and more effective it appears in serving its ends, the more it will be called upon to serve other ends. And the more it brings nations into deeper integration with one another, the more they will care about others' practices on issues stretching well beyond impediments to the free movement of goods and services.

The U.S. Congress feels the cross-pressures from this integration process, particularly as this process proceeds in North America, but also as it advances globally. Failure to resolve these pressures constructively will not reverse the process of globalization. It will not bring back Smoot-Hawley. Nor will it undo NAFTA, despite oft-virulent criticism emanating from Capitol Hill. But it will impede Congress's ability to back further trade liberalization, and hence for the United States to join its North American partners in the move toward hemisphere-wide integration.

Notes

1. See I. M. Destler, *American Trade Politics,* 3d ed. (Washington, D.C.: Institute for International Economics and Twentieth Century Fund, 1995), esp. chap. 2, and Robert Pastor, "The Cry-and-Sigh Syndrome: Congress and Trade Policy," in Allen Schick, ed., *Making Economic Policy in Congress* (Washington, D.C.: American Enterprise Institute, 1983).

2. The measure employed here takes the average of total exports and total imports of goods and services for the year, then divides that average by GDP. This and other percentages were calculated from Commerce Department and International Monetary Fund statistics.

3. For the history of the fast-track procedure, see my *Renewing Fast Track Legislation,* policy analysis no. 50 (Washington, D.C.: Institute for International Economics, September 1997). This essay draws upon that work.

4. The themes of this section are spelled out in greater detail in my *American Trade Politics,* esp. chaps. 2 and 4, and "Delegating Trade Policy," in Paul E. Peterson, ed., *The President, Congress, and the Making of Foreign Policy* (Oklahoma University Press, 1994), pp. 228–45.

5. "Super 301," actually Section 310 of the Omnibus Trade and Competitiveness Act of 1988, required the USTR to identify (in 1989 and 1990) "priority foreign countries," taking into account "the number and pervasiveness" of their trade-restrictive "acts, policies, and practices." Taken literally, the language called for a full-court press against Japan, unnamed but universally understood to be the target. Hills named Japan in 1989, but only for specific restrictions in three product sectors, and did not rename Japan in 1990 on the grounds that satisfactory solutions were being reached for these sectors.

6. Susan C. Schwab, *Trade-Offs: Negotiating the Omnibus Trade and Competitiveness Act* (Harvard Business School Press, 1994), p. 74. Schwab was legislative director to Senator John Danforth of Missouri, chairman of the Finance Subcommittee on Trade, from 1981 to 1989.

7. At a June 1990 academic conference on trade held in Mexico City, a former Canadian negotiator regaled his amused trilateral audience with tales of how hard it was to negotiate when almost no one in USTR was aware of what was going on. His lesson—that Mexicans could expect likewise—proved rather wide of the mark.

8. In fact, the Trade Act of 1974 included a provision endorsing negotiation of "a free trade area covering the United States and Canada," although it did not authorize fast-track consideration of the results (Section 612).

9. See chap. 2 of this volume.

10. For a superb treatment of this and the full range of NAFTA-related political issues, see Frederick W. Mayer, *Interpreting NAFTA: The Science and Art of Political Analysis* (Columbia University Press, 1998).

11. For a nice critique of both sides, see Paul Blustein, "NAFTA: Free Trade Bought and Oversold," *Washington Post,* September 30, 1996.

12. For much more extended treatment of congressional action on the Uruguay Round (and NAFTA), see Destler, *American Trade Politics,* esp. chap. 9.

13. The same seems to have been true in Europe. See Martin H. Wolf, "The Dog That Failed to Bark: The Climate for Trade Policy in the European Union," in Jeffrey J. Schott, ed., *The World Trading System: Challenges Ahead* (Washington, D.C.: Institute for International Economics, 1996), pp. 125–39.

14. An antidumping case against Mexican producers of tomatoes led to a minimum price agreement in October 1996; an "escape clause" action against broomcorn brooms led to U.S. imposition of a tariff rate quota a month later, as well as Mexican retaliation against selected U.S. products.

15. U.S. International Trade Commission, *The Year in Trade 1996: Operation of the Trade Agreements Program,* 48th report, USITC Publication 3024, April 1997, pp. 70–71.

16. In fact, despite the drastic devaluation and the deep recession, both of which cut deeply into sales of U.S. products, U.S. exports to Mexico grew substantially faster between 1993 and 1997 (by 71.7 percent) than U.S. global exports (48.5 percent). About half of the increase took place in 1997 as the Mexican economy rebounded.

17. In September 1997, a *Los Angeles Times* poll yielded a dead heat, 39 percent to 39 percent, on whether NAFTA "has been a good thing or a bad thing for the United States" (*National Journal,* October 4, 1997, p. 1984). The same source reported an NBC–*Wall Street Journal* survey done the same month that found 56 percent of Americans opposed to "having Congress grant the President fast-track authority to negotiate new free-trade agreements."

18. Richard E. Feinberg, *Summitry in the Americas: A Progress Report* (Washington, D.C.: Institute for International Economics, April 1997), p. 177. Feinberg served as senior director for Western Hemisphere issues on the National Security Council staff in 1993–95.

19. Ibid., p. 178.

20. The quotations are from an interview with a staff official involved, as part of my research for *Renewing Fast-Track Legislation.*

21. *Congressional Record,* daily ed., November 3, 1995, S16695.

22. The book was Ross Perot (with Pat Choate), *Save Your Job, Save Our Country: Why NAFTA Must Be Stopped—Now!* (New York: Hyperion, 1993).

23. The pages that follow draw substantially on my *Renewing Fast-Track Legislation.*

24. Ben Wildavsky, "Trade Fatigue," *National Journal,* January 18, 1997, p. 117.

25. See, for example, John Maggs, "Trading Places: The Gore-Gephardt Minuet," *New Republic,* April 14, 1997, pp. 15–16.

26. Bill Archer to William J. Clinton, reprinted in *Inside U.S. Trade,* May 23, 1997.

27. Quoted in *Inside U.S. Trade,* June 6, 1997, pp. 4, 6. Finance's new energy continued into the fall, with the committee voting out its own version of the legislation two weeks after Clinton submitted his fast-track proposal and one week before its House counterpart (which traditionally and constitutionally has the lead on trade policy).

28. Following the advice of congressional allies, trade policy officials had long since stopped speaking of "NAFTA expansion" as a fast-track goal. In fact, Barshefsky's prepared testimony at the Senate Finance Committee hearing of June 3 mentioned the "N-Word" just once, to say that it should not be the issue: "Our competitors would like nothing better than for us to sideline ourselves, debating NAFTA and our relationship with Mexico for years to come while they move ahead." But the report requirement forced USTR to address NAFTA, knowing that critics would scrutinize every word.

29. USTR, "Study on the Operation and Effect of the North American Free Trade Agreement (NAFTA)," July 11, 1997: http://www.ustr.gov/reports/index.html.

30. The report was issued on June 26, 1997. Other sponsoring organizations were the Economic Policy Institute, the Institute for Policy Studies, the International Labor Rights Fund, the Sierra Club, and the U.S. Business and Industrial Council Educational Foundation.

31. This quotation was taken from the web-page of Public Citizen's Global Trade Watch project: http://www.citizen.org/pctrade/tradehome.html.

32. By contrast, in an early 1997 conversation with me, a leading free trade Democrat had estimated the support likely among his colleagues at between 60 and 100 votes (out of 206), with the outcome likely on the lower side of the range. In 1993, 102 House Democrats (out of 258) had backed NAFTA.

33. The representative was Barney Frank. He used the phrase in an interview with *Washington Post* columnist E. J. Dionne and repeated it at a February 3, 1998, conference sponsored by the Institute for International Economics.

34. On this, see I. M. Destler, "The Political Economy of International Competition Policy," *Brookings Trade Forum* (Brookings, forthcoming).

35. The pejorative argument is "Why should we grant special trade privileges to a country that abuses its own citizens?" In fact, they are not special at all: 99.97 percent of imports now enter the United States on terms no less favorable than what is labeled MFN status.

36. For a perceptive critical look at issues on a worldwide scale, see Dani Rodrik, *Has Globalization Gone Too Far?* (Washington, D.C.: Institute for International Economics, 1997).

37. They will, on occasion, supplement these with arguments that trade liberalization buttresses U.S. leadership, an important Clinton argument for fast-track renewal. But they will be wary of pushing this argument too far lest skeptical congressmen interpret it as risking long-term commercial advantages for short-term diplomatic gains. Hence, for example, the importance of strengthening relations with Mexico was underemphasized by pro-NAFTA forces until the final days of the November 1993 debate.

Chapter 7

Trinational Perceptions

Neil Nevitte and Miguel Basañez

FROM A PURELY economic standpoint, a central puzzle is not why the North American Free Trade Agreement (NAFTA) emerged, but why this particular trade agreement took so long to forge. Part of the answer to the question of timing may well have to do with shifts in the global economic environment and, most particularly, the formation and consolidation of trading blocs in other parts of the world. But free trade agreements are also about politics, and any explanation of the timing of NAFTA has to take into account continental historical-cultural forces. Economic logic pulls the three countries of North America together, but political-historical logic has pushed them apart. The nation-building projects of both Mexico and Canada formed around the idea that U.S. influence should be resisted. That impulse has been grounded in the long-standing belief that the cultural orientations and interests of the three countries was fundamentally different and that they need to be protected. For these reasons the domestic politics surrounding NAFTA in each of the three countries were particularly contentious, and the eventual signing of the agreement represented a profound turning point in the political history of relations among the three countries.

This chapter is concerned with national values and public opinion, and it considers three broad sets of questions. First, to what extent do the publics in the three countries have different or compatible values? Second, how do citizens in the three countries view each other? And third, how are these mutual perceptions related to support for or opposition to free trade?

Culture and Values: The Survey Evidence

For a century or more politicians in Mexico and Canada have believed that the values of their people so differed from those of the United States that there was no sense in pursuing closer relations and considerable wisdom in defining the "limits to friendship."[1] Certainly, the weight of the historical evidence leads some to assume that the three countries are not compatible.[2] The gulf between the values of the Mexican people on the one hand and those held by Americans and Canadians on the other appears to be particularly wide. One influential historical explanation of North American cultural variation argues that the three societies were settled by three very different founding peoples, and these circumstances have profoundly shaped contemporary cultural orientations.[3]

This absence of a cultural consensus, however, is not just a question of the differences between Mexico and her two northern neighbors. Seymour Martin Lipset, perhaps the foremost comparative analyst of the political cultures of the United States and Canada, in a series of studies carried out over a period of nearly three decades, has argued that the United States and Canada experience a continental divide that is attributable to enduring differences in basic values and political styles.[4] Whether cultural variations qualify as "fundamentally different" or "essentially similar" or whether civilizations are "in conflict" or are compatible is difficult to determine conclusively. Viewed up close and seen in isolation, the "culture" of any country appears to be unique. Similarly, two-country comparisons, such as Lipset's, inevitably end up highlighting contrasts.[5] Mexico, the United States, and Canada undoubtedly did experience very different founding circumstances, but this is no guarantee that the contemporary value characteristics of the three populations are the same as those exhibited by their forebears some two or three centuries ago. Major changes have swept across all three societies since their founding moments. Cultures change.

Directly comparable evidence of the prevailing values of citizens in the three countries is in remarkably short supply. The richest and most systematic cross-temporal evidence available is provided by the World Values Surveys, national random sample surveys that were undertaken in 1981 and repeated in 1990. Detailed investigations of the data collected provide strong indications that all three societies are changing—in some respects quite rapidly. The values systems of the three North

American societies are gradually shifting, and significantly the directions of these values changes are entirely consistent with the broad
transformations that are taking place in most advanced industrial
states.

A large portion of the World Values evidence is summarized in
table 7-1, which reports the trajectories of values changes in sixteen
different domains. The values in nearly all these domains are measured
by multiple items that, through factor analysis, can be summarized as
value clusters (see the appendix for the wording of the questions).
Detailed cross-temporal comparisons of where the publics of the three
countries are located in these domains are revealing. For example,
norms related to sexual restrictiveness are becoming more relaxed in all
three countries. When it comes to child rearing, the publics in all three
countries are placing greater emphasis on such values as independence
and imagination rather than obedience and good manners. Respect for
authority is declining. In all three countries religious outlooks are becoming more secular, and church attendance rates are falling. Civil
permissiveness is rising, and confidence in government institutions is
falling. There is less support for state ownership of industry, and national pride is waning, whereas in all three countries levels of uncon-
ventional political participation are increasing.

The trajectories of change are strikingly similar—so similar that it is
hard to imagine that the causes of these shifts could be unique in each
national context. One interpretation is that these changes may be related to an increasing sense of security due to high levels of social
supports provided by the welfare state. The fate of most people is no
longer so heavily influenced by unpredictable forces as it was in agrar-
ian society and during early industrialism.[6] These changes are con-
ducive to orientations that place less emphasis on traditional religious
and cultural norms—especially insofar as these norms conflict with
individual self-expression. Regardless of their precise interpretation,
the central point to underscore here is that in twelve of the sixteen
domains considered the net result of these shifts is convergence of
values between the three countries; North Americans have become
significantly more alike. In three of the remaining four domains the
scale of the shifts was too small to be statistically significant, and in
the other domain, religiosity, the three countries were moving along the
same trajectory but then diverged simply because of the different rates
of secularization.

TABLE 7-1. *Converging Values in North America, 1981–90*

Value domain	Trajectory
Materialist/postmaterialist values	All moving in the same direction
Sexual restrictiveness	All moving in the same direction
Emphasis on autonomy over obedience for children	All moving in the same direction
Favor of greater respect for authority	All moving in the same direction
Emphasis on family duty	Mexico is moving in opposite direction from the United States and Canada, but converging
Civil permissiveness	All moving in the same direction
Religiosity	All moving in the same direction
Church attendance	All moving in the same direction
Confidence in government institutions	All moving in the same direction
Confidence in nongovernment institutions	Mexico is moving in opposite direction from the United States and Canada, but converging
National pride	All moving in the same direction
Conventional political participation	All moving in the same direction
Unconventional political participation	All moving in the same direction
Support for state ownership of industry	All moving in the same direction
Support for employee participation in management	Mexico is moving in opposite direction from the United States and Canada, but converging
Following instructions at work	Mexico is moving in opposite direction from the United States and Canada, but converging

Source: 1981 and 1990 World Values Surveys. The World Values Surveys are archived at the Inter-University Consortium for Political and Social Research, University of Michigan.

Given historical concerns about the influence of American values, it is reasonable to suspect that these values shifts might reflect the Americanization of Canadian and Mexican cultures.[7] To confirm this argument, the cross-temporal World Values data would have to show that American values changes lead those taking place in the other two countries. The thesis is plausible, but the survey evidence provides no support for it. Across the sixteen separate value domains examined, Canadian values actually lead American ones in thirteen cases, and in three of the other cases the evidence is indeterminate; it is statistically too close to call. Rather than suggesting an "Americanization" model of North American values change, the evidence is that all three countries are changing for similar reasons. Over the period for which we have directly comparable cross-temporal data, either the Canadians or the Americans led these changes, but the Mexicans were moving along the same trajectory and doing so at a faster pace. The net result is movement toward an overall convergence in North American values.

Detailed analysis of these data demonstrates that these changes in attitudes and behavior are systematically related to a combination of structural and intergenerational factors. There are clear generational differences, for example, in attitudes toward the value of autonomy. Increasingly people place a higher value on independence, and publics behave in elite-challenging ways.[8] Confidence in established political and societal institutions is eroding. At the same time the participation potential of Americans, Canadians, and Mexicans is gradually rising. The consistency of the pattern is unmistakable: more than 90 percent of the time the values shifts are correlated with age, education, and an underlying shift toward postmaterial values orientations.[9] The fact that the same values shifts are taking place in twenty-two countries for which we have cross-temporal World Values Surveys data; that shifts in the economic, political, and social domains are systematically connected; and that they are all similarly related to the background variables (generation and occupation) suggests that the change in North American values is part of a global pattern. North America is another stage upon which coherent and structurally driven values shifts are taking place.

The implications of these shifts are far reaching: the erosion of institutional authority and the rising levels of citizen intervention in politics mean that the established institutions that have shaped the societies for generations are losing their authority over average citizens. Public confidence is declining not only in key governmental institutions such as Parliament (and Congress), the police, civil service, and armed forces, but also in churches, educational systems, and the press. And there is evidence of a weakening sense of attachment to that most basic of all western institutions, the state itself. These changes are sometimes attributed to the fact that the specific administrator in office at the particular time a measure was taken was simply less effective or honest than previous ones. Certainly unpopular governments do evoke less confidence than popular ones. But a massive body of cross-temporal data demonstrates that these fluctuations cannot be linked to specific office holders. The same general trend is found in more than twenty-two different countries over a period of time that spans more than a decade; the transformations seem to be linked to a combination of factors, including structural factors associated with the expansion and increasing sophistication of the middle classes.

That North American values have shifted along a common trajectory and that they have converged helps to explain why, given the historical record of resistance to greater continental integration, Americans, Canadians, and Mexicans might have found continental free trade more acceptable than before—or perhaps less unacceptable—by the early 1990s.[10] No one doubts that the founding traditions of each of the three countries were different. The contemporary evidence is that the values have changed; North Americans increasingly want the same things out of life.

Mutual Perceptions

Core values shift, but they change quite slowly. Does the same hold true when it comes to mutual perceptions, that is, how Americans, Mexicans, and Canadians view each other? Table 7-2 reports American perceptions of some twenty countries across two dimensions—"favorability" and "vital interest" (see notes at bottom of table for an explanation of these terms). These data are useful because they situate American views about Mexico and Canada in a much larger cross-national and cross-temporal perspective. In the favorability dimension, table 7-2 reports standard "feeling thermometer" ratings for a sixteen-year period. In this scheme of things, a score of 50 signifies a neutral rating. The "warmth" of a respondent's feelings about any particular country is indicated by how much the score exceeds 50. "Coolness" is rated on the same principle, but in the opposite direction. Two basic findings are noteworthy. First, there is remarkably little variation in favorability ratings across the entire sixteen-year period. There are a couple of notable exceptions. Predictably, the scores for the Soviet Union/Russia "warmed up" at the end of the cold war, and just as predictably, they "cooled down" in the case of Iran between 1978 and 1982. These cases aside, the prevailing pattern was one of stability; ratings inched up or down, but the scope of the variation was small.

Second, Americans gave both Canada and Mexico relatively high favorability ratings. In fact, Americans gave Canada the highest ratings of all (on average, about 74 degrees), whereas they gave Mexico ratings (on average, 58) as high as those they gave to Germany (58), France (58), and Italy (57), America's allies in the North Atlantic Treaty Organization. Significantly, Americans gave Mexico ratings that were substantially higher than those assigned to other countries with similar levels of economic development. These comparatively strong favorability ratings seem to signify some sort of proximity dividend; perhaps it is presence, not absence, that makes the American heart grow fonder.

The percentages of respondents saying that the United States has a vital interest in each of the countries are also reported in table 7-2, and the clear finding here is that American respondents can and do discriminate among countries that they like and that they see to be of vital interest to the United States. For instance, the vast majority of Americans (80 percent) saw the United States as having a vital interest in Japan and Saudi Arabia. Notice, however, that the favorability ratings given those countries were neutral or just "lukewarm." The Soviet Union/Russia got high "vital interest" scores, but relatively low favorability ratings. On balance, Americans not only give both Canada and Mexico high favorability ratings, but they also see those countries as being of vital interest to the United States.

Favorability and vital interest ratings provide a useful overview, but they say little about the content of mutual feelings between citizens in the three countries of North America. Data on such feelings are less even, but they yield intriguing findings. That Americans hold "warm" feelings toward Mexico is a finding that is replicated in a variety of studies, but public opinion data also show that Americans see Mexico as a source of problems, particularly with respect to drugs and illegal immigration. According to Harris and Yankelovich data, for instance, some 60 percent of Americans think that illegal drugs from Mexico contribute "a great deal" to America's drug problem; 80 percent want to increase border controls.[11]

How do Mexicans view the United States? The data available indicate that Mexicans have generally favorable attitudes toward their northern neighbor. A 1989 Gaither Internacional survey, for instance, showed

TABLE 7-2. *U.S. Citizens' Favorability and Vital Interest Ratings of Twenty Countries, 1978–94*
"Feeling thermometer" degrees and percentages[a]

Country	1978 Favorability rating[b]	1978 Vital interest rating[c]	1982 Favorability rating	1982 Vital interest rating	1986 Favorability rating	1986 Vital interest rating	1990 Favorability rating	1990 Vital interest rating	1994 Favorability rating	1994 Vital interest rating	Average Favorability rating	Average Vital interest rating
Japan	56	78	53	82	61	78	52	79	53	85	55	80
Saudi Arabia	48	80	52	77	50	77	53	83	48	83	50	80
Canada	**72**	**69**	**74**	**82**	**77**	**78**	**76**	**77**	**73**	**71**	**74**	**75**
Great Britain	67	66	68	80	73	83	74	79	69	69	70	75
W. Germany/ Germany	57	69	59	76	62	77	62	73	57	66	59	72
Israel	61	78	55	75	59	76	54	67	54	64	57	72
Mexico	**58**	**60**	**60**	**74**	**59**	**74**	**56**	**63**	**57**	**76**	**58**	**69**
China	44	70	47	64	53	61	45	47	46	68	47	62
Brazil	52	38	54	45	54	45	54	39	54	35	54	40
India	49	37	48	30	48	36	48	…	48	31	48	33
Soviet Union/ Russia	34	74	26	…	31	…	59	83	54	79	41	79

France	62	54	60	58	58	56	56	45	55	39	58	50
Italy	56	36	55	35	58	41	59	:	58	:	57	37
Poland	50	28	52	43	53	35	57	43	52	31	53	36
South Korea	48	61	44	43	50	58	47	49	48	65	47	55
South Africa	46	63	45	38	47	54	51	53	52	57	48	53
Iran	50	67	28	51	22	50	27	:	28	:	31	42
Taiwan	51	53	49	51	52	53	48	46	48	49	50	50
Nigeria	47	42	44	32	46	31	47	29	:	46	34	
Egypt	53	75	52	66	49	61	52	53	:	41	60	50

Source: The 1979, 1983, 1987, 1991, and 1995 American Public Opinion and U.S. Foreign Policy data sets. The American Public Opinion and U.S. Foreign Policy data sets are archived at the Inter-University Consortium for Political and Social Research, University of Michigan.

a. See notes b and c for explanations.

b. The following wording was used to obtain these ratings: *Favorability toward Countries:* "Next I'd like you to rate the same countries on this feeling thermometer. If you feel neutral toward a country, give it a temperature of 50 degrees. If you have a warm feeling toward a country, give it a temperature higher than 50 degrees. If you have a cool feeling toward a country, give it a temperature lower than 50 degrees."

c. The following wording was used to obtain these ratings: *Vital Interests:* "Many people believe the United States has a vital interest in certain areas of the world and not in other areas. That is, certain countries of the world are important to the U.S. for political, economic, or security reasons. I'm going to read a list of countries. For each, tell me whether you feel the U.S. does or does not have a vital interest in that country." The numbers are percentages of respondents who answered that the United States does have a vital interest in the countries listed.

that 74 percent of Mexicans expressed favorable feelings toward the United States. Mexicans also admired the U.S. political system. Not surprisingly, an overwhelming majority of Mexicans surveyed (81 percent) thought that the United States exercised the greatest influence of any country on the Mexican way of life. Far more surprising is the fact that two-thirds of the Mexicans polled (67 percent) said that the influence was a positive one. Part of the reason for that finding may have to do with the fact that a substantial portion of Mexicans did not see Mexican and American interests as being at odds with each other; 67 percent viewed Mexican and American interests as being in agreement. Nonetheless, there are pockets of suspicion among the Mexican public. For example, Mexicans saw inequities in the relationships between the two countries; about half of the Mexicans surveyed viewed their own country as open to goods and services flowing from the United States, but more than two-thirds believed that the United States imposed restrictions on imports in order to protect American jobs. On balance, the Mexicans saw the United States as getting most of the benefits that come from closer trade relations between the two countries.

The mutual perceptions of Americans and Canadians exhibit asymmetries of a different sort. Public opinion data indicate that Canadians and Americans like each other, perhaps because they recognize the similarities between the two countries. For example, a 1989 poll showed that 78 percent of Americans thought of the two peoples as "mainly the same"; a majority of Canadians (56 percent) shared this view. Some 58 percent of Americans said they would send their children to study at a Canadian university; 41 percent of Canadians said they would send their children to study at American universities. There appear to be similar levels of mutual affection but not information. Americans tend to know less about their Canadian neighbors than vice versa. For example, only 12 percent of Americans correctly identified Canada as America's largest trading partner; 70 percent of Americans thought Japan was the United States' largest trading partner. Only 57 percent of American respondents indicated an awareness of the free trade agreement between Canada and the United States, but 97 percent of Canadians knew about the agreement. Fewer than 20 percent of Americans could identify Canada's prime minister, but 35 percent of Canadians could correctly identify the name of the U.S. vice president.[12]

These mutual knowledge asymmetries between the United States and Canada might be attributable to a variety of factors, including different geographic distributions of their respective populations. Over 90 percent of the Canadian population lives within 100 miles of the U.S. border, but less than 5 percent of the American population lives that close to the Canadian border; there are corresponding differences in media exposure. Over 90 percent of Canadian households have access to the three major U.S. television networks, whereas only a tiny fraction of U.S. households have comparable access to Canadian networks. These knowledge asymmetries may well reflect the reality that the United States is of more "vital interest" to Canada than vice versa; Canadians have greater incentives to know more about the United States than Americans have to know about Canada—and it costs them less.

Changing Attitudes toward NAFTA

The results of a survey about public attitudes toward NAFTA suggest that public opinions are volatile. According to the summary evidence reported in figures 7-1 and 7-2, Canadian and Mexican support for NAFTA has been moving in different directions since 1990. Throughout much of the early 1990s a clear majority of Canadians were opposed to the idea of free trade "between Canada, the U.S., and Mexico." In early 1992 opponents of the idea outnumbered supporters by a clear margin of about 3 to 1. Since 1992 Canadian support for continental free trade has been on a fairly consistent upward trajectory, and by 1996 supporters of continental free trade outnumbered opponents by a margin of more than 2 to 1. The Mexican data from MORI de Mexico show a gradual erosion in support for NAFTA from 1990 through 1994. Then came the depression of 1995 after the peso crisis. The most recent Mexican data indicate that public support for NAFTA is recovering. Figure 7-3 reflects changes in American attitudes toward NAFTA over roughly the same period. There are reasons to be more cautious about interpreting these data. Unlike the findings presented in figures 7-1 and 7-2, the American data come from different public opinion organizations using slightly different questions, so some of the variations might be attributable to differences in

FIGURE 7-1. *Changing Canadian Support for NAFTA, 1990–96[a]*

Percent

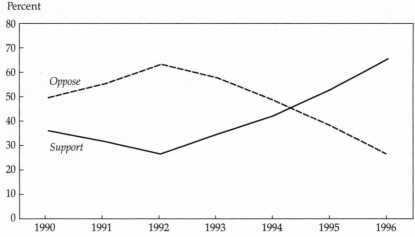

Source: Environics 1996. Available on request from Environics, Toronto.

a. Those surveyed responded to the following question: "Do you strongly agree, somewhat agree, somewhat disagree, or strongly disagree that there should be free trade between Canada, the U.S., and Mexico?"

FIGURE 7-2. *Changing Mexican Support for NAFTA, 1990–96[a]*

Percent

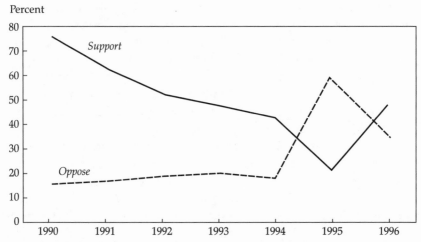

Source: MORI de Mexico Surveys 1990–96. Available from the Inter-University Consortium for Political and Social Research, University of Michigan.

a. Those surveyed responded to the following question: "Are you personally in favor of or against NAFTA?"

FIGURE 7-3. *Changing U.S. Support for NAFTA, 1991–97*[a]

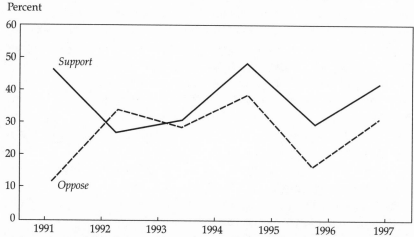

Percent

Sources: 1991—Roper Organization, December 1991; 1992—NBS/*Wall Street Journal*, September–October 1992; 1993—NBS/*Wall Street Journal*, August 1993; 1995—Harris, April 1995; 1996—CBS News, October 1996; 1997—American Viewpoint and Greenberg Quinlan Research, August 1997. Data are available from the respective organizations.

a. Those surveyed responded to the following questions: 1991—"All things considered, are you generally in favor of or opposed to a North American Free Trade Agreement involving the U.S., Canada, and Mexico?" 1992—"Do you favor or oppose the North American Free Trade Agreement with Mexico and Canada that eliminates nearly all restrictions on imports, exports, and business investment between the U.S., Mexico, and Canada?" 1993—"Do you favor or oppose the North American Free Trade Agreement with Mexico and Canada that eliminates nearly all restrictions on imports, exports, and business investment between the U.S., Mexico, and Canada?" 1995—"Do you favor or oppose NAFTA, the North American Free Trade Agreement signed by Canada, Mexico, and the United States?" 1996—"Do you favor or oppose NAFTA—the North American Free Trade Agreement between Mexico, Canada, and the U.S. (United States)?" 1997—Question wording is not available.

measurement and research design. Still, the essential message of these data is the same: in all three countries public opinion about NAFTA has changed.

Data from the World Values Surveys and other sources consistently show that the publics of all three North American countries enthusiastically support the principle of free trade.[13] That general enthusiasm, however, becomes far more muted when it comes to the specific case of NAFTA. What accounts for these striking variations in public attitudes?

There are a number of possibilities. Undoubtedly some variations might be grounded in country-specific characteristics. In the Canadian case, for example, limp support for free trade in 1992 might reflect the fact that NAFTA issues were crowded off the Canadian domestic agenda. In 1992 Canadians were preoccupied with Quebec and the referendum crisis. Leadership factors may also matter. Canadian Prime Minister Mulroney hitched his political wagon to free trade in 1988.[14] After the debate about the 1988 Canada–U.S. Free Trade Agreement, Prime Minister Mulroney's popularity gradually dropped off. By 1992 it was in free fall and slumped to the lowest level ever recorded for any Canadian prime minister in history. In Mexico the peso crisis undoubtedly shook public confidence and undermined support for free trade in that country (see figure 7-2).

But the more challenging task is to determine whether there might be more general explanations of variations in public support for NAFTA, ones that go beyond such idiosyncratic country-specific wrinkles and apply across different national settings. There are reasons to suppose that economic performance counts; a mountain of evidence demonstrates that economic considerations have a powerful impact on public opinion.[15] This idea has common-sense appeal. After all, the low point in Canadian support for NAFTA (see figure 7-1) coincided with the economic slowdown of late 1991 and early 1992, and the shift in Mexican support for NAFTA (see figure 7-2) could be related to the fallout from the peso crisis.

The key issue, however, may not be aggregate economic performance; economic upswings and downturns can benefit or hurt some people more than others, so these dynamics have the potential to stiffen opposition to, or boost support for, free trade in different ways. There is evidence indicating that what matters for public opinion is people's subjective evaluations of those conditions; these can be based on judgments about past economic performance (retrospective), or they may be forward looking (prospective). Expectations about the economic future or past may be shaped either by personal considerations (egocentric) or communitywide considerations (soiciotropic).[16] Variations in support for NAFTA may also be attributable to social location, because the costs and benefits associated with expanding trade environments are unevenly distributed throughout populations.[17] That explanation is plausible given repeated evidence of significant sociodemographic variations in support for NAFTA.[18]

Other plausible explanations are rooted in ideological factors or basic values orientations. Some evidence indicates that public support for free trade is driven by affect, shaped by feelings toward the particular countries involved.[19] On balance the research record is that people's feelings toward other nationalities are relatively stable; if changes do occur, the pace is usually gradual. Then again, these affective orientations, feelings, might be complemented by principle. For instance, people who are "free traders" by economic inclination are, all things being equal, more likely than others to support free trade in particular circumstances. Yet another possibility is that, when it comes to foreign policy questions about trade, people reason from consequences. Research demonstrates that on some policy matters people "arrive" at their particular positions neither via affect nor via principle but by way of mental experiment.[20] That may entail, in the case considered here, speculating about what the world would be like should NAFTA be passed, trying that world on "for size," and reaching a decision about supporting or opposing NAFTA after weighing these speculative likes and dislikes.

In some respects this "reasoning from consequences" model of citizen decisionmaking mimics public rhetoric around NAFTA fairly well. Not surprisingly, the speculative worlds constructed by supporters and opponents of free trade looked quite different depending on national context. NAFTA supporters in the United States, for example, appealed to a "new era of prosperity," whereas opponents were encouraged to imagine a "great sucking sound" of American jobs being vacuumed up by the low-wage Mexican environment. In Canada opponents described free trade with the United States as a "slippery slope" to total dependence, to the loss of policymaking autonomy. At issue was the worry that freer trade would induce policy convergence, particularly that free trade would undermine those public policy choices—for instance, the choice to offer more expansive state benefits such as health care—that historically set Canadians apart from their American cousins. Most Canadian supporters of free trade, on the other hand, viewed NAFTA as strategically prudent, as an institutional mechanism to help ensure Canadian access to U.S. markets while reducing the chances of Canadian business's getting sideswiped by the unpredictable turns of American policymakers.

No single post-NAFTA data set is adequately configured to allow one to evaluate all these propositions together and to do so for each

TABLE 7-3. *Sociopolitical Correlates of Support for Free Trade, 1993*

Individual characteristic	Gamma[a]
Sociodemographic characteristics	
Age	−0.08
Education	0.06
Gender	−0.23
Income	0.06
Work in public sector	−0.004
Rural	−0.02
Born in Canada	0.02
Income	0.07
Economic evaluations	
Retrospective personal evaluations	0.11
Prospective personal evaluations	0.10
Retrospective national evaluations	0.14
Prospective national evaluations	0.18
Attitudinal profile	
Economic individualism	0.27
Support for welfare state	−0.20
Positive feeling about U.S.	0.35

Source: 1993 Canadian Election Study. The study results are archived at the Institute for Social Research, York University.

a. Gamma coefficients measure the correlation, or strength, of the relationships between suppport for free trade and the sociodemographic items. Large gamma values represent strong relationships whereas small gamma values represent weak relationships. A negative sign indicates the presence of an inverse relationship.

country at the same time. This is a significant obstacle, but there are enough pockets of comparable data from a variety of sources (commercial surveys, elections studies, and the World Values Surveys) to allow us to evaluate the plausibility of most of these explanations.

The data in table 7-3 come from 1993, after the passage of NAFTA, and rely on a national random sample of Canadians. Critical for present purposes, these data include a number of items that are comparable with earlier measures (see figures 7-1 and 7-2) of attitudes toward free trade with Mexico and the United States, a cluster of economic indicators that capture both prospective and retrospective evaluations as well as personal (egocentric) and sociotropic (national) ones, and a variety of measures that allow us to look simultaneously at the impact of some plausible affective and ideological orientations.

That sociodemographic variables emerge as significant comes as no surprise at all. The data show that younger people are slightly more likely to support free trade, and so are those with higher levels of formal education and higher levels of income. Women, those working in the public sector, and nonimmigrants are less likely to support free trade than males, those working in the private sector, and immigrants. All correlations are statistically significant, and the results corroborate findings reported in earlier investigations. It is also clear that economic evaluations count for something—at least they do for the Canadian public. Each of the four economic evaluations is consistently and positively related to support for free trade. Canadian support for free trade increases if respondents reckon that they are "better off" now than in the past, that they will be better off in the future, and that these judgments apply both to themselves personally and to the country as a whole.

The attitudinal multi-item indicators tapping affective orientations (feelings) and ideological orientations (principled positions) are well-tested measures. The essential finding is that principles and feelings have an impressive impact on views about free trade—and that this impact is in the predicted direction. Principle is an important indicator. People who are "economic individualists," the hypothesis runs, should be more likely than others to support free trade.[21] According to the data, they do. The affective dimension is also a very powerful one: those with warm feelings about the United States are more likely than others to want free trade with the United States. There also some indications that attitudes toward the welfare state matter to Canadians. But the vital point here is that the direction of the relationships corresponds to expectations. These findings are heartening, but they indicate nothing about which of these explanations is most powerful. From the standpoint of explanation, the critical question is this: Of all these factors, which is doing most of the explanatory legwork?

To answer these questions we must turn to more powerful statistical strategies; the results of one such set of tests are summarized in table 7-4.

The first part of the analysis reports the coefficients for the impact of sociodemographic factors alone. We know that most of these sociodemographic variables are significantly correlated with support for NAFTA (see table 7-3). The regression estimates reported in table 7-4

TABLE 7-4. *Sociopolitical Predictors of Support for Free Trade in Canada, 1993*

Standardized regression coefficients

Predictor	Beta[a]	Beta	Beta
Sociodemographic characteristics			
Gender	−0.18**	−0.16**	−0.10*
Education	0.04	0.03	−0.01
Age	0.02	0.01	. . .
Born in Canada	0.02	0.02	0.02
Income	0.002	0.01	0.02
Employment in public sector	−0.002	0.02	0.005
Rural residence	−0.005	. . .	0.007
Economic evaluations			
Retrospective personal evaluations	. . .	0.07*	0.05
Prospective personal evaluations	. . .	0.05	0.04
Retrospective national evaluations	. . .	0.08*	0.02
Prospective national evaluations	. . .	0.12**	0.10*
Attitudinal profile			
Economic individualism	. . .	. . .	0.20**
Positive feeling about U.S.	. . .	. . .	0.31**
Support for welfare state	. . .	. . .	−0.09*
Constant	5.95	4.23	0.62
Adjusted R-square	.03	.06	.23
N	826	815	552

Source: 1993 Canadian Election Study. The study results are archived at the Institute for Social Research, York University.

*Significant at $p < .05$.

**Significant at $p < .01$.

a. Beta coefficients reported in the multivariate regression analysis measure the strength of each predictor variable (i.e., sociodemographic items) in determining support for free trade in Canada.

clearly show that, for Canadians, gender is the only sociodemographic indicator that remains significant after all factors are statistically considered together. Notice, however, that the amount of variation collectively "explained" by these sociodemographic factors is extremely modest (adjusted R-square = .03). At least for Canadians in 1993, demographic factors "mattered," but they did not count for much.

The second part of the analysis fixes on the middle column of betas, and it allows one to evaluate the relative impact of the four different kinds of economic evaluations. The results are fairly impressive. The amount of explained variance doubles, and three out of the four economic evaluations are statistically significant. As it happens, prospective national economic evaluations (the expectation that the country will "do well" economically in the future) have the biggest effect on free trade orientations, whereas the effects of personal retrospective evaluations (how well one did during the past year) are negligible.

The comprehensive test of the entire model produces several noteworthy findings. First, of all the sociodemographic factors only one remains statistically significant: women are more likely than men to oppose free trade in 1993. Second, all the economic evaluations except one disappear from the model. When everything is considered together, only prospective national economic considerations produce significant variations in support for free trade: respondents who are optimistic about the economic future of the country are significantly more likely to support free trade than those who are not optimistic.

Most striking of all is the impact of the broader set of attitudinal variables. In the Canadian case, the two most powerful determinants of attitudes toward free trade are economic individualism and feelings toward the United States. Economic individualists are far more likely to support free trade, and those with warmer "feelings about the United States" are far more likely than others to support free trade. The welfare state dimension also resonates within the Canadian public: those who want to maintain or expand social supports are significantly more likely than others to oppose free trade with the United States.

What do these findings mean collectively? First, that economic individualism and feelings toward the United States have independent effects means that each has a significant effect on free trade orientations after all the other factors have been taken into account. This implies that anyone seeking comprehensive explanations of variations in support for free trade should scrutinize these two predictors very closely. If these Canadian findings are generalizable, the clear implication is that variations in support for NAFTA may well be attributable to the combined effects of both a cross-temporal shift in such basic economic orientations as economic individualism or to warmer feelings toward NAFTA partner countries. Gender and prospective economic evaluations do matter, but they matter far less than economic individualism and feelings toward other NAFTA countries.

These results also suggest that reported sociodemographic variations in support for freer trade may simply reflect the uneven distribution of orientations toward economic individualism values or feelings toward other countries within and between different sociodemographic groups of the population. How plausible is it that the changes in support for free trade (see figures 7-1, 7-2, and 7-3) could be results of shifting demographics alone? A more compelling explanation requires both unpacking these data and turning to other data sources. To determine whether these findings are country specific or whether they apply more broadly entails looking at comparable data from other settings

Unpacking the Data

Previous analyses have shown that economic individualism was on the rise in Canada and Mexico during the 1980s, in the period before NAFTA.[22] To test the generalizability of the proposition that economic individualism and feelings toward the United States determine variations in support for NAFTA, we can turn to the 1990 World Values Surveys data for Canada and Mexico for 1990. Consider the results reported in table 7-5. The variables in these cross-national comparisons are not always measured in precisely the same ways as the earlier data, but they provide an important methodological check. Table 7-5 not only serves as a proximate test of the generalizability of the explanatory model that emerged from our initial analysis, but it also provides a foundation for a more discriminating perspective on attitudes toward the United States.

For both the Mexican and the Canadian publics, income and gender are significant predictors of free trade support. In both countries men are more likely than women to support free trade and those with higher incomes are greater supporters of free trade, although the combined effects of these sociodemographic factors are still very modest. When the World Values Surveys proxy for economic evaluations ("How satisfied are you with your personal finances?") is entered into the analysis, there is little change, a finding that is not so surprising given that the indicator is conceptually closer to egocentric evaluations than the prospective sociotropic considerations that appeared earlier as the prime mover.

TABLE 7-5. *Sociopolitical Predictors of Support for Free Trade in Canada and Mexico, 1990* Standardized regression coefficients

Predictor	Canada			Mexico		
	Beta[a]	Beta	Beta	Beta	Beta	Beta
Sociodemographic characteristics						
Gender	-0.10**	-0.10**	-0.11**	-0.09*	-0.10*	-0.09*
Education	0.002	0.004	-0.006	0.01	0.004	-0.01
Age	0.06	0.04	0.001	0.01	0.001	-0.02
Income	0.10**	0.08*	0.08*	0.08*	0.08*	0.06
Occupation	-0.01	-0.01	-0.01	...	0.002	-0.01
Economic evaluations						
Satisfaction with personal finances	...	0.05	0.02	...	0.02	-0.01
Attitudinal profile						
Economic individualism	...	...	0.06*	...	...	0.11**
Trust in Americans	...	...	0.24**	...	...	0.27**
National pride	...	...	-0.05	...	...	-0.02
Cosmopolitanism	...	...	0.08*	...	...	0.02
Constant	5.40	4.29	4.39	5.92	5.88	4.59
Adjusted R-square	.02	.02	.09	.01	.01	.10
N	1,028	1,022	968	612	599	497

Source: 1990 World Values Surveys. The World Values Surveys are archived at the Inter-University Consortium for Political and Social Research, University of Michigan.

*Significant at $p < .05$.

**Significant at $p < .01$.

a. See note a to table 7-4 for the definition of beta.

When it comes to the impact of the broader attitudinal indicators, the evidence underscores the earlier results. As before, these indicators have a very substantial impact on attitudes toward free trade, and they work in similar, although not identical, ways in both settings. Economic individualism has a pronounced impact on support for free trade in Canada and Mexico. In 1990 these orientations operated in the same direction in both countries: the greater the levels of economic individualism, the higher the support for free trade.

And what about general feelings toward other countries? More specifically, what is it about these general "feelings" toward the United States that matters most? There are several possibilities. One is that support for free trade with the United States may have to do with levels of national pride. People with high levels of national pride might have more difficulty supporting free trade with the United States for historical reasons. Conversely, those who do not have much national pride may have less difficulty in arriving at a pro–free trade position. The same may apply in the case of trust. Then again, globalization may well correspond to expanding cognitive horizons among publics: those who identify with North America or some higher-level aggregation might well be more inclined to support free trade with the United States than those who are more parochial in their identifications. In a sense, support for free trade might be conceptualized as an economic analogue of cosmopolitanism.

It turns out that trust in Americans is the most important of the three items considered—and it has about the same impact in Canada and in Mexico. Surprisingly, perhaps, levels of national pride contribute very little to the explained variance in both countries. The directions of the effects are consistent with expectations—those with higher levels of national pride display lower levels of support for free trade—but the impact is small and statistically insignificant. Mexican and Canadian responses differ in the cosmopolitanism dimension: Canadians who qualify as "cosmopolitan" are significantly more likely than those who do not to support free trade. For Mexicans there is no evidence of a comparable effect.

What about the status of demographics factors in this model? At the end of the day, nearly all the demographics factors wash out; they disappear in the final equation. The major exception—and it applies to the publics of both countries—is the matter of gender. Mexican and Canadian women are less likely than men to support free trade with the

United States. Moreover, these gender differences cannot be attributable to differences in education, age, or occupation, and when there are modest income effects (in the same direction in both countries), there are still significant gender effects that are over and above those of income.

Significantly, the findings concerning affective orientations toward other countries also apply equally to Mexicans and Canadians. A detailed probing of these data plainly indicates that what is most central to feelings toward the United States is trust. That finding raises yet another issue: if trust of Americans is crucial to explaining greater support for free trade with the United States, what factors influence Mexican and Canadian levels of trust toward Americans?

The findings reported in table 7-6 summarize how the same independent variables explain variations in Canadian and Mexican levels of trust in Americans. For Mexican respondents (right side of the table) the results are absolutely clear: there is only one factor that has a significant impact on levels of trust in Americans—orientation toward economic individualism. Striking here are the nonfindings: levels of interpersonal trust are irrelevant, and so are levels of national pride and cosmopolitanism. As it happens, personal financial satisfaction has no impact either. Notice that in the first and second iterations of the stepwise model, income does feature as a significant predictor. But the impact of income disappears once economic individualism is introduced; this is more important than objective income levels.

The results of the Canadian data are more complex, but they are striking for very different reasons. Of the sociodemographic factors, age matters: older Canadians are significantly more likely to trust Americans than are younger ones. Interpersonal trust significantly affects levels of trust in Americans: if Canadians are trusting of others, they are more likely to trust Americans. And national pride counts, but according to these data the direction of the impact of national pride is counterintuitive: Canadians with high levels of national pride are more inclined to trust Americans than those with less such pride. National pride, it seems, does not carry the connotations that conventional wisdom in Canada usually attributes to it. Pride in Canada does not necessarily signify distrust of Americans. Nevertheless, as in the case for Mexico, levels of economic individualism in Canada also feature prominently as predictors of trust in Americans.

One interpretation of these findings is that Mexicans and Canadians share one perspective in common: they both see the United States as a

TABLE 7-6. *Sociopolitical Predictors of Trust in Americans in Canada and Mexico, 1990*
Standardized regression coefficients

	Canada			Mexico		
Predictor	Beta[a]	Beta	Beta	Beta	Beta	Beta
Sociodemographic characteristics						
Gender	0.07*	0.06*	0.04	0.001	0.006	0.02
Education	0.02	0.02	0.003	0.02	0.02	−0.01
Age	0.18**	0.16*	0.14**	0.06	0.05	0.04
Income	0.05	0.02	0.002	0.11**	0.10*	0.08
Occupation	−0.005	...	0.003	−0.05	−0.06	−0.06
Economic evaluations						
Satisfaction with personal life	...	0.04	0.02	...	0.06	0.05
Satisfaction with personal finances	...	0.08*	0.06	...	0.05	0.006
Attitudinal profile						
Economic individualism	...	...	0.07**	...	...	0.10*
Interpersonal trust	...	...	0.17**	...	...	0.04
National pride	...	...	0.11**	...	...	0.02
Cosmopolitanism	...	...	−0.01	...	...	−0.004
Constant	2.80	2.43	4.39	2.12	1.79	1.44
Adjusted R-square	.03	.04	.09	.01	.01	.01
N	1,279	1,272	1,188	732	716	576

Source: 1990 World Values Surveys. The World Values Surveys are archived at the Inter-University Consortium for Political and Social Research, University of Michigan.
*Significant at $p < .05$.
**Significant at $p < .01$.
a. See note a to table 7-4 for the definition of beta.

symbol of economic individualism. Those who score high on this orientation also score high on trust in Americans. That interpretation is consistent with our earlier analysis, indicating that rising support for economic individualism is powerfully related to support for free trade with the United States.

To what extent do the same attitude structures emerge when we focus on trust in Mexicans rather than trust in Americans? That is, when levels of trust in Mexicans are the focus, are similar predictors as significant for Americans and Canadians? Table 7-7 summarizes findings in this area.

Among Canadians the one sociodemographic indicator that significantly predicts levels of trust in Mexicans is age: older Canadians are more trusting of Mexicans. For American respondents occupation matters, and that finding is consistent with the rhetoric of NAFTA in the United States. Americans with high-status jobs are more likely to trust Mexicans than those in low-status occupations. Americans with low occupational status were more worried about the impact that NAFTA would have on their livelihoods. Satisfaction with personal finances is also significant. Interpersonal trust is the most powerful predictor of trust in Mexicans: Americans (and Canadians) exhibiting high levels of interpersonal trust are far more likely to trust Mexicans than those who do not trust others. And for Americans national pride matters: those with higher levels of "pride in country" are significantly less likely to trust Mexicans than those with less national pride. The significant nonfinding for both Americans and Canadians is that levels of economic individualism do not feature as determinants of trust in Mexicans. And that finding provides additional support for the earlier interpretation concerning Canadian and Mexican trust in Americans: in those two countries trust in Americans *is* woven into orientations toward economic individualism; these values are more powerful determinants of attitudes toward free trade than income, occupation, or any other characteristic considered.

Conclusions

What conclusions can we draw from the data reported in this chapter? First, there is no question that all three NAFTA partners experienced values shifts throughout the course of the 1980s, the period be-

TABLE 7-7. *Sociopolitical Predictors of Trust in Mexicans in Canada and the United States, 1990*
Standardized regression coefficients

Predictor	Canada				Mexico	
	Beta[a]	*Beta*	*Beta*	*Beta*	*Beta*	*Beta*
Sociodemographic characteristics						
Gender	0.05*	0.05	0.03	-0.03	-0.02	-0.05
Education	0.06*	0.07*	0.03	0.04	0.04	0.03
Age	0.10**	0.09**	0.06*	0.06*	0.04	0.01
Income	0.06*	0.05	0.02	0.04	0.01	0.02
Occupation	...	...	-0.01	0.10**	0.09**	0.08*
Economic evaluations						
Satisfaction with personal life	...	...	-0.04	...	.08**	.05
Satisfaction with personal finances	...	0.05*	.07*	...	.08*	.06*
Attitudinal profile						
Economic individualism	...	...	0.01	...	...	-0.02
Interpersonal trust	...	...	0.25**	...	...	0.22**
National pride	...	...	0.05	...	...	0.08**
Cosmopolitanism	...	...	0.02	...	...	0.03
Constant	2.54	2.41	1.87	3.13	2.75	2.69
Adjusted R-square	.02	.02	.07	.02	.03	.09
N	1,213	1,207	1,127	1,268	1,263	1,139

Source: 1990 World Values Surveys. The World Values Surveys are archived at the Inter-University Consortium for Political and Social Research, University of Michigan.
*Significant at *p* < .05.
**Significant at *p* < .01.
a. See note a to table 7-4 for the definition of beta.

fore NAFTA. The most striking features of these shifts are their scope and their connectedness. They apply to the economic, political, and social domains, and in each national setting the same patterns of change are replicated. The values shifts were more rapid in Mexico than in either of the other two countries, but they are equally coherent in all three countries, and the trajectories of the values changes produced, at the end of the period studied, three North American publics with more in common than they had before. These changes, however, cannot be explained satisfactorily in terms of the "Americanization" of Canada or Mexico. Rather, these North American transformations mirror the shifts that have been taking place in virtually all other countries for which systematic data are available.

The second broad theme to emerge concerns evidence of shifting attitudes toward free trade in the three countries of North America. Public opinion toward NAFTA is volatile. Some of the variations might be attributed to country-specific events or characteristics. But our analyses of a variety of data sources in this chapter also show that there are commonalities. It turns out that such sociodemographic factors as education, age, and income have limited explanatory reach. At one level it is not difficult to demonstrate that there are sociodemographic correlates of support for and opposition to NAFTA. But the impact of these factors disappears when the search is expanded to include other considerations.

The key findings in this respect are that individual variations in support for NAFTA are best explained by two factors—trust and economic individualism. Research demonstrates that trust is a relatively stable attribute. It is conceptually close to favorability ratings, which, as we have also demonstrated, are also stable attributes. Levels of trust between the three North American peoples have changed marginally; they have risen. There are almost no data illustrating Canadian attitudes toward trade with Mexico or vice versa. But the data probing Canadian-American and Mexican-American orientations plainly show that trust is a crucial factor mediating attitudes toward NAFTA (see tables 7-6 and 7-7).

Economic individualism is also central, but it operates in a slightly different way. Canadian and Mexican attitudes toward NAFTA—and toward freer trade with the United States—are powerfully shaped by the extent to which Canadians and Mexicans support the values of economic individualism. Economic individualism is a significantly less powerful predictor of American attitudes toward NAFTA than trust, but it is more variable.

Some of the values changes documented in the first section of this analysis illustrate that North American levels of economic individualism have risen over the past decade or so, and that leads to the expectation that aggregate support for NAFTA should increase. But it is also clear that people "reason from consequences" and that their support for NAFTA is geared to and contingent on other considerations. Our analysis in this chapter shows that it is shaped by prospective economic evaluations, among other things, and these in turn are affected by material conditions. Many of the dire warnings floated by opponents of free trade have not materialized, and the post-NAFTA period, for the most part, has been a time of economic prosperity. The implication of our analysis is that the joint effects of rising levels of mutual trust and rising levels of shared perspectives about economic individualism, together with the experience of economic prosperity, contribute to increasing support for NAFTA. Recessions and currency crises have the reverse effect.

Appendix: Methodology

Variables used in this analysis have been created on the basis of items contained in the 1990 World Values Surveys and the 1993 Canadian Election Study. The items have been recoded and, in some cases, combined into indexes. The following describes the coding and index-building procedures employed in this analysis.

World Values Surveys

Support for Closer Economic Ties (additive scale): "Should Canada/Mexico have closer economic ties with the United States?" (much more distant = 1; much closer = 4).

"Should Canada/Mexico have closer economic ties with Mexico/Canada?" (much more distant = 1; much closer = 4).

Economic Individualism (additive scale)

1. Incomes should be made more equal (1).   There should be greater incentive for individual effort (10).

2. Government ownership of business and industry should be increased (1).

Private ownership of business and industry should be increased (10).

3. The government should take more responsibility to ensure that everyone is provided for (1).

Individuals should take more responsibility for providing for themselves (10).

4. Competition is harmful. It brings out the worst in people (1).

Competition is good. It stimulates people to work hard and develop new ideas (10).

5. Hard work doesn't generally bring success—it's more a matter of luck and connections (1).

In the long run, hard work usually brings a better life (10).

Satisfaction with Personal Finances: "How satisfied are you with the financial situation of your household?" (very dissatisfied = 1; very satisfied = 10).

National Pride: "How proud are you to be Canadian/Mexican?" (not at all = 1; very proud = 4).

Cosmopolitanism: "Which of these geographical groups do you belong to first of all?" (country = 0; locality/town = 1; the world as whole = 4).

Trust in Americans: "How much do you trust Americans?" (do not trust at all = 1; trust completely = 5).

Gender: Sex of respondent (male = 0; female = 1).

Income: "Here is a scale of incomes, and we would like to know in what group your household is, counting all wages, salaries, pensions, and other incomes that come in" (1 = lowest; 10 = highest).

Education: "At what age did you (or will you) complete your full-time education, either at school or at an institution of higher education?" (< 12 years = 1; 13–20 years = 2; 21 and over = 3).

Age: "Can you tell me the date of your birth? This means that you are ____ years old" (15–34 = 1; 35–54 = 2; 55 and over = 3).

Canadian Election Study

Support for Free Trade (additive scale): "Should Canada's ties with the United States be much closer, somewhat closer, about the same as now, more distant, much more distant, or haven't you thought much about this?" (much more distant = 1; much closer = 5).

"In 1988 Canada signed a free trade agreement with the United States. All things considered, do you support the agreement or do you oppose it?" (1 = oppose; 5 = support).

Economic Individualism (additive scale):

"Most people who don't get ahead should not blame the system; they have only themselves to blame" (strongly disagree = 1; strongly agree = 4).

"One of the big problems in this country is that we don't give everyone an equal chance" (strongly agree = 1; strongly disagree = 4).

"If people work hard they almost always get what they want" (strongly disagree = 1; strongly agree = 4).

"It is not really that big a problem if some people have more of a chance in life than others" (strongly disagree = 1; strongly agree = 4).

"The government must do more to reduce the income gap between rich and poor Canadians" (strongly agree = 1; strongly disagree = 4).

"Under the private enterprise system, working people do not get their fair share of what they produce" (strongly agree = 1; strongly disagree = 4).

"When businesses are allowed to make as much money as they can, everyone profits in the long run, including the poor" (strongly disagree = 1; strongly agree = 4).

"The welfare state makes people nowadays less willing to look after themselves" (strongly disagree = 1; strongly agree = 4).

The fact that some regions in Canada are poorer than others:

1. Means that governments should give incentives for firms to create jobs in the poorer regions.

2. Should be accepted as the normal result of market forces.

A person's wages should depend on:

1. How much he or she needs to live decently.

2. The importance of the job.

If the system of private enterprise were abolished:

1. Most people would work hard.

2. Very few people would do their best anyway.

Competition:

1. Brings out the worst in human nature.

2. Leads to excellence.

Welfare State (additive scale):

On the deficit, which comes closest to your own view?

1. Reduce deficits.

2. Maintain programs.

Should welfare be cut a lot, some, or not at all? (a lot = 1; not at all = 5).
Should health care be cut a lot, some, or not at all? (a lot = 1; not at all = 5).
Should unemployment insurance be cut a lot, some, or not at all? (a lot = 1; not at all = 5).

Which comes closer to your own view:

One: If people had to pay a fee each time they go to [a doctor/a hospital], there would be less waste in the health care system.
or
Two: If people had to pay a fee, [low-income/some] people would not be able to get the health care they need.

1. Less waste.

2. Not get the health care.

Feeling about the U.S.: Thermometer scale (very negative = 0; very positive = 100).

Retrospective Personal Economic Evaluations: "Would you say that you are better off or worse off financially than you were a year ago?" (much worse = 1; much better = 5).

Retrospective National Economic Evaluations: "Would you say that over the past year, Canada's economy has gotten better, stayed about the same, or gotten worse?" (much worse = 1; much better = 5).

Personal Economic Expectations: "Do you think that a year from now you will be better off financially, worse off, or just about the same as now?" (much worse = 1; much better = 5).

National Economic Expectations: "What about the next 12 months? Do you expect Canada's economy to get better, stay about the same, or get worse?" (much worse = 1; much better = 5).

Gender: Sex of respondent (male = 0; female = 1).

Income: "What was your total household income before taxes and other deductions for 1992 (in thousands of dollars)?" (less than 11 = low; 56 and over = high).

Education: "What is the highest level of education that you have completed?" (elementary = 1; secondary = 2; college/degree = 3).

Age: "In what year were you born?" (18–29 = 1; 30–48 = 2; 49 and over = 3).

Employment in Public Sector: "Do you work for a . . . ?" (private company = 0; government-owned company = 1).

Country Born: "In what country were you born?" (other country = 0; Canada = 1).

Rural Residence: Area of residence (urban = 0; rural = 1).

Notes

1. Robert Pastor and Jorge Castenada, *Limits to Friendship: The United States and Mexico* (Knopf, 1988).

2. See, for example, Laurence Harrison, *Who Prospers: How Cultural Values Shape Economic and Political Success* (Basic Books, 1992).

3. Louis Hart, *The Founding of New Societies* (Harcourt Brace, 1964).

4. Seymour Martin Lipset, *The First New Nation* (Norton, 1963); and *Continental Divide: The Values and Institutions of the United States and Canada* (Toronto and Washington, D.C.: C. D. Howe Institutes and National Planning Association, 1990).

5. Lipset, *Continental Divide.*

6. Ronald Inglehart, *Culture Shift in Advanced Industrial Society* (Princeton University Press, 1990).

7. Gad Horowitz, "Notes on 'Conservatism, Liberalism and Socialism in Canada,'" *Canadian Journal of Political Science,* vol. 32 (June 1978), pp. 143–70.

8. Neil Nevitte, *The Decline of Deference* (Toronto: Broadview Press, 1996).

9. Ronald Inglehart, Neil Nevitte, and Miguel Basañez, *The North American Trajectory: Cultural, Economic, and Political Ties among the United States, Canada, and Mexico* (New York: Aldine de Gruyter, 1996).

10. Ibid.

11. Louis Harris, "Mexico Is Friendly but Has Serious Problems," *The Harris Survey*, vol. 44 (August 1986), p. 1; Clancy Schulman Yankelovich, "Poll Findings on Mexico," *Memorandum to Time Magazine* (August 1986), p. 1.

12. *Maclean's*/Decima Poll, *Maclean's*, July 1989, pp. 48–50.

13. Edward Sarpolus, "Polls Show Growing Support for Free Trade," Clearinghouse on State International Policies, September 1997.

14. There are reasons to be cautious about the issue of comparable timing. Core Canadian economic interests in continental free trade were largely addressed in the 1988 Canada–U.S. Free Trade Agreement (CUFTA), which preceded NAFTA. Within Canada, NAFTA was far less contentious than CUFTA. The volumes of trade between Canada and Mexico are relatively small.

15. John Zaller, *The Nature and Origins of Mass Opinion* (New York: Cambridge University Press, 1992).

16. Morris P. Fiorina, *Retrospective Voting in American National Elections* (Yale University Press, 1981); Donald R. Kinder and D. Roderick Kiewiet, "Economic Grievances and Political Behavior: The Role of Personal Discontents and Collective Judgments in Congressional Voting," *American Journal of Political Science*, vol. 23 (August 1979), pp. 495–527; Kinder and Kiewiet, "Sociotropic Politics," *British Journal of Political Science*, vol. 11 (April 1981), pp. 129–61.

17. Ronald Rogowski, *Commerce and Coalitions: How Trade Affects Domestic Political Alignments* (Princeton University Press, 1989); Stephen Weatherford, "Economic Stagflation and Public Support for the Political System," *British Journal of Political Science*, vol. 14 (January 1984), pp. 187–205.

18. Describing the correlations between sociodemographic characteristics and support for or opposition to free trade is a fairly simple task. But showing that income, for instance, is related to support for free trade does not take the analysis very far. The more substantial challenge is to establish the precise reasons that lie behind such correlations.

19. This is a variation on the notion of "groupthink"; respondents evaluate a message differently when different group identifications are engaged. See Paul M. Sniderman, Richard A. Brody, and Philip Tetlock, *Reasoning and Choice: Explorations in Political Psychology* (New York: Cambridge University Press, 1991).

20. Zaller, *The Nature and Origins of Mass Opinion*.

21. Economic individualists have values that are closely akin to what are sometimes called a cluster of "capitalist values." See Herbert McCloskey and John Zaller, *The American Ethos: Public Attitudes towards Capitalism and Democracy* (Harvard University Press, 1984). The scale used in this analysis is not identical to the content of the McCloskey and Zaller scale, but it comes close enough to share a label.

22. Inglehart, Nevitte, and Basañez, *The North American Trajectory*.

Chapter 8

Replacing Paternalism with Partnership

Robert A. Pastor and Rafael Fernandez de Castro

"IF WE COULD look down at the earth from a distant planet," said Samuel Berger, President Bill Clinton's national security adviser, "one of the most powerful phenomena we would observe are the effects of economic integration—reinforced by a communications and technological revolution that telescopes time and distance." The new order, said Berger, "increasingly is shaped by the forces of integration."[1]

Berger recognizes that integration is "not without downsides," including growing economic vulnerability, worsening disparities within and between nations, and terrorists and drug traffickers taking advantage of free movement. One dimension that he omits, but which is both inherent and, paradoxically, subversive of the integration process, is the "Newtonian conundrum," which posits that every movement toward integration evokes an opposite, though not always an equal, reaction.

The Newtonian conundrum can be seen in many forms. As the volume and value of trade increased, the pressures to slow or stop some imports—for example, of winter vegetables—increased. As immigration to the United States from Mexico swelled, Californians approved Proposition 187 to stop providing public services for children of illegal aliens. In south Florida, a veritable cauldron of bilingualism, people voted to make English the "official language." These reactions are hardly unique to the United States. Indeed, for 100 years the anticipated fear of being overrun by Americans or their goods or influence kept Canadians and Mexicans from considering the establishment of a free trade area with the United States. Canadians and Mexicans fear American cultural influence, and individual industries, farmers, and fishermen in those countries fear competition from their more powerful neighbor.

Newton's conundrum means that integration will not proceed in a fashion that can be plotted by a straight line; indeed, it has slowed the integration process in the United States, and some question whether it has hastened a process of *dis*integration in Canada and Mexico. Quebeçois separatism has a long history, but the movement seems to have picked up steam in recent years. Separatists have said that they want to be part of the North American Free Trade Agreement (NAFTA), although not of Canada, and this parallels the views of north Italian separatists, who prefer to be governed by Brussels rather than by Rome. The Mexican philosopher Luis Villoro has written of a paradox at the end of the twentieth century in which a tendency toward globalization has coincided with a resurgence of ethnic and cultural identities.[2]

A different but not unrelated phenomenon seems to have occurred in Chiapas in southern Mexico. The Zapatista rebellion was launched on January 1, 1994, the day that NAFTA began to be implemented, to protest the effect of the trade agreement on poor Indians. Few analysts believe there is any serious connection between NAFTA and Chiapas, but there is no doubting the fear of NAFTA felt by many groups, especially the poor.

What is new today is that all three countries of North America are subject to similar fears, and the interacting anxieties lead each to think that the others might bend, break, or abandon the rules of NAFTA if it suits them. This keeps the integration process tenuous and fragile. Although NAFTA was supposed to engender respect and accelerate integration, the Newtonian conundrum produces the opposite result.

This is not just a NAFTA problem; it is the essence of the global challenge of integration. The community as a whole benefits from global competition, but that is not true of everyone, and some are hurt. The process of integration can advance only if those who fear losing a job or an identity can be reassured. The collective decisionmaking process of aggregating hopes and fears affects whether a country moves forward or backward—or does not move at all. That brings us to Congress.

Congress: Why Is It the Pivot?

The fears that subvert the integration process reside in the bodies politic of the three countries, but they are given the most concrete and effective expression by legislatures that respond to their constituents' needs and concerns. The Canadian parliamentary system channels these concerns into the executive's private deliberations. The Mexican Congress, although beginning to display some independence, has a considerable distance to travel before its voice is heard loud enough to affect Mexico, let alone trilateral relations. The members of the U.S. Congress are the loudest and most aggressive legislators in North America, and that is one reason we have chosen it as this book's focus.

There are some who view this congressional behavior as new and different, but rather than accept that proposition we decided to investigate it systematically and historically, first by looking at Congress's effect on Mexico and Canada and then by looking at the way the governments of those two countries have approached the U.S. Congress. What we found in chapters 2 and 3 was that Congress has had a substantial effect on both countries on most issues since the middle of the nineteenth century. The U.S. Congress played a critical role in the setting of Mexican and Canadian territorial borders in the nineteenth century. Today it defines U.S. trade policy toward Canada and Mexico.

Members of the U.S. Congress not only lack the political or systemic restraints of their colleagues across the borders; incentives are built into the U.S. political and electoral systems that encourage more aggressive behavior by Congress. Among other things, the work of Congress is public. Members need to impress their constitutents, often at the price of gratuitous criticism of foreign governments. Ironically, congressional hearings on Mexico and Canada are covered sensationally in Mexico City and Ottawa and usually not at all in the United States.

Throughout history the U.S. Congress has asserted particular interests, often at the expense of the general interests of the United States. As Kim Richard Nossal puts it in chapter 3, Congress's decisions often take "the form of a careful calculation of the public interest that is unabashedly local in definition" or represents "electoral self-interest." This is not new, nor is it necessarily undesirable. Congress has often shaped the national agenda by emphasizing a particular interest or issue. In the 1960s Congress pressed U.S. interests in protecting U.S. investments overseas despite a reluctant executive branch of the government; in the mid-1970s Congress pressed U.S. interests in human rights; and in the 1980s and 1990s it insisted on new steps to curb drug trafficking. In each case the initial response of the executive branch was that Congress should not try to micromanage U.S. foreign policy and that U.S. interests were wider than any single set of interests. In the end,

U.S. priorities were reshaped. This pattern has long reflected congressional involvement in foreign policymaking.

The influence of the U.S. Congress on Mexican and Canadian affairs evinces some other patterns. Congress's behavior has been more moderate on U.S.-Mexican security issues, more assertive on economic and trade issues. With regard to Canada, the U.S. Congress's action is contradictory: at times the members of Congress are, in Nossal's words, "careless, self-indulgent, shortsighted, and myopically parochial toward their northern neighbor"; at other times they have "proven to be farsighted, statesmanlike, and endowed with a regional vision." A similar pattern is at work in congressional-Mexican relations, except that there seems to be a sharper edge in the acerbic way that Congress treats Mexico than in the way it treats Canada.

In chapter 5 Norman Ornstein shows that the new members of Congress have much in common with their predecessors at the end of World War I and, to a slightly lesser degree, after World War II. Their focus is on domestic concerns, and they have little or no experience abroad. What is new is that the United States is now the center of an emerging region in which an integration process is increasingly important; however, because of the asymmetry of the three nations, it is also very shaky.

In chapter 4 George Grayson demonstrates that Mexico and Canada have revised traditional approaches to deal with the United States and integration. Both governments had long approached the U.S. government diplomatically through the Department of State. In the mid-1980s, as it began to contemplate a Free Trade Agreement (FTA) with the United States, Canada first awoke to the importance of Congress. A few years later Mexico developed a full-court strategy for influencing the views of Congress and the American public on NAFTA. In the course of lobbying Congress, both governments learned about the concerns of the American public and the intricacies of the congressional process. By adapting to the congressional process, both succeeded in getting the agreements approved.

Canada with the FTA in the mid-1980s and Mexico with NAFTA in the early 1990s started to play the Washington game. Both governments began to actively seek to make their case on Capitol Hill, and they have continued to play active roles on economic issues. This activism has not completely replaced the traditional defensive nationalism sometimes displayed by Mexican and, less so, by Canadian officials when the United States responds aggressively on bilateral issues such as drug trafficking and migration in the case of Mexico and cultural issues in the case of Canada.

Our study of the history of congressional policy toward Mexico and Canada demonstrated that the U.S. approach to its neighbors has not changed. The problem, in brief, is not that Congress treats Mexico and Canada worse than before. It is that Congress does not treat them better, and there is a new compelling reason to do so. A North American region has emerged. The movement of people, although not free, has been proceeding among the three countries of the region at a rapid clip. During the past three decades Mexico has been more than twice as large a source of legal and illegal immigrants to the United States than has any other country. North Americans travel more to their neighbors than elsewhere. In 1996 some 33 million Americans visited Canada and Mexico; about a third of that number visited Europe.[3] Because of the language and the cultural similarities between Canada and the United States, Canadians already play a large but often unrecognized role in business and the arts in the United States.

Economic integration among the three countries of North America has been accelerating since the passage of NAFTA in 1993. Trade increased from a third of their total trade in 1980 to nearly half in 1996. By 1997 Mexico had surpassed Japan as the second largest market for U.S. exports. Many of the largest corporations in the United States, Canada, and Mexico have begun to reorganize and restructure their units so as to function as North American entities. Sidney Weintraub has noted that "NAFTA institutionalized industrial co-production between Mexico and the United States across the board,"[4] but it is equally important that large corporations are thinking continentally, not just nationally or binationally.

The opportunities presented by a successful process of integration, combined with the dangers of a failed process, argue for a more deliberate approach to the phenomenon.

A Regional Identity: Options and Implications

The United States does not view itself as part of a region in the way that France and Germany view themselves as part of the European Union (EU), but the idea of a European identity did not spring up fully formed in 1957 when the Treaty of Rome was signed. Although the initial motive for unity was different in Europe than it is in North America, the consequences were similar to that of NAFTA.

The combined product of the three countries of North America is virtually the same as that of the fifteen members of the EU, and both regions grapple with the challenge of integration; however, with concerns born of different origins, the three governments of North America have shied away from the idea of trying to construct a regional identity. Even the terms used to describe the residents of this region are confusing. Mexicans have long used the word *Norteamericano* to refer to people from the United States. Mexican diplomats and scholars have begun to refer to U.S. citizens as *estadounidense*, but the term has not caught on in Mexico, and it does not translate well into English. Citizens of the United States refer to themselves as Americans, which is both true and pretentious at the same time, although the same could be said about a number of utterances of the region's great power.

During the negotiations for NAFTA and subsequently during the U.S. congressional debate, some scholars and policymakers began to refer to a North American Community.[5] The term applied to a new economic area and a disposition of the three nations to cooperate in a new spirit of mutual respect. The phrase was barely used before it almost vanished. The year that NAFTA came into effect, 1994, was also a year that began with the Chiapas rebellion and ended with Mexico's economic crisis.

Partly because of these two incidents, the initial interest in creating a trilateral community succumbed to more traditional ways of operating—that is, two intense bilateral relationships, the United States-Canada and the United States-Mexico, with a weak relationship between Mexico and Canada. During the NAFTA negotiations Canadians showed a relatively greater interest than their partners in the concept of a North American Community, but that, too, soon diminished.

The absence of a single word to describe all the people of North America is only one sign of an absence of a regional identity. Perhaps this is to be expected; after all, NAFTA is a business agreement aimed to reduce trade and investment barriers. However, NAFTA is also the centerpiece of a dynamic integration process between three very different countries. The question is whether NAFTA is an end in itself or a means to either a hemispheric free trade area or an integrated North America built on a new, respectful trilateral partnership.

In December 1994 in Miami, thirty-four heads of governments of the Americas declared that the establishment of a Free Trade Area of the

Americas (FTAA) was a goal to be achieved by 2005. As negotiations for an FTAA proceed, some may see NAFTA as just a building block for the larger trade area. We view that as a mistaken view for several reasons.

First, four years after the promise of an FTAA the United States still has not obtained fast-track trade negotiation authority from Congress. Without that the United States cannot assume leadership, and the FTAA's goal of 2005 will slip. Second, an FTAA, whenever it is established, will look very different from NAFTA because the rate of integration in the hemisphere is very low compared with that in North America. Roughly half of U.S. trade with the thirty-three nations of Latin America and the Caribbean is with just Mexico.

Third, North America has too many overlapping problems for one to believe that these will disappear as we remove trade and investment barriers. Indeed many more problems will emerge as integration proceeds. If an FTAA is to have any chance of success, the United States and Canada will have to devise mechanisms to facilitate integration with Mexico first.

So one needs to start in North America, and there consider which of three options is most viable for addressing the challenge of integration: an arm's-length relationship that relies on the market, a confederation that aims to construct a more unified political response, or a set of procedural and institutional mechanisms that could generate the benefits of integration while minimizing the costs.

Option 1, the market option, is essentially the status quo: remove trade and investment barriers and cross our fingers. This is clearly the most likely option simply because of inertia or fatigue. It is also the most problematic in the sense that it is the least able to cope with either the windfall or the fallout of integration. The business cycle will carry the three economies through periods of growth and decline, but NAFTA will be oblivious to the distributional effects. Thus far the weakest of the three economies, Mexico, has predictably experienced the widest swings in the cycle, and that is likely to continue. The United States will continue to pay part of the burden of the negative swing, as it does in absorbing large flows of illegal migration or coming to the rescue of debt-ridden banks. The implication of the "let the market work" option is that U.S. policy will remain decentralized and reactive, often driven by congressional bursts of frustration or rage. Canada and Mexico will react as they have in the past.

If the "status quo" option seems the most likely, the establishment of a North American Confederation seems the least likely. Generally the strongest party to a free trade agreement would advocate the kind of comprehensive political package envisaged in this option, but the United States does not fit this model. Since the Republican Senate failed to approve the League of Nations, there has been a strong element in the party that has viewed international organizations and agreements as undesirable restraints on the unilateral actions of the United States. This position has sometimes been confused with isolationism, but it is quite different. It accepts that the United States cannot be isolationist, but it sees international obligations as anchors that weigh down the United States and prevent it from fulfilling its correct role. More than the protectionism that is reflected by legislators from both parties, especially the Democrats, this unilateral internationalism would hamper any efforts to establish a supranational body to guide or plan the integration process.

The EU has been working on this question for four decades, and it has created a rather extensive set of institutions that have been harmonizing and subsequently unifying the domestic and foreign policies of its members into a single set of European policies. In contrast to the EU, NAFTA avoided not only any political institutions such as the European Commission or Parliament, but even any professional secretariat that is able to analyze issues and connect officials from the member countries.

Without a planning body, all three governments of North America were surprised by the suddenness and magnitude of the peso crisis of December 1994. Nor have the three governments understood the relationship between uneven development in Mexico and immigration and drug trafficking to the United States. The three governments of North America would need a much more serious crisis than the peso devaluation and a graver threat than illegal immigration before they contemplated the kinds of supranational institutions that could anticipate and prevent future crises or plan for the best ways to take advantage of integration.

The third option for effecting integration recognizes that NAFTA is inadequate and that confederation is implausible. Then what is needed? First, a new attitude is needed that can begin to influence the way that the three nations approach their common problems. Second, new institutions are needed to assess transnational problems from a trinational perspective and offer proposals. This requires a capability for planning and a sensitivity to the interrelationships of the various issues affected by the integration process. Third, all three governments need some bureaucratic rearrangements in order to relate to each other and to their common problems more effectively than in the past. One could argue that these three conditions—attitude, institutions, and governmental reorganization—were implicitly accepted by the three governments during the NAFTA negotiations. Nevertheless, once the NAFTA negotiating euphoria had evaporated, the three governments largely returned to business as usual.

Finally we return to the role of the U.S. Congress, and we propose procedures and mechanisms that could increase the prospects that the farsighted, statesmanlike side of its dual personality will be more prevalent than the myopic, angry side. As a general rule, in proposing new ideas in each of these areas in the next section, we look at what has worked in the past instead of trying to reinvent the wheel.

A Trilateral Partnership

For much of the past 200 years North American relations have largely been two sides of the triangle—U.S.-Canadian and U.S.-Mexican relations. Canada and Mexico had the most minimal relations. The addition of the third side of the triangle has been like adding the third leg of a stool; it has offered stability and enhanced the overall value of the stool. Both Mexico and Canada have found it easier talking to the United States if the other was present. Together the three countries will each find its position strengthened internationally. The United States benefits because Canada and Mexico have already demonstrated their independence and integrity in international forums, and Canada and Mexico benefit from the reach and power of the United States. If all three governments could agree on a strategy, that would likely be more effective than if any of the three pursues its policy independently.

In this section we propose some ideas for a North American approach, but first we try to extract some lessons from the bilateral relationships that already exist. A useful point of departure in considering the best attitudes on which to build a new identity is to compare the very different approaches that two U.S. states, Texas and California, have taken toward Mexico.

Identity

Perhaps nothing better illustrates the difference in approaches than the actions of the two governors during the early stages of the 1996 U.S. presidential campaign. In August 1995 Texas Governor George W. Bush warned prospective U.S. presidential candidates that he would not permit them to engage in immigrant bashing while campaigning in Texas. "Mexico," he said, "is too important a partner to be used as a scapegoat in a political race."[6] At the same time California Governor Pete Wilson, having ridden an anti-Mexican issue, Proposition 187, to reelection in California, based part of his presidential bid on anti-immigrant rhetoric.

What accounts for the striking differences in the positions taken by the politicians of these two important U.S. border states? What explains the fact that Texas behaves like a partner, whereas California acts as an insensitive bully? The explanations range from the historic to the economic. Although both states were originally Mexican territories, Texas was the first to secede, and it inherited a larger Mexican population, which has grown comfortably and well in the state. It is not a coincidence that many of the most prominent Mexican-American political leaders have been from Texas. In contrast, the largest flow of migration from Mexico to California has occurred in the past three decades, and many of these immigrants have not been assimilated as were those who migrated to Texas. Instead they live in Mexican barrios in the city of Los Angeles, or they return to Mexico after earning some money.

Monterrey and Saltillo, the most important northern Mexican cities from a commercial and cultural perspective, have been connected to Texas cities, whereas California is remote from the centers of Mexico's cultural life. Both states are linked economically to Mexico, but Texas sits astride the traditional overland route into the heart of Mexico and is more dependent on its southern neighbor than California is. In 1994 more than 247,000 Texans had jobs directly related to Texas exports to Mexico, and another 217,000 jobs were indirectly affected by this trade.[7] John Sharp, the Texas comptroller, wrote that "from the Texas perspective, it made sense for the U.S. to co-sign $20 billion worth of emergency loans to help Mexico overcome the devaluation of the peso. . . . Before 2010, Texas-Mexico trade could pass $150 billion—a level equal to the current U.S. trade with Japan. That's why what happens in Mexico matters to Texas."[8] In contrast, California sees itself more as a part of the Pacific Rim, with Japan and China as its natural trading partners.

Texans and their state government elicit from Mexico more cooperation than California because of their more respectful approach to Mexico. The findings of Neil Nevitte and Miguel Basáñez described in chapter 7 suggest that a regional North American identity can build from a foundation of mutual affection, even admiration. These authors collected a considerable amount of survey data over a long period that showed that Mexicans, Canadians, and Americans not only like each other, but they also have a real admiration for each other. Although it was not a surprise to learn that Mexicans believed that the United States exercises a great deal of influence on their country, it was a surprise to discover that two-thirds of the Mexicans surveyed viewed U.S. influence as positive and that the same proportion see U.S. and Mexican interests as overlapping.

U.S. citizens and Canadians have an affection based on their perceived similarities, although the degree of their knowledge of each other reflects the economic asymmetry. For example, only 12 percent of us know that Canada is our most important trading partner, and only 57 percent are aware of the free trade agreement with Canada, whereas 97 percent of Canadians are aware of it. Nevitte and Basáñez believe that the converging value systems of the three countries help explain why NAFTA has become more acceptable in the three countries, or at least less unacceptable, over time.

Certainly the polls show a public that is far less stridently nationalistic than many of the politicians and members of the U.S. Congress. It is possible that the politicians are following the voices of angry voters, who reside in areas that experience the concentrated assault of integration, and that they cannot hear the quieter support among the people of the three countries for a new regional relationship. In some ways public opinion in all three countries seems considerably in front of that of the leadership in looking toward the development of North America.

Trilateral Institutions

The need for a formal mechanism for consultation between the United States and Mexico was first recognized two decades ago when Presidents Jimmy Carter and Jose Lopez Portillo established a U.S.-Mexican Consultative Commission. The commission linked the domestic agencies of the two governments more closely with each other. Presidents Ronald Reagan and Lopez Portillo maintained the group, although they changed the name to Binational Commission.

The real breakthrough, of course, occurred during the administrations of George Bush and Carlos Salinas. In 1990 the commission was expanded to include more than ten cabinet officials from each country and fifteen working groups. Given the complexity of the relationship, good coordination is essential. Currently composed of sixteen working groups, the Binational Commission needs a permanent secretariat, which could give continuity to agreements and proposals made in the groups during the annual meetings.

Apart from this bilateral mechanism for consultation, there exist organizations for dealing with specific problems. Perhaps the most effective of these is the International Boundary and Water Commission (IBWC), which was established in 1889 but has been improved since then. Its success is due to the expertise that it attracts from both sides of the border and to its specialization.

During the 1992 presidential campaign Bill Clinton promised that he would improve NAFTA by negotiating side agreements on labor and the environment. These two parallel agreements established the first trilateral institutions. The ministers (or, in the United States, the secretaries of) labor and the environment are required to meet periodically to discuss ways to promote better labor and environmental conditions in all three countries. Two commissions were established to enforce the agreement—the North American Environmental Commission in Montreal, Canada, and the North American Labor Commission based in Dallas, Texas. Each of the labor ministers has set up a National Administrative Office that serves as a liaison with the other labor ministries. In addition, a North American Development Bank has been established to promote environmental projects on the U.S.-Mexican border.

These three institutions are minimally funded and were slow to begin work. The Environmental Commission has pursued a number of cases in Mexico and has succeeded in persuading the Mexican government to make some changes in its regulatory framework and to prosecute a few violations of the environmental law. It has made some progress, but the Labor Commission has been weaker and more bureaucratic.

What is needed is a North American secretariat with some independence from the governments. The secretariat should approach the region's problems from a trinational perspective, planning for the infrastructural, economic, and political futures of North America and seeking to understand the relationships of different phenomena—such as drugs, migration, and the exchange rate—to each other and to the integration process. The secretariat would have broader responsibilities to reach the publics of the three countries and would help educate them in a manner that could permit the emergence of a North American perspective, if not an identity.

The North American secretariat could play other needed roles as well. For example, it could be the catalyst for the three countries to begin to coordinate their trade and foreign policies. It is remarkable but true that Mexico, Canada, and the United States have not yet coordinated their trade policies with regard to Asia and the FTAA.

Bureaucratic Reorganization

To be able to respond to the secretariat's proposals, each of the three governments needs to undertake some reorganization. In January 1998 the new foreign minister of Mexico repeated one mistake long made by the United States by establishing an undersecretary of state for North American and European affairs. The United States has an assistant secretary of state, but the point is that both governments place North America and Europe in the same bureaucratic box, which suggests that neither government understands the significance of the North American region. Canada's two pertinent ministries, Foreign Affairs and Commerce, each has only one undersecretary with a functional responsibility. Many of the personnel in both ministries give a considerable amount of time to U.S. affairs; fewer, naturally, to Mexican affairs.

An undersecretary in each of the countries dedicated exclusively to North American affairs would be able to coordinate the more than a dozen agencies dealing with North American issues within each government. In addition, he or she could coordinate the two main mechanisms of North American consultation, the U.S.-Mexico Binational Commission, and the Mexico-Canada Ministerial Meeting.[9] The undersecretaries could also give continuity to the decisions made by the binational commissions—and, even better, they could make the binational commissions trinational.

Integrating Congress

Even if one could change attitudes, establish new trilateral mechanisms, and reorganize the foreign affairs bureaucracies to give concentrated attention to North American issues, one would still need to address the central theme of this book and the pivot of the trinational relationships—the U.S. Congress. The issue is how to elicit the best from the Congress and discourage offensive comments or actions. We propose three suggestions as to how Congress could reorganize itself, restructure its hearings, and revitalize and trilateralize the Interparliamentary Conference (IPC).

First, Congress is organized and politically constituted to focus on issues in U.S.-Canadian and U.S.-Mexican relations in their most narrow and often most sensational sense. A newspaper article leaks an unsubstantiated report that the governor of a small northern Mexican state might have had a relationship with a major drug trafficker. A member of Congress responds with a speech and a resolution seeking the decertification of Mexico. U.S. Customs reacts by slowing traffic on the border, and then Mexican newspapers and politicians react. This type of incident is hardly news anymore, although it continues to elicit the same unproductive behavior on both sides of the border.

There are alternative ways for Congress to behave. Instead of reacting to newspaper headlines, Congress can begin to study the long-term North American relationships and propose alternative futures. Congress does not need to wait for the U.S. president or the other countries to begin contemplating the parameters of a long-term North American entity. Within Congress, one good place to undertake such a study would be under the auspices of the Joint Economic Committee (JEC). Perhaps the JEC could establish a subcommittee on North American Affairs and define a five-year work plan in which the subcommittee could commission research from institutions in all three countries and encourage the institutions to do the research together. Instead of asking how well NAFTA did in the past year, these institutions could be encouraged to turn to the future and broaden their horizons to include economic, social, and political issues. Following are some of the questions that could be considered:

—How could one restructure and combine the economies of the three North American countries to ensure sustained prosperity over the next twenty years? What should be done about lagging regions, sectors, and groups? How could the income gap be narrowed within and among the three countries?

—What joint steps could be taken within each country to ensure that the immigrants and minorities in that country are treated with respect? What joint steps could be taken to deal more effectively with both the supply and the demand sides of the problem with illegal drugs?

—What political or consultative institutions should be established to ensure that the voices of each of the countries are heard in the others and that the policies consider more systematically the effect on one's neighbors?

Aside from the establishment of a special subcommittee on North American affairs of the JEC, Norman Ornstein suggests that the trade committees in both houses expand beyond their current jurisdiction to take into account the increasing interest in "ancillary" issues such as labor, the environment, and human rights. I. M. Destler notes that two reasons for the trade policy stalemate are the declining interest and expertise in trade issues in Congress and the rising interest and expertise in these ancillary issues. He suggests that one way to break the stalemate is to connect the two debates, and the trade committees should take the lead in doing that.

To whom should Congress listen? The subcommittee on North American affairs of the JEC could hold hearings on its commissioned research in Mexico, Canada, and throughout the United States. The subcommittee could also testify before other committees of Congress dealing with specific issues of concern to Mexico and Canada, and it could encourage other committees to seek—or at least receive—briefings from officials in the other two countries. In brief, the subcommittee could serve as a kind of catalyst or ombudsman to the rest of Congress to make sure that North American issues are handled in a thoughtful fashion.

In considering how Congress can play a more constructive role in North American relations, a good point of departure is to review the U.S.-Mexico IPC. Created in 1960, the IPC is the oldest binational mechanism of consultation in use. Meeting once a year, alternately in the United States and Mexico, the IPC's goal is to establish an ongoing dialogue between U.S. and Mexican legislators.

The mechanism enjoyed its best moments during the 1960s and early 1970s. In 1964 and 1973 the IPC played a key role in settling the dispute over the El Chamizal region on the border (the U.S. returned it to Mexico) and the Colorado salinity problem. The fact that Mike Mansfield, then the Senate majority leader, had a personal interest in the IPC as a complementary mechanism to that of the diplomats, in part explains the success of the meetings.

Beginning in the mid-1970s the mechanism began to lose its effectiveness, mostly because of the decline in the level and number of influential U.S. legislators. The 1985 assassination of Enrique Camarena, the U.S. Drug Enforcement Administration agent, generated new but not very constructive interest in the IPC. Paradoxically, during the Salinas and Bush administrations, when many other bilateral mechanisms were strengthened, the influence of the IPC diminished.

There was some improvement in the thirty-fifth meeting, held in Zacatecas, Mexico, in 1996. Discussions among the legislators were direct and honest. The legislators reached two conclusions as to the cause of the IPC's weakness in the past and its potential in the future. First, the lack of autonomy of the Mexican Congress had diminished the meetings' importance. Because Mexican legislators cannot serve consecutive terms, parliamentary careers do not exist in Mexico as they do in the United States. The Zacatecas meeting was unusual in the active role that Mexico's opposition parties played. This could be a good signal for the future.

Second, since the mid-1970s few members of the U.S. delegation have wielded real influence in the two houses of Congress. Mike Mansfield's departure from the IPC in the late 1970s hurt the conference, and it began to recover only in 1996 when Jim Kolbe replaced "Kika" de la Garza, who had led the U.S. House delegation for twenty-one years. Kolbe, a dynamic and forceful chairman, is a specialist on trade issues.

The increased representation of the opposition in Mexico's Congress could improve the debate. If the Mexican Constitution cannot be changed to permit legislators to run for reelection, perhaps former legislators might be permitted to join the delegation for extended periods of time. In brief, the first step is to improve the representation of both sides. Next the IPC needs to agree to a substantive agenda and try to negotiate some agreements. Finally, if each side can ensure that the agreements are implemented, the IPC will become a new transnational arena for building partnership.

There have been some sporadic initiatives to link the Mexican and the U.S. Congresses through specific interests or regional groups. This was the case in the early 1990s with the border caucus. Under the leadership of Representative Ron Coleman from Texas, the group had various meetings with Mexican officials and some of their Mexican border counterparts. The efforts ended when the Republicans gained control of both houses of Congress in November 1994 because only one of the border legislators who had met with the Mexicans was a Republican. The relationship between the Mexican government and the Hispanic caucus in Congress has always proven difficult. When this organization was led by a member of Congress who was interested in Mexican affairs, the relationship improved, as was the case with Bill Richardson and Xavier Bonilla.

For all the reasons already mentioned when discussing the importance of trilateralism, the IPC could be significantly enhanced if both Mexico and the United States invited Canadian parliamentarians to join. In fact, the United States first established an interparliamentary conference with Canada a few months after approving the U.S.-Mexican conference. Mexico and Canada have had an interparliamentary group since 1974, and this group has met ten times since then, although it is not at all clear what has been accomplished. Similarly, U.S. legislators, particularly from the northern states, have met with their counterparts in Canada but not to great effect.

It seems obvious and logical to integrate these various parliamentary bodies. No doubt it would broaden the horizons of all three legislatures, but it would probably have the greatest and most positive impact on those border-state legislators who have previously concentrated on a single leg of the "relationship triangle." Of course there remains the problem of generating interest and participation on the U.S. side. In October 1997 the Canadian government hosted a Parliamentary Assembly of the Americas with legislators from virtually every country in the hemisphere—except the United States. The Mexican contingent was very large and included state as well as federal legislators. The Canadian leaders had invited and contacted a number of U.S. legislators, but the Americans did not attend. If the United States saw the IPC as a first step toward a North American parliamentary body, some might be frightened to participate, but we suspect that a good number of U.S. legislators would be intrigued.

As Kim Richard Nossal pointed out in chapter 3, Mexico and Canada discarded their traditional passivity in dealing with the U.S. Congress when their free trade agreements were being debated. Both launched very effective lobbying campaigns. In their approach to the U.S. Congress Mexico and Canada should not look for friends, but for allies, legislators with a common constituent interest. The behavior of Senator Robert Torricelli of New Jersey illustrates the importance of this point. Two weeks before the U.S. Senate considered the issue of whether Mexico cooperated with the United States to stop drug trafficking, he came to the Mexican Embassy to thank the ambassador for his help in securing the extradition of a New Jersey citizen. As the story was told by a Mexican diplomat, Torricelli was charming and grateful, and some Mexican diplomats thought he would support Mexico on the drug issue, but when the vote on certification came to the floor on March 26, 1988, Torricelli voted to decertify Mexico.[10]

Canada has had more experience in dealing with the U.S. Congress than Mexico. The Canadian Embassy liaison office was established earlier than the Mexican one and has more personnel and resources. Mexico should reinforce its congressional liaison office. In addition, Mexican and Canadian diplomats should work more together and should visit Capitol Hill more. In policy areas such as drug trafficking or human rights, or even on foreign policy, hiring professional lobbyists to make the Mexican or Canadian case in Congress is not as good as sending the ambassador or credible leaders from the country.

Conclusion

Beyond the style and behind the purpose of Congress's activities on Mexican issues is the intermestic nature of the issues that confront North America. Almost all the issues on the North American agenda are not considered foreign or external by Americans. The environment, trade, drugs, immigration, crime, jobs, interest rates, agriculture, copyright protection and intellectual property, regulations on banking, services, insurance, and investments—these are considered domestic issues by the U.S. Congress, but they are also the North American agenda. The job of representatives and senators is to look after their constitutents' interests on these issues—stopping illegal trafficking in people and drugs, protecting U.S. farmers and banks, and so on—so it is hardly a surprise that Congress's role in the North American relationship is pivotal.

The debates on migration might offer a clue to the future of the relationship. The main arena for the debates has always been Congress. All the fears, hopes, and interests of the United States that are generated by immigration are collected and sorted by members of Congress. Of all the issues that Congress addresses, immigration is one of the most difficult. That might be because the central question of immigration policy—Who should be allowed to come to the United States?—is at the core of what it means to be "American," and that idea is easier to grasp in the abstract than in the real world. Congress, not surprisingly, has taken longer to approve laws on immigration than on most other important issues. The 1921 and 1924 laws, for example, were the product of fifteen years of debate; the 1986 law also took fifteen years to pass.

Although some of NAFTA's proponents argued that it would reduce migration, they were wrong in the short and the medium terms. Until the income gap between the United States and Mexico narrows significantly—and under the best of circumstances that won't happen for decades—the U.S.-Mexican border will function as a powerful magnet. The more the two economies integrate, the more the two societies will combine.

NAFTA will continue to foster greater social and economic integration, and tensions are inevitable under these conditions. These tensions will be transmitted to Congress, which could, as it has in the past, step on the brakes of integration. Unless the congressional process is modified in some way, the partnership implicit in the NAFTA idea will prove elusive.

If one compares the integration of North America with that of Europe, it seems that North America has made a mistake the opposite of Europe's. Whereas Europe has overbureaucratized, North America has underinstitutionalized; it has relied solely on the market, and that is inadequate between three such disparate economies. The peso crisis was not an accident, nor will it be unique unless concerted steps that involve the U.S. Congress are taken to forge a North American entity that can take full advantage of the opportunity of integration.

Notes

1. Samuel Berger, "A Foreign Policy Agenda for the Second Term," Center for Strategic and International Studies, Washington, D.C., March 27, 1997, pp. 1–2.

2. Luis Villoro, "Sobre Derechos Humanos y Derechos de los Pueblos," in *Isonomia, Review of Theory and Philosophy of Law,* no. 3 (October 1995), p. 7.

3. Barbara Crosette, "Surprises in the Global Tourist Boom," *New York Times*, April 12, 1998, p. E5.

4. Sidney Weintraub, "The Depth of Economic Integration between Mexico and the United States," *Washington Quarterly* (Autumn 1995), p. 178.

5. The idea of a North American or a hemispheric community has been developed by a number of authors, including Robert A. Pastor, *Whirlpool: U.S. Foreign Policy toward Latin America and the Caribbean* (Princeton University Press, 1992), chaps. 14–15; Jerry M. Rosenberg, *The New American Community* (New York: Praeger, 1992); Michael Hawes, "Construyendo una Nueva Casa," *Observador Internacional*, vol. 1, no. 20 (February 1994), pp. 40–42.

6. George W. Bush, "Don't Let Rhetoric Alienate Mexico," *Austin American Statesman*, August 8, 1995, p. 9.

7. John Sharp, Texas comptroller of public accounts, "We Need a Strong Mexico," Fiscal Notes, March 1995, p. 2, as quoted by Jan Gilbreath, "La Relacion Mexico-Texas: Redefinicion del Regionalismo," in Rafael Fernandez de Castro, Monica Verea, and Sidney Weintraub, eds., *Nueva Agenda Bilateral en la Relacion Mexico–Estados Unidos* (Mexico, D.F.: Fondo de Cultura Económica, 1998), p. 301.

8. Ibid.

9. Established in 1988, the Mexico-Canada Ministerial was modeled after the U.S.-Mexican Binational Commission. It does not have working groups, but a similar number of cabinet members participate.

10. Interview by Rafael Fernandez de Castro with Federico Salas, former Minister for Congressional Affairs at the Mexican Embassy, Washington, D.C., April 1998.

About the Authors

Miguel Basañez is senior vice president and director of international research at MORI International in Princeton, N.J. He is the coauthor of *The North American Trajectory: Cultural, Economic, and Political Ties among the United States, Canada, and Mexico* (Aldine de Guyter, 1996) and *Human Values and Beliefs* (Michigan State University Press, 1998). He worked with the government of Mexico as a pollster and served as attorney general of the State of Mexico. He was a professor of public opinion at the Instituto Tecnológico Autónomo de México, publisher of *Este Pais*, and president of MORI-USA.

I. M. Destler is director of the Center for International and Security Studies at the School of Public Affairs of the University of Maryland and visiting fellow at the Institute for International Economics. He is the author of *American Trade Politics* (Institute for International Economics and Twentieth Century Fund, 3d ed., 1995) and other books on U.S. foreign and trade policymaking and coauthor of *Misreading the Public: The Myth of a New Isolationism* (Brookings, 1998). He has been a senior associate at the Carnegie Endowment for International Peace and the Brookings Institution and a visiting lecturer at Princeton University and the International University of Japan.

Rafael Fernandez de Castro is chairman of the Department of International Studies and professor of international relations at the Instituto Tecnológico Autónomo de México. He is coeditor of *U.S.–Mexico: The New Agenda* (University of Texas Press, forthcoming) and editor of *¿Qué son los Estados Unidos? (What Are the United States?)* (McGraw-Hill, 1996). He was one of ten scholars from the United States and Mexico who wrote *Binational Study on Migration,* the first conducted by the Mexican and U.S. governments (1995–97). He is a visiting fellow at the Brookings Institution.

George W. Grayson is the Class of 1938 Professor of Government at the College of William and Mary. His writings include *Mexico: Corporatism to Pluralism?* (Harcourt-Brace, 1997) and *The North American Free Trade Agreement: Regional Community and the New World Order* (University Press of America, 1995). He lectures regularly at the National Defense University, the Army War College, and the Foreign Service Institute. He has served as a member of the Virginia state legislature since 1974.

Neil Nevitte is professor of political science at the University of Toronto. He is the author of *The Decline of Deference: Canadian Value Change in Cross-National Pespective* (Broadview Press, 1996) and co-author of *The North American Trajectory: Cultural, Economic, and Political Ties among the United States, Canada, and Mexico* (Aldine de Guyter, 1996) and *New Elites in Old States* (Oxford University Press, 1990).

Kim Richard Nossal is professor of political science at McMaster University. He is the author of *The Patterns of World Politics* (Prentice Hall, 1998), *The Politics of Canadian Foreign Policy* (Prentice Hall, 3d ed., 1997), and *Rain Dancing: Sanctions in Canadian and Australian Foreign Policy* (University of Toronto Press, 1994). He served for five years as the editor of *International Journal*, the quarterly of the Canadian Institute of International Affairs.

Norman J. Ornstein is a resident scholar at the American Enterprise Institute for Policy Research and an election analyst for CBS News. He cochairs the Presidential Advisory Committee on the Public Interest Obligations of Digital Television Broadcasters. He writes a column about Congress for *Roll Call*, has worked as a commentator and pollster for the Comedy Central Television Network, and is senior advisor to the Pew Research Center for the People and the Press. He is codirector of the Renewing Congress Project. He has written or contributed to many books and coedited *Intensive Care: How Congress Shapes Health Policy* (Brookings, 1995).

Robert A. Pastor is the Goodrich C. White Professor of Political Science at Emory University. He was director of the Latin American and Caribbean Program at the Carter Center (1985–98) and is the Ralph Straus Visiting Professor at the Kennedy School of Government and the Center for International Affairs at Harvard University (1998–99). He is the author of ten books, including *Congress and the Politics of U.S. Foreign Economic Policy* (University of California Press, 1980) and *Integration with Mexico: Options for U.S. Policy* (Twentieth Century Fund, 1993). He was director of Latin American affairs on the U.S. National Security Council from 1977 to 1981.

Index